THE NEW REFLECTIONISM IN COGNITIVE PSYCHOLOGY

Over the past two decades, psychologists have increasingly emphasized the role of intuition and emotion in human cognition and behavior. Some have even argued that we are so governed by our intuitions that analytic thinking merely facilitates confirmation bias and motivated reasoning. However, a recent trend in thinking and reasoning research has called this position into question, indicating that just being willing to engage in analytic reasoning is a meaningful predictor of key psychological outcomes in diverse areas of everyday life.

The New Reflectionism in Cognitive Psychology reviews the evidence for the most recent theories on human thinking and reasoning, exploring how analytic thinking plays an important role in human morality and creativity. Featuring contributions from leading researchers, the volume also considers research on religious, paranormal, and conspiratorial beliefs.

An essential volume for all students and researchers of thinking and reasoning, *The New Reflectionism in Cognitive Psychology* emphasizes the role that analytic thinking plays in everyday life and the importance of reason in the modern technological age.

Gordon Pennycook is a Banting Postdoctoral Fellow at Yale University, USA.

Current Issues in Thinking and Reasoning
Series Editor: Linden Ball

Current Issues in Thinking and Reasoning is a series of edited books which will reflect the state of the art in areas of current and emerging interest in the psychological study of thinking processes.

Each volume will be tightly focussed on a particular topic and will consist of from seven to ten chapters contributed by international experts. The editors of individual volumes will be leading figures in their areas and will provide an introductory overview.

Example topics include thinking and working memory, visual imagery in problem solving, evolutionary approaches to thinking, cognitive processes in planning, creative thinking, decision making processes, pathologies of thinking, individual differences, neuropsychological approaches and applications of thinking research.

Aberrant Beliefs and Reasoning
Edited by Niall Galbraith

Reasoning as Memory
Edited by Aidan Feeney and Valerie A. Thompson

Individual Differences in Judgement and Decision Making
Edited by Maggie E. Toplak and Joshua Weller

Moral Inferences
Edited by Jean-François Bonnefon and Bastien Trémolière

Dual Process Theory 2.0
Edited by Wim De Neys

The New Reflectionism in Cognitive Psychology
Edited by Gordon Pennycook

Insight and Creativity in Problem Solving
Edited by Kenneth J. Gilhooly, Linden J. Ball and Laura Macchi

THE NEW REFLECTIONISM IN COGNITIVE PSYCHOLOGY

Why Reason Matters

Edited by Gordon Pennycook

Taylor & Francis Group
LONDON AND NEW YORK

First published 2018
by Routledge
2 Park Square, Milton Park, Abingdon, Oxon OX14 4RN

and by Routledge
711 Third Avenue, New York, NY 10017

Routledge is an imprint of the Taylor & Francis Group, an informa business

© 2018 selection and editorial matter, Gordon Pennycook; individual chapters, the contributors

The right of the editor to be identified as the author of the editorial material, and of the authors for their individual chapters, has been asserted in accordance with sections 77 and 78 of the Copyright, Designs and Patents Act 1988.

All rights reserved. No part of this book may be reprinted or reproduced or utilised in any form or by any electronic, mechanical, or other means, now known or hereafter invented, including photocopying and recording, or in any information storage or retrieval system, without permission in writing from the publishers.

Trademark notice: Product or corporate names may be trademarks or registered trademarks, and are used only for identification and explanation without intent to infringe.

British Library Cataloguing in Publication Data
A catalogue record for this book is available from the British Library

Library of Congress Cataloging in Publication Data
A catalog record for this book has been requested

ISBN: 978-1-138-20808-7 (hbk)
ISBN: 978-1-138-20809-4 (pbk)
ISBN: 978-1-315-46017-8 (ebk)

Typeset in Bembo
by Taylor & Francis Books

CONTENTS

List of contributors   vi

1   Why reason matters: An introduction   1
    Gordon Pennycook

2   Reflective thought, religious belief, and the social foundations hypothesis   10
    Jonathan Morgan, Connor Wood, and Catherine Caldwell-Harris

3   Towards understanding intuition and reason in paranormal beliefs   33
    Marjaana Lindeman

4   The Earth is flat! Or is it?: How thinking analytically might just convince you the Earth isn't flat   56
    Viren Swami

5   The Moral Myopia Model: Why and how reasoning matters in moral judgment   70
    Justin F. Landy and Edward B. Royzman

6   Intuition, reason, and creativity: An integrative dual-process perspective   93
    Nathaniel Barr

7   Why reason matters: Connecting research on human reason to the challenges of the Anthropocene   119
    Nathaniel Barr and Gordon Pennycook

Index   *143*

CONTRIBUTORS

Nathaniel Barr, School of Humanities and Creativity, Sheridan College, 407 Iroquois Shore Road, Oakville, Ontario, L6H 1M3, Canada

Catherine Caldwell-Harris, Department of Psychological and Brain Sciences, Boston University, 64 Cummington Mall, Boston, MA, 02215, USA

Justin F. Landy, Center for Decision Research, Booth School of Business, University of Chicago, 5807 S. Woodlawn Avenue, Chicago, IL, 60637, USA

Marjaana Lindeman, Department of Psychology and Logopedics, University of Helsinki, PO Box 21, FI-00014, Finland

Jonathan Morgan, Graduate Division of Religious Studies, Boston University, 145 Bay State Road, Boston, MA, 02215, USA

Gordon Pennycook, Department of Psychology, Yale University, 2 Hillhouse Avenue, New Haven, CT, 06511, USA

Edward B. Royzman, Department of Psychology, University of Pennsylvania, 425 S. University Avenue, Stephen A. Levin Building, Philadelphia, PA, 19104–6241, USA

Viren Swami, Department of Psychology, Anglia Ruskin University, East Road, Cambridge, CB1 1PT, UK

Connor Wood, Center for Mind and Culture, 566 Commonwealth Ave, Suite M-2, Boston, MA, 02215, USA

1
WHY REASON MATTERS

An introduction

Gordon Pennycook

A long-standing and important tension commonly encountered in psychology is illustrated using the following two quotations:

> Thought constitutes the greatness of man.
>
> *Blaise Pascal,* Thoughts

> A great many people think they are thinking when they are merely rearranging their prejudices.
>
> *Attributed to William James (Greene & Haidt, 2002, p. 517)*

Are humans defined by our analytic, logical, and reflective thought processes, as implied by Pascal, or are we prisoners to our intuitions and biases, as implied by James? What role does analytic thinking really play in determining our beliefs and behaviors? This edited volume brings together a diverse body of work that strongly supports the following conclusion: *Reason matters*.

In this introductory chapter, I will provide a brief (and non-comprehensive) historical overview of the clash between what I refer to as "intuitionist" and "reflectionist" perspectives in cognitive and social psychology. I will then use this context to introduce the chapters that follow.

Historical context

The human capacity to reason has long been held up as one of our most important and cherished evolutionary milestones. Indeed, from Socrates to Descartes to Russell, reasoning could verily be considered one of the primary obsessions of philosophy. It is hardly a surprise, then, that some of the earliest work in cognitive psychology emphasized the importance of reason (Haidt, 2012). For example,

Piaget (1932) and, later, Kohlberg (1969) argued that abstract and logical reasoning represents the pinnacle of cognitive development.

In the 1970s, Kahneman and Tversky began publishing findings that would later comprise the "heuristics and biases" program of research (Kahneman, Slovic, & Tversky, 1982). This work, which ultimately won Kahneman a Nobel Prize (Kahneman, 2002) and that was the focus of his bestseller, *Thinking, Fast and Slow* (Kahneman, 2011), illustrated the many pitfalls of human reasoning. Namely, in lieu of reasoning in a cold and rational way, people tend to rely on simple rules (heuristics) and prior beliefs when making judgments. Consider, for example, the now famous lawyer-engineer problem:

> A panel of psychologists have interviewed and administered personality tests to 30 engineers and 70 lawyers, all successful in their respective fields. On the basis of this information, thumbnail descriptions of the 30 engineers and 70 lawyers have been written. You will find on your forms a description, chosen at random from the 100 available descriptions. Please indicate your probability that the person described is an engineer, on a scale from 0 to 100.
>
> The same task has been performed by a panel of experts, who were highly accurate in assigning probabilities to the various descriptions. You will be paid a bonus to the extent that your estimate comes close to those of the expert panel.
>
> [...] [Here is the description:] Jack is a 45-year-old man. He is married and has four children. He is generally conservative, careful, and ambitious. He shows no interest in political and social issues and spends most of his free time on his many hobbies, which include home carpentry, sailing, and mathematical puzzles.
>
> The probability that Jack is one of the 30 engineers in the sample of 100 is ___%.
>
> (Kahneman & Tversky, 1973, p. 241)

The key to this problem is the inclusion of stereotypical information that is strongly representative of one of the groups (in this case, engineers) but that is also inconsistent with the probability of group membership according to the base rate (in this case, 70% of the sample consists of lawyers). Kahneman and Tversky found that people tend to neglect or underweight the base rate and, instead, respond according to the stereotypical information (a finding that has been replicated many times; see Pennycook & Thompson, 2016, for a review). Remarkably, participants typically respond according to the stereotypes even in cases where extreme base rates (e.g., 997 lawyers and 3 engineers) are used (De Neys & Glumicic, 2008; Pennycook, Fugelsang, & Koehler, 2012; Pennycook & Thompson, 2012). The tendency to rely on simple heuristics (in this case, the representativeness heuristic) in the face of more appropriate information is, apparently, quite strong.

Similar results emerged from investigations of belief bias in the 1980s. For example, Evans, Barston, and Pollard (1983) found that the majority of participants accepted as valid a conclusion that was believable but that did not follow necessarily from the stated premises. For example: All flowers need water; roses need water; therefore, roses are flowers (this is an invalid syllogism). Findings of this sort formed the earliest support for dual-process theories of reasoning (e.g., Evans, 1989; see Frankish & Evans, 2009, for a historical overview), which distinguish between Type 1 (or "System 1") processes that are autonomous, fast, and associative and Type 2 (or "System 2") processes that are working memory dependent, slow, and serial (although there are many different perspectives on dual-process theory; see: De Neys, 2012; Evans, 2008; Evans & Stanovich, 2013; Pennycook, Fugelsang, & Koehler, 2015b; Sloman, 2014; Stanovich, 2005; Thompson, Prowse Turner, & Pennycook, 2011). The reason why humans fall prey to heuristics, biases, belief bias, and the like is because these effects are driven by intuitive cognitive processes that precede – and often supersede – more analytic ways of thinking. Dual-process theories also proliferated in social psychology (Chaiken & Trope, 1999).

An intuitionist backlash

The 1990s and early 2000s saw the emergence of some notable alternative perspectives on the previously assumed power of human reasoning. Perhaps ironically, one such broad perspective arose due to a backlash against Kahneman and Tversky's heuristics and biases program of research (which, at least in my view, played a large role in the breakdown of the idea that human reasoning is some awe-inspiring faculty that keeps us rational). In the "great rationality debate" (Tetlock & Mellers, 2002), detractors argued that the heuristics and biases program focused on a "very narrow normative view" of rationality (Gigerenzer, 1991, p. 83) and that heuristics are actually quite smart (Gigerenzer, 2007; Gigerenzer, Todd, & the ABC Research Group, 1999). Ultimately, the debate was more about terminology than a dispute over the reality of the effects that Kahneman and Tversky (among others) uncovered.[1] Regardless, the emphasis on the "intelligence" of our gut feelings represents a strong intuitionist position that became popular in the 1990s (and continues today).

The intuitionist backlash was perhaps strongest in social (as opposed to cognitive) psychology. I will allow Paul Bloom to summarize:

> There are countless demonstrations of how we are influenced by factors beyond our conscious control.
> […] College students who fill out a questionnaire about their political opinions when standing next to a dispenser of hand sanitizer become, at least for a moment, more politically conservative than those standing next to an empty wall. Those who fill out a survey in a room that smells bad become more disapproving of gay men. Shoppers walking past a good-smelling bakery are more likely to make change for a stranger. Subjects favor job applicants whose résumés are presented to them on heavy clipboards. Supposedly egalitarian white people who are under time pressure are more likely to misidentify a tool as a gun after being shown a photo of a black male face. People are

more likely to vote for sales taxes that will fund education when the polling place is in a school.

(2017, pp. 221–222)

The emergence of subtle counterintuitive effects in social psychology (however unlikely their replication may be; Open Science Collaboration, 2015) led to a gradual diminishing of the presumed role of reflective processes (Bloom, 2014). This is perhaps most strongly exemplified by Jonathan Haidt's social-intuitionist model wherein reflective reasoning processes are thought to be used *primarily* for motivated reasoning and rationalization (Haidt, 2001, 2012). According to Haidt (2001), human reasoning is "more like a lawyer defending a client than a judge or scientist seeking truth" (p. 820).

The new reflectionism

It is becoming increasingly apparent than the pendulum has swung too far toward intuitionism (Baumeister, Masicampo, & Vohs, 2011; Evans, 2013; Evans & Stanovich, 2013; Kahneman, 2011; Newell & Shanks, 2014; Stanovich, 2005; Weber & Johnson, 2009). For example, research on conflict detection during reasoning has demonstrated that people can recognize (if implicitly) that they might be making an error on Kahneman and Tversky's classic heuristics and biases tasks (De Neys, 2012, 2014). For Bloom (2017), our capacity to think analytically allows us to, at least, recognize errors when they are pointed out to us (this is precisely why the examples offered above are so interesting!). Moreover, the capacity to think analytically (intelligence) is predictive of a wide range of outcomes, from school grades to job performance to longevity (Ritchie, 2015). The death of reason has been overstated.

The present volume focuses on some of the more surprising avenues where reason matters (Pennycook, Fugelsang, & Koehler, 2015a). One could argue that, for example, intelligence correlates with a number of important life-outcomes because it merely facilitates the development of smart intuitions. Or, perhaps, that conflict detection during reasoning may only trigger analytic thought that leads to rationalization and motivated reasoning (for a more detailed review of this issue, see Pennycook, Fugelsang, & Koehler, 2015b). Moreover, people may recognize their errors when told, but there are some errors that people do not appear to be aware of (Pennycook, Ross, Koehler, & Fugelsang, 2017). Take, for example, the now famous bat-and-ball problem: "A bat and a ball cost $1.10 in total. The bat costs $1.00 more than the ball. How much does the ball cost?" (Frederick, 2005, p. 26).

This problem reveals some important features of our cognitive architecture. First, the problem appears to be very simple, but it is actually quite difficult. Most people respond with "10 cents," which comes to mind automatically and intuitively (Campitelli & Gerrans, 2014; Pennycook, Cheyne, Koehler, & Fugelsang, 2016). However, this is not the correct answer (if the ball was

10 cents, the bat would cost $1.10 and together they would cost $1.20). The math required to realize that the intuitive answer of "10 cents" is incorrect is not at all advanced and, once explained, obvious to anyone who has basic mathematical knowledge.

The key to the bat-and-ball problem (and others like it) is that the reasoner must question their intuition. That is, insofar as the intuitive response comes to mind for most people, getting the correct answer requires the participant to stop and question a response that, at least initially, *seems* correct. As a consequence, the problem indexes (to some degree) a willingness or propensity to think analytically (as opposed to mere numeracy or intelligence; see Pennycook & Ross, 2016; Toplak, West, & Stanovich, 2011). According to the rationalist perspective, this is an incredibly important faculty. The question, then, is how well do problems such as the bat-and-ball problem predict psychological outcomes that people care about (Pennycook, Fugelsang, & Koehler, 2015a)? Does the mere propensity to reason matter? This is the focus of the present volume.

Brief chapter overviews

Chapter 2: Reflective thought, religious belief, and the social foundations hypothesis (Jonathan Morgan, Connor Wood, & Catherine Caldwell-Harris, Boston University)

Morgan, Wood, and Caldwell-Harris review research indicating that the propensity to think analytically is negatively associated with religious belief. They also report additional evidence that triggering analytic thought actually decreases religious belief. A novel explanation of this association is offered: The social foundations hypothesis. The authors argue that social density plays an important role in whether it is socially acceptable to question religious beliefs. In short, socially dense societies do not provide the conditions under which reflection is likely to undermine religious belief. Evidence for the social foundations hypothesis is discussed.

Chapter 3: Towards understanding intuition and reason in paranormal beliefs (Marjaana Lindeman, University of Helsinki)

This chapter provides an overview of dual-process accounts of paranormal and supernatural beliefs. Lindeman reviews evidence from both questionnaire and behavioral measures that show a negative correlation between analytic thinking and belief in the paranormal. Research on superstitious thinking is also reviewed along with the important topic of core knowledge confusions. For example, paranormal believers are more likely to use the properties of one ontological category (such as physical objects) to characterize an entity in a different ontological category (such as mental phenomenon). The links between analytic thinking, paranormal beliefs, and core knowledge confusions are elucidated.

Chapter 4: The Earth is flat! Or is it?: How thinking analytically might just convince you the Earth isn't flat (Viren Swami, Anglia Ruskin University)

Conspiratorial ideation offers a unique form of epistemically suspect belief: Many conspiracists form elaborate and complex narratives around an originally dubious claim. Although this may seem like a typical case where analytic thinking goes awry, Swami argues otherwise. The available evidence suggests that analytic thinking protects against conspiracist ideation. This chapter also reviews other factors that play a role in why people believe conspiracy theories and develops a "conspiracist profile" by integrating various lines of independent research. Interventions to reduce conspiracist ideation are also discussed.

Chapter 5: The Moral Myopia Model: Why and how reasoning matters in moral judgment (Justin F. Landy, University of Chicago, & Edward B. Royzman, University of Pennsylvania)

Landy and Royzman review a diverse body of work on the role of analytic thinking in moral judgments and values. They propose a novel theoretical perspective that integrates several lines of (sometimes conflicting) research: The Moral Myopia Model. According to the model, analytic thinking allows complex representations of moral problem spaces and supports attentiveness to multiple normative considerations, whereas intuitive (non-analytic) thinking is associated with a myopic focus on a single, salient concern (such as, deontological constraint or conventional norms). A myriad of supportive evidence is reviewed, and the Moral Myopia Model is contrasted with other accounts of moral judgment.

Chapter 6: Intuition, reason, and creativity: An integrative dual-process perspective (Nathaniel Barr, Sheridan College)

Creativity is an area where the dispute over the potential positive influence of reflective reasoning is particularly salient. Whereas some studies indicate that executive functioning and intelligence facilitate creativity, others show that too much thinking might actually hinder creativity. Barr develops a dual-process account that allows for the integration of seemingly contradictory lines of evidence. He provides a mechanistic approach that accords with both behavioral and neuroscientific evidence and offers a common language which may facilitate the integration of future research on creativity with multiple seemingly disparate approaches from past work.

Chapter 7: Why reason matters: Connecting research on human reason to the challenges of the Anthropocene (Nathaniel Barr, Sheridan College, & Gordon Pennycook, Yale University)

The human capacity to reason has led to such powerful innovation that the current era has been called the Anthropocene; that is, an era defined by the impact of human activity on the planet. Although advanced reasoning affords inarguable benefits, it is also the cause of many new challenges (e.g., globalization, climate change). In this chapter, Barr and Pennycook connect research on reasoning to such problems and argue that basic and applied research on human reason holds special promise in our pursuit to ensure a prosperous future. Reason matters for it is both cause of and solution to many of our contemporary problems.

Note

1 The following is an excerpt from Kahneman and Tversky (1996, p. 589) that, in my opinion, does a good job of summarizing the dispute:

> Gigerenzer's polemics obscure a surprising fact: There is less psychological substance to his disagreement with our position than meets the eye. Aside from the terminological question of whether terms such as "error" or "bias" can be applied to statements of subjective probability, the major empirical point made by Gigerenzer is that the use of frequency reliably makes cognitive illusions "disappear." Taken at face value, this statement is just wrong. Because Gigerenzer must be aware of the evidence that judgments of frequency and judgments based on frequency are subject to systematic error, a charitable interpretation of his position is that he has overstated his case by omitting relevant quantifiers. Thus, some cognitive illusions (not all) are sometimes reduced (not made to disappear) in judgments of frequency.

References

Baumeister, R. F., Masicampo, E. J., & Vohs, K. D. (2011). Do conscious thoughts cause behavior? *Annual Review of Psychology*, 62, 331–361. doi:00A0;10.1146/annurev.psych.093008.131126

Bloom, P. (2014). The war on reason. *The Atlantic*. Retrieved July 25, 2017, from https://www.theatlantic.com/magazine/archive/2014/03/the-war-on-reason/357561/

Bloom, P. (2017). *Against empathy: The case for rational compassion*. London: The Bodley Head.

Campitelli, G., & Gerrans, P. (2014). Does the cognitive reflection test measure cognitive reflection? A mathematical modeling approach. *Memory & Cognition*, 42(3), 434–447. doi:00A0;10.3758/s13421-013-0367-9

Chaiken, S., & Trope, Y. (1999). *Dual-process theories in social psychology*. New York: Guilford.

De Neys, W. (2012). Bias and conflict: A case for logical intuitions. *Perspectives on Psychological Science*, 7(1), 28–38. doi:00A0;10.1177/1745691611429354

De Neys, W. (2014). Conflict detection, dual processes, and logical intuitions: Some clarifications. *Thinking & Reasoning*, 20(2), 169–187. doi:00A0;10.1080/13546783.2013.854725

De Neys, W., & Glumicic, T. (2008). Conflict monitoring in dual process theories of thinking. *Cognition*, 106(3), 1248–1299. doi:00A0;10.1016/j.cognition.2007.06.002

Evans, J. St. B. T. (1989). *Bias in human reasoning: Causes and consequences*. Brighton, UK: Erlbaum.

Evans, J. St. B. T. (2008). Dual-processing accounts of reasoning, judgment, and social cognition. *Annual Review of Psychology*, 59, 255–278. doi:00A0;10.1146/annurev.psych.59.103006.093629

Evans, J. St. B. T. (2013). Two minds rationality. *Thinking & Reasoning*, 20(2), 1–18. doi:00A0;10.1080/13546783.2013.845605

Evans, J. St. B. T., Barston, J. L., & Pollard, P. (1983). On the conflict between logic and belief in syllogistic reasoning. *Memory & Cognition*, 11(3), 295–306. doi:00A0;10.3758/BF03196976

Evans, J. St. B. T., & Stanovich, K. E. (2013). Dual-process theories of higher cognition: Advancing the debate. *Perspectives on Psychological Science*, 8(3), 223–241. doi:10.1177/1745691612460685

Frankish, K., & Evans, J. St. B. T. (2009). The duality of mind: An historical perspective. In J. St. B. T. Evans and K. Frankish (Eds.), *In two minds: Dual processes and beyond* (pp. 1–30). Oxford, UK: Oxford University Press.

Frederick, S. (2005). Cognitive reflection and decision making. *Journal of Economic Perspectives*, 19(4), 25–42. doi:00A0;10.1257/089533005775196732

Gigerenzer, G. (1991). How to make cognitive illusions disappear: Beyond "heuristics and biases." *European Review of Social Psychology*, 2(1), 83–115.

Gigerenzer, G. (2007). *Gut feelings: The intelligence of the unconscious*. New York: Viking.

Gigerenzer, G., Todd, P., & the ABC Research Group. (1999). *Simple heuristics that make us smart*. New York: Oxford University Press.

Greene, J., & Haidt, J. (2002) How (and where) does moral judgment work? *Trends in Cognitive Sciences*, 6(12), 517–523.

Haidt, J. (2001). The emotional dog and its rational tail: A social intuitionist approach to moral judgment. *Psychological Review*, 108(4), 814–834. doi:00A0;10.1037//0033-295X

Haidt, J. (2012). *The righteous mind: Why good people are divided by politics and religion*. New York: Pantheon.

Kahneman, D. (2002). Maps of bounded rationality: A perspective on intuitive judgment and choice. *The Sveriges Riksbank Prize in Economic Sciences in Memory of Alfred Nobel*, (December), 449–489. doi:00A0;10.1037/0003-066X.58.9.697

Kahneman, D. (2011). *Thinking, fast and slow*. New York, NY: Farrar, Straus and Giroux.

Kahneman, D., Slovic, P., & Tversky, A. (1982). *Judgments under uncertainty: Heuristics and biases*. Cambridge: Cambridge University Press.

Kahneman, D., & Tversky, A. (1973). On the psychology of prediction. *Psychological Review*, 80(4), 237–251.

Kahneman, D., & Tversky, A. (1996). On the reality of cognitive illusions. *Psychological Review*, 103(3), 582–591. doi:00A0;10.1037/0033-295X.103.3.582

Kohlberg, L. (1969). Stage and sequence: The cognitive-developmental approach to socialization. In D. A. Goslin (Ed.), *Handbook of socialization theory and research* (pp. 347–480). Chicago: Rand McNally.

Newell, B. R., & Shanks, D. R. (2014). Unconscious influences on decision making: A critical review. *The Behavioral and Brain Sciences*, 37(1), 1–19. doi:00A0;10.1017/S0140525X12003214

Open Science Collaboration. (2015). Estimating the reproducibility of psychological science. *Science*, 349(6251). doi:00A0;10.1126/science.aac4716

Pennycook, G., Cheyne, J. A., Koehler, D. J., & Fugelsang, J. A. (2016). Is the cognitive reflection test a measure of both reflection and intuition? *Behavior Research Methods*, 48(1). doi:00A0;10.3758/s13428-015-0576-1

Pennycook, G., Fugelsang, J. A., & Koehler, D. J. (2012). Are we good at detecting conflict during reasoning? *Cognition*, 124(1), 101–106. doi:00A0;10.1016/j.cognition.2012.04.004

Pennycook, G., Fugelsang, J. A., & Koehler, D. J. (2015a). Everyday consequences of analytic thinking. *Current Directions in Psychological Science*, 24(6). doi:00A0;10.1177/0963721415604610

Pennycook, G., Fugelsang, J. A., & Koehler, D. J. (2015b). What makes us think? A three-stage dual-process model of analytic engagement. *Cognitive Psychology*, 80. doi:00A0;10.1016/j.cogpsych.2015.05.001

Pennycook, G., & Ross, R. M. (2016). Commentary on: Cognitive reflection vs. calculation in decision making. *Frontiers in Psychology*, 6: 936. doi:00A0;10.3389/fpsyg.2015.00532

Pennycook, G., Ross, R. M., Koehler, D. J., & Fugelsang, J. A. (2017). Dunning–Kruger effects in reasoning: Theoretical implications of the failure to recognize incompetence. *Psychonomic Bulletin & Review*. doi:00A0;10.3758/s13423-017-1242-7

Pennycook, G., & Thompson, V. (2012). Reasoning with base rates is routine, relatively effortless, and context dependent. *Psychonomic Bulletin & Review*, 19(3), 528–534. doi:10.3758/s13423-012-0249-3

Pennycook, G., & Thompson, V. (2016). Base rate neglect. In R. F. Pohl (Ed.), *Cognitive Illusions* (pp. 44–61). London: Routledge.

Piaget, J. (1932). *The moral judgment of the child*. London: Routledge Kegan Paul.

Ritchie, S. (2015). *Intelligence: All that matters*. London: Hodder & Stoughton.

Sloman, S. A. (2014). Two systems of reasoning: An update. In J. Sherman, B. Gawronski, & Y. Trope (Eds.), *Dual process theories of the social mind* (pp. 69–79). New York: Guilford Press.

Stanovich, K. (2005). *The robot's rebellion: Finding meaning in the age of Darwin*. Chicago: The University of Chicago Press.

Tetlock, P. E., & Mellers, B. A. (2002). The great rationality debate. *Psychological Science*, 13(1), 94–99.

Thompson, V. A., Prowse Turner, J. A., & Pennycook, G. (2011). Intuition, reason, and metacognition. *Cognitive Psychology*, 63(3), 107–140. doi:00A0;10.1016/j.cogpsych.2011.06.001

Toplak, M., West, R., & Stanovich, K. (2011). The Cognitive Reflection Test as a predictor of performance on heuristics-and-biases tasks. *Memory & Cognition*, 39(7), 1275–1289. doi:00A0;10.3758/s13421-011-0104-1

Weber, E. U., & Johnson, E. J. (2009). Mindful judgment and decision making. *Annual Review of Psychology*, 60, 53–85. doi:00A0;10.1146/annurev.psych.60.110707.16363

2
REFLECTIVE THOUGHT, RELIGIOUS BELIEF, AND THE SOCIAL FOUNDATIONS HYPOTHESIS

Jonathan Morgan, Connor Wood, and Catherine Caldwell-Harris

Introduction

The past five years have seen a growing interest in the relationship between cognitive styles and religious belief. At the heart of this research lies a consistently positive association between reflective thought and religious disbelief. Numerous correlational studies and even a few experimental priming studies support this relationship, but it is not uncontested. Beyond empirical disputes or adjustments to this association, however, a key challenge is to explain why this relationship holds. In this chapter, we will review the documented associations between religious belief and cognitive style along with the most common interpretations of these relationships. From there, we will explore open questions and present a novel interpretation: the social foundations hypothesis.

The empirical work

Empirical work on religiosity and cognitive style originated with Aarnio and Lindeman's (2005, 2007) surveys of students in Finland. With measures including religious and paranormal belief, Aarnio and Lindeman found mixed results connecting religiosity to thinking styles. Their 2005 study demonstrated that analytical thinking was negatively related to paranormal beliefs, but not significantly predictive of religious beliefs. But their 2007 follow-up found a reliable preference for intuitive thought among religious believers. This early work on cognitive style and religiosity relied on the Rational-Experiential Inventory (Pacini & Epstein, 1999), a self-report measure of an individual's preference for intuitive or analytical thought, but nevertheless set the stage for later research.

In the past five years, there has been a stronger and more consistent research effort tracking the relationship between religiosity and cognitive style. Many of these studies used the Cognitive Reflection Test (CRT; Frederick, 2005) as a measure of cognitive style. The CRT consists of three math problems with intuitively compelling, but incorrect, answers. For example: "A bat and a ball cost $1.10 in total. The bat costs $1.00 more than the ball. How much does the ball cost?" (Frederick, 2005, p. 26). The immediate and intuitively compelling response is 10 cents, but pausing to reflect will reveal this is wrong. This test suggests that those participants with a preference for reflective thought will pause, override the quick intuitive answer, and use analysis to determine the correct response. The CRT therefore serves as a proxy measure of cognitive style, because the more correct answers a participant gives, the greater her preference for reflective thought.

Shenhav, Rand, and Greene (2012) used the CRT in a series of studies that found support for the connection between religious belief and preference for intuitive thought. In the first of their studies, participants who gave more intuitive answers were more confident in their belief in God ($r = 0.18$; Shenhav et al., 2012, p. 424). This relationship held while controlling for age, gender, education, income, IQ, and conservatism (which has been shown to strongly predict belief in God; Layman & Carmines, 1997). Including conservatism dropped the correlation to 0.08, but intuitive thought remained significant in relation to religious belief.

This relationship was further supported by an empirical study in which the researchers used a writing task to induce a temporary preference for intuitive or reflective thought. In this task, some participants were asked to describe "a time when your intuition led you in the right direction and resulted in a good outcome"; these individuals later reported stronger belief in God, compared to those who were asked to describe "carefully reasoning through a situation" (Shenhav et al., 2012, p. 426). In a complementary set of studies, Gervais and Norenzayan (2012) showed that priming individuals to favor reflective processing tended to promote religious disbelief.

Additional studies have clarified these findings by examining specific aspects of the relationship between cognitive style and religious belief. For example, Pennycook, Cheyne, Seli, Koehler, and Fugelsang (2012) included measures of the type of religious belief rather than simply focusing on the strength of belief. As before, the more correct answers participants gave on the CRT, the less likely they were to believe in a personal, anthropomorphic God. But these more analytical thinkers were not only atheists, but endorsed a variety of less conventional views of God, such as deism, pantheism, or different forms of agnosticism.

To assess cognitive style beyond the CRT, Pennycook, Cheyne, Koehler, and Fugelsang (2013) used a series of syllogisms designed to elicit belief bias, or the tendency to prefer intuitively appealing but technically invalid conclusions (cf. Markovits & Nantel, 1989). The conclusions of the syllogisms are logically valid but contradict our common understanding of the world. For example, "All mammals can walk. Whales are mammals. Therefore, whales can walk. Logically valid or invalid?" (Pennycook et al., 2013, p. 806). Although the intuitive answer is "false" (since in reality whales cannot walk), in this test the correct answer is "true," because the conclusion logically follows from the given premises. Similar to the CRT, correct answers on this test indicate a tendency to engage in careful, analytical processing when faced with a novel problem. Confirming the established relationship, religious skeptics tended to make fewer errors on this task. Furthermore, religious skeptics also spent more time on the problems than religious believers, a finding that fits the conception of reflective processing as slower and more effortful.

Further advancing our understanding of this dynamic, Browne, Pennycook, Goodwin, and McHenry (2014) tested the relationship between the CRT and religious beliefs, but included a one-item measure of "spiritual epistemology." This measure gauged an individual's willingness to accept spiritual experiences as important sources of knowledge. Analytical scores on the CRT were negatively associated with participants' willingness to accept spiritual experiences, and in turn the spiritual epistemology item predicted the strength of participants' faith ($r = 0.42$). Browne and colleagues argued that this mediating role of spiritual epistemology demonstrates that the pathway from cognitive style to religiosity partially depends on the types of knowledge people favor when constructing their worldviews.

This interpretation is further supported by a study from Pennycook, Cheyne, Barr, Koehler, and Fugelsang (2014) on the role of conflict sensitivity. That team used a base-rate neglect task, which tests subjects' propensity to overestimate the likelihood of scenarios that are intuitively appealing but which are less probable than a logically simpler scenario. In this case, the intuitive/reflective conflict focused on salient stereotypes about social groups. De Neys and Glumicic (2008) provide an example:

> In a study 1000 people were tested. Among the participants there were 4 men and 996 women. Jo is a randomly chosen participant of this study.
>
> Jo is 23 years old and is finishing a degree in engineering. On Friday nights, Jo likes to go out cruising with friends while listening to loud music and drinking beer.
>
> What is most likely?
> a. Jo is a man
> b. Jo is a woman
>
> *(p. 1252)*

Even though the personal information offered seems more stereotypically appropriate for a man, analytical thinkers were more efficient than intuitive thinkers at using the base-rate information to select the correct answer: b. This conflict sensitivity also predicted religious belief: the more likely individuals were to detect conflicts while reasoning, the less likely they were to be religious. Based on these findings, Pennycook and colleagues suggest that a mechanism driving the relationship between analytical thought and religious disbelief may be "the likelihood of implicitly detecting conflict between nonmaterial religious beliefs and our understanding of the material world" (2014, p. 9). This interpretation stands alongside that from Browne et al.'s (2014) research. Both focus on the propositional, cognitive content of religious beliefs and the degree to which individuals assess this content as reliable or conflicting with other, more naturalistic, worldviews. We will explore this interpretation in more detail below, but first we will review some of the empirical work that challenges the relationships we have described so far.

Empirical challenges

Our review thus far could give the impression that a coherent consensus exists regarding the connection between analytical thought and religious disbelief, but – as usual in science – there is in fact considerable disagreement among researchers. For example, Razmyar and Reeve (2013) suggest that cognitive ability, not cognitive style, is the primary driver in this relationship. An individual's cognitive ability describes her capacity to use analytical reasoning in solving problems, while her cognitive style refers to her tendency to engage those analytical processes (Stanovich & West, 2008). With this difference in mind, Razmyar and Reeve (2013) found that cognitive ability had a moderate to strong inverse relationship to religiosity. If cognitive ability was controlled for, the relationship between religiosity and cognitive style was small or nonexistent.

This connection between cognitive ability and religiosity integrates well with the broader literature suggesting a negative relationship between religiosity and intelligence (Zuckerman, Silberman, & Hall, 2013). But it directly contradicts the many other studies that have controlled for cognitive ability (e.g., Pennycook et al., 2013; Pennycook et al., 2012; Shenhav et al., 2012). Furthermore, much of the research connecting intelligence and religious belief equates intelligence per se with analytical intelligence (cf. Zuckerman et al., 2013). The problem this poses is apparent in Pennycook et al.'s (2012) study, in which controlling for analytical cognitive style dropped the correlation coefficients between intelligence and religious belief from $r = 0.24$ ($p < 0.05$) to $r = -0.02$ ($p > 0.28$) (as cited in Zuckerman et al., 2013, p. 342). The weight of evidence would suggest that cognitive style – that is, the proclivity to engage in reflective thought – is related to religious beliefs above and beyond intelligence or cognitive ability.

As Pennycook (2014) argues, this discrepancy could be attributed to a number of differences across these studies. Most likely, the discrepancy arises from the different measures used to assess cognitive ability and religiosity. Razmyar and Reeve (2013) assessed religiosity through a range of measures that included overall religiosity and spirituality, religious attendance, religious practices, and prayer frequency along with fundamentalism and scriptural acceptance. All the other studies focused on the cognitive content of religiosity – that is, religious beliefs. Therefore, it is possible that Razmyar and Reeve (2013) have exposed a more complex dynamic between an individual's rationality and his religiosity, of which the cognitive style/religious belief dimension is just one part.

Another challenge came more recently from Finley, Tang, and Schmeichel (2015), who suggested that the association between analytical thought and religious belief may be more fragile than it seems. They found that the order in which the measures were given had a strong effect on whether the relationship emerged. In one study, they administered the CRT before assessing religious belief, and the established trend emerged: higher CRT scores corresponded with disbelief. In a second study, however, they measured religious belief first and then administered the CRT afterward. The result was non-significance (Finley et al., 2015, p. 56). Together, these studies hinted that the established relationship between analytical thought and religious disbelief may be primarily the result of an order effect and, therefore, may not be as robust as previously thought.

However, Pennycook, Ross, Koehler, and Fugelsang (2016) responded with a comprehensive meta-analysis, which included 35 studies and a total sample size of 15,078 subjects. This survey reaffirmed the relationship between religious disbelief and analytical thought, with an overall $r = -0.183$. In order to affirm that this relationship was not a product of order effects, they also included another series of experiments in which the CRT and measures of religious belief were administered in separate sessions, finding similar associations to the meta-analysis (Pennycook et al., 2016). This response suggests that regardless of the modest correlation coefficients, the association between religiosity and cognitive style is a consistent phenomenon, not a product of measurement order. This relationship has also been found among a Muslim majority sample (Yilmaz, Karadöller, & Sofuoglu, 2016), and studies are beginning to trace individual and demographic differences that may moderate the relationship (Yonker, Edman, Cresswell, & Barrett, 2016). The open question therefore is not *if* the relationship exists, but rather *why*.

Interpretations

The early interpretations of this relationship (e.g., Shenhav et al., 2012) argued that religious beliefs emerge from intuitive cognitive biases in favor of mind/body dualism (Bering, 2011), anthropomorphism (Waytz, Cacioppo, & Epley, 2014), and teleology (Kelemen, 2004), to name a few. Relying on a version of dual-process theory in which analytical and intuitive processes are reciprocally inhibitory, these interpretations suggest that analytical cognitive processes override the intuitive biases that underlie spiritual worldviews, thus resulting in disbelief.

This interpretation has been commonplace within the cognitive science of religion, informing works such as McCauley's (2011) *Why Religion is Natural and Science is Not*, which argues that "default" cognitive tendencies foster religious beliefs. In a slightly more nuanced account, Baumard and Boyer (2013) acknowledge that while religious beliefs likely arise from natural intuitions, the beliefs themselves have the character of reflective thought. Therefore, Baumard and Boyer suggest, religious beliefs are not simply intuitive impulses, but instead are reflective explanations for common intuitions. Despite some variations between researchers, this family of explanations argues that religious belief rests on intuitive foundations that can be undermined by analytical processing (see also Oviedo, 2013).

Pennycook et al.'s (2014) analysis extends beyond this hypothesis to explicitly argue that the supernatural content of religious beliefs is the primary target of the nonbelievers' reflective processing. As highlighted above, Pennycook suggests that the analytically minded are more likely to sense and attempt to resolve conflicts between religious beliefs and a naturalistic view of the material world (Pennycook et al., 2014). This supposition fits with Browne et al.'s (2014) interpretation that an individual's "spiritual epistemology" partially mediates the relationship between reflective thought and religious disbelief. Rather than assuming that reflective thought undermines intuitive foundations, both of these accounts focus on the representational conflict between intuitive cognitive outputs that leads to further reflection among analytically inclined individuals.

Expanding the interpretation: social density and cognitive styles

One important finding that has been largely overlooked in the literature surveyed thus far is that rather than being merely a factor of individual differences, cognitive styles vary across large-scale cultures in predictable ways. North Atlantic (Western European) societies exhibit analytical cognitive preferences compared with the rest of the world (Henrich, Heine, & Norenzayan, 2010). Members of these "WEIRD" – Western, Educated, Industrialized, Rich, and Democratic – societies prioritize individual autonomy, deprioritize social context, and focus on isolated elements rather than relationships in both perception and cognition. Meanwhile, inhabitants of East Asian cultures such as China and Japan are more holistic in their cognitive styles (Nisbett, Peng, Choi, & Norenzayan, 2001). Members of these societies typically attend more carefully to social context, see wholes more quickly than parts, and focus on relations between elements. Members of WEIRD societies tend to be *field-independent*, while East Asians are more likely to be *field-dependent* (Witkin & Goodenough, 1977). Moreover, even within specific societies, cognitive styles vary among subgroups. For example, Talhelm et al. (2015) found that political liberals had more analytical cognitive styles than political conservatives in both the United States and China. In a separate study, inhabitants of rice-growing regions in China were found to have more holistic cognitive styles than residents of wheat-growing regions (Talhelm et al., 2014).

Why would individual-level cognitive differences track such apparently unrelated macro-level phenomena? Varnum, Grossmann, Kitayama, and Nisbett (2010) offer a concise explanation: *social orientation*. That is, people who are more socially interdependent exhibit more holistic cognitive styles, while people who are more socially independent think more analytically. Since rice agriculture requires more intensive interdependent coordination than wheat farming, rice farmers develop holistic, less analytical cognitive preferences (Talhelm et al., 2014). Along similar lines, political conservatives tend to be more socially collectivistic, or "hivish," while liberals are more individualistic (Haidt, 2013). It is therefore not surprising that conservatives think more holistically.[1]

In these cases, a single key discriminator – social orientation – explains large-scale differences between the WEIRD world and East Asia; between political liberals and conservatives; and between wheat farmers and rice farmers in China (Varnum et al., 2010). In each instance, the more individualistic group is more cognitively analytic, while the more collectivistic group is more cognitively holistic. Taken together, these studies demonstrate a tight relationship between social density and cognitive style. Importantly, the relationship here is likely reciprocal: an analytically minded person will often seek out more individualistic groups. But, of course, that new social context will influence his preference for a particular cognitive style in turn.

It is important to point out that the instruments used in the cross-cultural literature on thinking dispositions and religion are different from those typically used to study religion and cognitive style. The CRT – used in most studies of religion and cognitive style – is intended to measure *reflection*, or the effortful overriding of intuitive cognitive responses (Frederick, 2005). It is thus a measure of deliberate, "Type II" processing, or how well test-takers deliberate and effortfully use working memory – which is distinguished from implicit and intuitive "Type I" processing (Evans & Stanovich, 2013; Morgan, 2016). By contrast, the instruments used to measure thinking dispositions in most cross-cultural studies (e.g., Nisbett et al., 2001) are more properly measures of cognitive *mode* (Evans & Stanovich, 2013). For instance, Talhelm et al. (2015) used the Triad Task (Ji, Zhang, & Nisbett, 2004) to discriminate between holistic/relational and analytical/categorical thinkers. The Triad Task consists of groups of three related words from which subjects select the two that they feel most belong together. *Categorical* pairings (e.g., "train" + "bus") are considered analytical and abstract, while *relational* pairings ("train" + "tracks") reflect a more holistic and concrete cognitive mode. However, note that neither choice necessarily involves effortfully overriding intuition.

Because it indexes thinking dispositions without requiring that an intuitive response be overridden by an analytical response, the Triad Task may be quite useful for understanding how cognitive styles are connected to religious belief. For instance, Talhelm et al. (2015) found that conservatives made more relational pairings on the Triad Task than liberals did. Social and political conservatives have also been found to offer more intuitive (less reflective) answers on the CRT than liberals (Deppe et al., 2015; Iyer, Koleva, Graham, Ditto, & Haidt, 2012). Similarly, in a study of religious ideology, two of the present authors found that theologically conservative religious believers made significantly more relational pairings on the Triad Task than respondents who were more liberal or agnostic (Wood & Morgan, 2017). The same demographic factors (i.e., religiousness and conservatism) thus serve as convergent predictors for both kinds of cognitive style measures. This suggests that the CRT and the Triad Task may be tracking similar (though not identical) underlying cognitive patterns.

On a theoretical level, analytic reflection requires rule-based thinking and formal logic, which in turn depends on strict categories rather than relational associations. Hence, people whose preferred cognitive mode is abstract categorization (the Triad Task) may also be more likely to override intuitive responses with rule-based cognitive effort (the CRT). In both cases, analytical people (liberals, the nonreligious, WEIRDs, etc.) are less likely to be deeply embedded in tight in-group-oriented social relationships than more holistic/intuitive people (conservatives, religious adherents, rice farmers, etc.). A key reason appears to be that "stronger social networks … produce a more holistic orientation toward the world" (Nisbett et al., 2001, p. 303). Thus, social density, in part influenced by religiosity, may predict both cognitive style and cognitive mode.

The social foundations hypothesis

The relationship between cognitive style and religious belief is most usefully understood as one strand of a larger social fabric. This means that religiosity may be correlated with intuitive style because a third variable causes both. A plausible third variable is whether the larger culture is *individualistic* or *collectivistic* (in the sense developed by cross-cultural psychologists; e.g., Triandis & Suh, 2002). Persons who have grown up with individualist values are likely to find it easy to adopt an analytical style, at least in some situations (Ji et al., 2004). But individualism is also associated with factors that promote secularity, such as skepticism, independent thought, and external locus of control. For instance, Twenge, Exline, Grubbs, Sastry, and Campbell (2015) noted that religiosity among American young adults has decreased in tandem with increasing individualism.

In principle, the culture in which a person is raised can be an independent third variable separately influencing religiosity and analytical style. In practice, however, many situations probably do not reflect simple, linear causality. Growing up in a household with individualist values means that children will be exposed to and acquire the values of analytical thinking and independent thinking. The values of independent thinking will, in turn, bring along with them implicit or explicit permission to choose a level of religiosity which accords with the child's temperament, cognitive style, and personal experiences. Thus, households that value *independent* thinking are at the same time statistically likely to be households that value *analytical* thinking – and ones that permit low religiosity.

The "third variable" argument, then, posits that possessing an analytical thinking style does not cause low religiosity through linear causality, but that analytical thinking, individualistic values, and permission to make up one's own mind about religion co-occur together in households and in the larger culture. This observation lies at the root of the view we advocate, which we call the *social foundations hypothesis*. We argue that a feedback loop exists between social density, religiosity, and cognitive styles (see Figure 2.1). Social density is a broad concept that subsumes many aspects of our sociality that vary cross-culturally. These include the relative tightness/looseness of social norms (Gelfand et al., 2011); the reliance on social roles with obligatory functions (Douglas, 1970); and the preference for independent versus interdependent social orientations (Varnum et al., 2010).

We refer to cultures with tight social norms, interdependent self-construal, respect for hierarchy, and obligations to in-groups as cultures high in social density. In socially dense societies, an intuitive cognitive style confers benefits that facilitate learning and adhering to social norms, respecting authority, and aligning one's own goals with expectations of parents and authority figures. By not questioning or

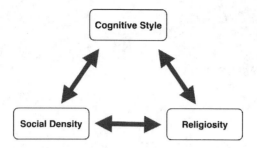

FIGURE 2.1 The social foundations hypothesis

analyzing rules and requirements, individuals fit into a social structure where respect for hierarchy and group harmony are necessary for smooth social functioning. These habits are particularly important under harsh and precarious living conditions, when natural disasters can strike and people must depend on an extensive social network of strong alliances. Hence, religiosity – a concomitant of social density – often increases following severe natural disasters or economic crises (Chen, 2010; Norris & Inglehart, 2011; Sibley & Bulbulia, 2012).

Importantly, an analytical cognitive style can be disadvantageous in a socially dense society. Analytical thinking encourages noting contradictions, including inspecting cultural teachings for self-relevance and questioning social mores. A consequence of an analytical thinking style may thus be less prosocial behavior, in terms of adherence to conventional norms and cooperating with others in uncalculating ways (Pennycook, Fugelsang, & Koehler, 2015; Rand, 2016). Individuals with an analytic cognitive style may tend to put their own goals before group goals. The result is that "the nail that sticks out is hammered flat"; that is, in a socially dense society, analytically minded individuals can be subject to group sanctions or may simply fail to establish beneficial cooperative relationships.

According to the social foundations hypothesis, then, the relationship between cognitive style and religious belief is not causal, but emerges as part of a more complex dynamic. In some contexts, the influence of cognitive style on religiosity may be mediated by social density variables. Additionally, religiosity may reciprocally influence cognitive style by promoting a more dense form of sociality that fosters intuitive processing. The weak form of the hypothesis suggests that this feedback loop exists and influences the relationship between cognitive style and religiosity. The strong form of the hypothesis argues that social density is the primary driver of this relationship.

Religious beliefs are not like other beliefs

As described above, the most common explanations for the inverse relationship between analytic cognition and religiousness have focused on the propositional content of religious beliefs. If religious beliefs arise naturally as byproducts of default cognitive processes such as agency detection or teleological reasoning, then analytical reflection may interrupt the intuitive processes that undergird those beliefs (Shenhav et al., 2012). Alternatively, if religious beliefs are ontologically problematic propositional claims, then analytical thinking may help people detect the inherent conflicts between natural causal reasoning and supernatural faith claims (Pennycook et al., 2014).

A drawback of the standard explanation is that, cognitively speaking, religious beliefs are not the same as other beliefs. Unlike everyday propositional beliefs, religious beliefs appear to be a special kind of social postulate or shared "as-if" statement (Seligman, Weller, Puett, & Simon, 2008; van Leeuwen, 2014). This imaginative character of religious beliefs is intimately related to their social functions, as Émile Durkheim (1912/2008) pointed out. From a Durkheimian perspective, when a Muslim believer recites the Shahada ("There is no god but Allah, and Muhammad is his prophet"), he is not just making a straightforward claim about how he thinks the world actually is. Instead, he is also making tacit statements about his identity, his social allegiances, and which authorities he accepts as legitimate. As van Leeuwen (2014) points out, these statements also have a perceived moral or normative force. That is, for Muslim believers, the Shahada not only indicates how things are but also points to how things *ought* to be.

A key piece of evidence for this claim is that religious beliefs depend on unique contexts and are influenced by social authority, while factual beliefs are not (van Leeuwen, 2014). Van Leeuwen defines "factual beliefs" as those that do not vary by setting; govern people's expectations about what will occur; and are vulnerable to or informed by empirical evidence. For instance, Sarah believes that if she drops a wafer, gravity will cause it to fall to the ground. This factual belief holds no matter where she is, what she is doing, or what her cultural identity is. She believes it because her lifetime of experience has shown her that things with mass reliably fall to the ground when dropped. However, Sarah also happens to believe that the particular wafer in question is the literal body of Christ, because it is a communion wafer, consecrated by a priest. Hence, Sarah's religious beliefs obtain for a narrower range of contexts than her factual beliefs do. Moreover, unlike factual beliefs, we can draw important inferences about her social identity from them – for example, that she is Catholic, not Protestant. And, finally, there is no empirical – that is, objectively measurable or observable – distinction between a consecrated wafer and an unconsecrated one. Her belief in the literal transubstantiation of the wafer is not subject to quotidian sensory evidence, but instead indexes her social identity and highlights the authorities she treats as legitimate (specifically, Catholic hierarchs and tradition). Unlike factual beliefs, then, belief in transubstantiation is "inferentially inert" – that is, not used by believers to draw actionable inferences about practical reality – outside very circumscribed contexts (Bulbulia, 2008, p. 97).

Thus, although neutral or instrumental propositions can be accepted or rejected based on objective evidence, a person's religious beliefs come loaded with subtext and rich associations that bear on group identity and moral norms (Atran & Ginges, 2012; Berger, 1967; Haidt & Kesebir, 2010). They also require imaginative assent. After all, a consecrated communion wafer does not look objectively different from other wafers. So it takes an act of imagination to affirm that it has indeed been transubstantiated into something divine. As Steadman and Palmer (2010) have argued, that imaginative affirmation links the parishioner with everyone else who shares it, while separating her from outsiders (for whom the wafer is really just a wafer).

Sharing an imaginative viewpoint therefore bonds people in a way that sharing straightforward facts does not, because an imaginative viewpoint can be *chosen*. This is why, as anthropologists have pointed out, religious beliefs serve as powerful tools for binding religious communities and instilling contingent moral norms (Geertz, 1993; Rappaport, 1999). Objective facts can be verified or falsified by anybody and therefore are not as practical for indicating group membership.[2] Only imaginative conventions – which have to be affirmed or chosen – can discriminate fellow believers from outsiders. Thus, religious beliefs function as a social signal of one's in-group. Because religious beliefs are not like factual beliefs, a religious person may decline to analyze them for contradictions with the natural world.[3] Our cognitive-anthropological framework thus posits a correlation between (1) imaginative or subjunctive postulates and (2) social affiliation. Affirming your group's imaginative claims is a form of motivated cognition that strengthens social ties within the in-group (Ditto, Pizarro, & Tannenbaum, 2009).

Preliminary evidence for the social foundations hypothesis

Recent research supports the social foundations hypothesis by investigating the interrelationship between analytical thought, social cognition, and religious belief. A growing number of studies have found an inverse correlation between analytical thought and social cognition (Baron-Cohen, Wheelwright, Spong, Scahill, & Lawson, 2001; Jack et al., 2013; Jack, Robbins, Friedman, & Meyers, 2014). A parallel line of research has demonstrated positive associations between religiosity and various aspects of social cognition, such as "mentalizing," or inferring others' mental states (Banerjee & Bloom, 2013; Caldwell-Harris, 2012; Gervais, 2013; Liu, 2010; Norenzayan, Gervais, & Trzesniewski, 2012). Considered together, these findings lend credibility to the social foundations hypothesis by suggesting that analytical thought may inherently conflict with the processing of *social* information and that this basic cognitive conflict may undergird the negative correlation between analytical cognitive modes and religiosity.

Jack, Friedman, Boyatzis, and Taylor (2016) recently published a series of eight studies that elucidate these relationships. Following previous work (e.g., Jack et al., 2013; Shamay-Tsoory, Aharon-Peretz, & Perry, 2009) Jack et al. (2016) first distinguished between two types of social cognition: mentalizing and moral concern. Mentalizing refers to Theory of Mind, or an individual's capacity to discern the intentional mental states of others. Past theorists (e.g., Norenzayan et al., 2012) have suggested that religious beliefs arise as an extension of our tendency to infer these mental states. Moral concern, on the other hand, is a "broad category which includes empathic concern, interpersonal connection, prosocial behavior and aspects of moral reasoning" (Jack et al., 2016, p. 2).

Building off of this distinction, Jack et al. (2016) examined the relationship between these different types of social cognition, religious belief, and analytical cognitive style, finding that moral concern – especially empathic concern – was the strongest predictor of religious belief ($r = 0.26$, $p < 0.001$) (Jack et al., 2016). Mentalizing, on the other hand, was *not* associated with belief – a finding that raises questions for the postulated link between Theory of Mind and religious belief (see also Lindeman, Svedholm-Häkkinen, & Lipsanen, 2015). Importantly, moral concern was also negatively related to analytical thought ($r = -0.11$, $p < 0.001$). Throughout these studies, Jack et al. (2016) found that controlling for this negative relationship between moral concern and analytical thought significantly weakened the link between analytical thought and religious belief, in some cases reducing it to non-significance. In the final pooled analysis, moral concern showed significantly greater bivariate and partial correlations with religious belief than did CRT scores, although both remained significant predictors (Jack et al., 2016).

These findings suggest that a third-variable explanation may illuminate the relationship between reflective thought and religious belief. As the social foundations hypothesis argues, the simple association between religiosity and cognitive style may be secondary to a more foundational relationship between religiosity and core social factors. Jack et al. (2016) posit that the association between religious belief and cognitive reflection, which holds across individuals, is subordinate to a more central, robust relationship between religious belief and empathic moral concern (overall $r = 0.24$). We extend this hypothesis to the between-groups level by positing that the number and extent of social obligations (i.e., moral claims on behavior) experienced by an average member of a society predicts both cognitive style and religiosity (see Bainbridge, 2005).

Further supporting this claim, substantial evidence indicates that cognitive profiles can be directly influenced by religious ideologies rooted in culture, such that different religious beliefs and practices are associated with differences in various cognitive processing styles (Hommel, Colzato, Scorolli, Borghi, & van den Wildenberg, 2011). One study, measuring perceptual styles, found that Italian Roman Catholics and Israeli Jews were more attuned to global features of their visual field than their nonreligious compatriots – an example of a holistic processing mode. However, in the Netherlands, this association was shown to be reversed: Dutch Calvinists were more analytically attuned to local specific features of their visual fields, while atheists were more holistic in their perceptual/cognitive styles (Colzato et al., 2010b). Importantly, both Catholic and Jewish beliefs prioritize collectivistic social values, while Calvinist theology is more individualistic.

Other studies have found similar reversals in regards to cognitive control processes, such as attention regulation (Colzato, Hommel, & Shapiro, 2010a; Colzato, van den Wildenberg, & Hommel, 2008), response selection and inhibition (Hommel et al., 2011), and delay of gratification behaviors (Paglieri, Borghi, Colzato, Hommel, & Scorolli, 2013), to name a few (cf. Hommel & Colzato, 2010). These cognitive processes are distinct from the reflective processes captured by the CRT, but the capacity to isolate specific factors during perception and cognition is a crucial aspect of analytical thinking. The research survey immediately above indicates that differences in this capacity are predicted by the differing types of religiosity, particularly individualistic or collectivistic forms of religion.

Reflective self-interest and intuitive cooperation

One benefit of the social foundations hypothesis is its capacity to connect with other branches of the cognitive science of religion. A prime example is the large and growing literature that has found a positive relationship between religion and prosociality, especially *parochial altruism* or costly help for in-group members (Ahmed, 2009; Norenzayan et al., 2016; Xygalatas, 2013). Why would religiosity benefit in-group prosociality? As discussed above, strong social ties appear to encourage motivated acceptance of social subjunctives or arbitrary beliefs, such as religious claims, that are often linked with moral norms by convention. Accepting these arbitrary conventions benefits parochial cooperation because it signals in-group membership in a way that agreeing on objective facts could not (Atran & Henrich, 2010). It thereby improves trust by boosting people's ability to predict one another's strategic decisions, since people can usually accurately predict what others will do when those others appear to accept the social norms of the in-group (Bulbulia, 2008). When everybody can successfully predict that everyone else will abide by norms in a given situation, trust and cooperation are likely to increase (e.g., Lewis & Weigert, 1985; Mayer, Davis, & Schoorman, 1995).

A further reason intuitive or holistic cognitive modes are beneficial for generating social coordination is because they place the control of social commitment signals *outside of conscious awareness* (Bulbulia & Sosis, 2011). From a game-theoretic perspective, putting affirmation of social subjunctives under the control of non-conscious processes is adaptive because holding up one's end of the social bargain does not always pay off. That is, there are often transient strategic motives for individuals to defect or renege on moral norms in specific circumstances. However, if enough people defect enough of the time, the social arrangements fall apart because no one trusts anyone else. Everybody ends up losing. Thus, tight social living provides a strong motivation to *unreflectively cooperate* most of the time, even if cheating could offer temporary benefits.

For example, say that Richard's neighbor has stacked bundled firewood for sale out by the road. The neighbor is a busy guy, so he leaves a coffee can next to the wood into which passersby can stuff $5 per bundle. Face to face, Richard would have a self-interested motive to play fairly with his neighbor, since they live next to each other and any foul play would harm their future relationship. But when the neighbor is nowhere to be seen, there is not as much immediate strategic incentive for Richard to pay the $5. Whether he pays or not, his relationship with the neighbor – and all the future benefits that might come with it – will probably remain unchanged. If Richard deliberates about the decision, he might well decide to take some free wood. But if he is simply committed to cooperation as a social norm, then he will probably just pay the $5 without any reflection. In a community of people where everyone is implicitly committed to the norm of cooperation, people will likely continue to be willing to trust their neighbors and leave wood untended. But in a community where people cooperate only when self-interested strategic calculation says they should, trust will quickly plummet. No one will leave out wood to buy by the road.

A significant body of work has provided theoretical and empirical evidence that religious commitments, sincerely displayed, serve as heuristic indicators that a person will be more likely to cooperate (with in-group members) reflexively, rather than deliberatively (Irons, 2001; Shaver & Bulbulia, 2016; Sosis & Bressler, 2003). That is, members of religious communities come to hold the cognitive heuristic that a co-religionist who exhibits credible displays of sincere religious belief will tend to follow through on her obligations *regardless of whether it benefits her in every precise instance* (Henrich, 2009; Rand, 2016). The reason that such a heuristic can become stabilized in a population, we argue, is precisely because holding sincere religious beliefs is a tautologically honest indicator that the person who holds them is likely not to critically question social conventions. To an extent, her socially normative responses will thus be *automatized* and, thus, out of the purview of analytical calculation − even if the socially normative action represents an uncompensated pure cost in the given instance. As a result, people exhibit higher levels of trust towards targets who display credible signals of religious commitment, sometimes even if their religious traditions do not match (Hall, Cohen, Meyer, Varley, & Brewer, 2015).

A recent body of research further supports this posited connection between intuitive cognition and implicit cooperation by demonstrating that analytical cognition tends to prompt strategically self-interested responses in strategic payoff interactions. In a meta-analysis of priming and economic cooperation games, Rand (2016) found that priming intuitive cognition induced subjects to be significantly more likely to cooperate even when doing so imposed a strategic cost. Analytical cognition, on the other hand, induced a more rational and calculating strategy: subjects who had been primed to think more analytically were more likely to only cooperate when doing so would benefit them in future rounds of the game.

In a set of evolutionary models, Bear and Rand (2016) showed that selection pressures were mathematically unlikely to stabilize a positive correlation between analytic reflection and greater likelihood of cooperation. In all realistic scenarios, reflection was correlated with opportunistic defection. That is, evolutionary logic implies that analytic cognition will be beneficial − and thus spread in a population − only when it is used to opportunistically override intuitive cooperative instincts, enabling its wielders "to evaluate more complex trade-offs between self-interest and altruistic concerns" (Pennycook et al., 2015, p. 430). The only type of cooperation that analytical cognition appears capable of motivating to a greater extent than intuition is low- or no-cost cooperation (Corgnet, Espín, & Hernán-González, 2015).

Therefore, it is reasonable to expect that only certain social contexts, such as cosmopolitan settings where most interactions are one-time engagements with strangers, will foster the spread of such forms of competitive association. Moreover, religious communities, which often foster tight implicit association through social conventions, will preclude such self-interested interactions. Of course, religious communities vary in the degree to which they require such tight associations, a variance which can explain the growth or stagnation of the communities (Iannaccone, 1994). The social foundations hypothesis therefore predicts that tighter religious communities will foster more intuitive cognitive styles, more holistic thinking dispositions, and a greater commitment to orthodox belief.

It is important to point out that in the sense we mean here, "cooperation" does not necessarily imply "behaving in an objectively moral or good fashion." Social conventions are often harmful or unfair. People who exhibit genuine commitment to the social heuristics of their in-group will follow such conventions – ones that harm outsiders, for instance – just as readily as those which benefit everyone. Thus, the fact that religious believers are more likely to be unreflectively cooperative does not constitute an argument in favor of religion (or at least not a very good one), because it leaves underdetermined what "being cooperative" actually *means* in any given religious context. Cooperation might mean suicide bombing, for instance (Atran, 2011). Conversely, it could mean tithing, feeding the poor, and volunteering. The content of religious conventions thus varies radically by context.

But regardless of context, unfalsifiable religious beliefs will tend to be supported by intuitive or heuristic cognition and weakened by analytical thinking. The social foundations hypothesis argues that this is not only because religious beliefs are cognitively natural products of teleological or anthropomorphic reasoning, but – more primarily – because they are social subjunctives that require motivated affirmation as signals of affiliation and moral commitment. As such, they credibly signal the believer's intention to automatically play by the agreed-upon rules of the social game – whatever game that happens to be.

Future directions

With the social foundations hypothesis, we posit a feedback loop between social density, religiosity, and cognitive style. By emphasizing the importance of various forms of social organization, this hypothesis also helps to connect the religion and cognitive style literature with other research, as we have demonstrated. The social foundations hypothesis remains an empirical claim requiring further corroboration. Therefore, we make the following predictions to demonstrate its heuristic potential:

- The endorsement of orthodox religious beliefs will be correlated with the density of an individual's social context.
- In turn, the tightness of an individual's social context will predict her cognitive style – the tighter the context, the more intuitive her thought will be.
- Social density will account for a substantial portion of the variance within the relationship between cognitive style and religious belief.

- Affirmation of religious beliefs will predict unreflective – that is, uncalculating – adherence to the contingent social norms of the religious in-group.
- Within individualistic cultures, preferences for reflective thought will be correlated with field-independent, thinking dispositions.
- Priming an individual with holistic and intuitive cognitive styles will increase an individual's tendency to sacralize, or impute sacredness to target concepts (e.g., Sheikh et al., 2012).
- In repeated instances of prosocial economic games, preference for intuitive thought will predict an individual's skill at detecting cheaters.
- The relationship between religion and self-regulation will be mediated by social density and preference for intuitive thought.

While we take the evidence for the social foundations hypothesis to be convincing, there are likely objections that could be raised.

One of our main points is that the relationship between cognitive style and religiosity is strongly, if not entirely, mediated by social density. This explanation does not directly contradict that of Browne et al. (2014) and Pennycook et al. (2014), which emphasizes the representational content of religious beliefs; but it does significantly challenge the strength of this direct association. However, it could be argued that analytical thought is still the primary driver even if social density mediates its relationship to religiosity. For instance, analytically minded individuals may tend to disaffiliate from socially dense communities, and those who prefer intuitive styles may tend to seek out and create dense social networks. Especially in individualistic societies, community membership is fluid, allowing a person's choice of community to be influenced by their cognitive style. Thus, social selection effects may be the driver of the association between social density and cognitive style. This possibility does not contradict the social foundations hypothesis, since the hypothesis is built around a feedback loop that permits cognitive style to reciprocally influence social density. However, the social foundations hypothesis maintains that social density is the primary driver of this feedback loop. Evidence in favor of this claim is offered by findings (e.g., Talhelm et al., 2014) that show historical geographical associations between economic modes and cognitive style. It is unlikely that Qing Dynasty villagers migrated to regions where the farming economies matched their cognitive styles. It is much more likely that particular farming styles – collectivistic rice farming or individualistic wheat farming – influenced the cognitive style of practitioners over the long term.

In a second possible objection, recent research has argued that systematic thinkers have better empathic accuracy than intuitive thinkers (Ma-Kellams & Lerner, 2016), contrary to our view that intuitive thinking sensitizes people to social and moral obligations. However, empathic accuracy, as measured by Ma-Kellams and Lerner (2016), is an aspect of social cognition closer to Theory of Mind than to moral concern, as described by Jack et al. (2016). Therefore it seems likely that different styles of social cognition relate to different cognitive styles, which in turn are advantageous in different social contexts. Importantly, the cooperative styles we highlighted above depend not on direct empathy (the ability to intuit what others' motivations and thoughts are), but instead on the *tacit or heuristic acceptance of subjunctive postulates, such as religious beliefs, which index social norms*. It may be the case that reflectively fostered empathy helps navigate social contexts involving mostly new interactions, where the social norms cannot be taken for granted. Future research should remain attentive to these various forms of social cognition and cooperative techniques.

Conclusion

A substantial body of evidence connects religious beliefs and cognitive styles. The consistent finding is a modest but reliable association between reflective thought and religious disbelief. The explanations for this association vary. Early interpretations suggested that religious beliefs depend on intuitive cognitive defaults, which are undermined by reflective thought (Baumard & Boyer, 2013). More recent interpretations suggest that the relationship between reflective thought and religious disbelief emerges from the heightened conflict sensitivity associated with reflective cognition, which would detect dissonance between a naturalistic worldview and the supernatural claims of religious beliefs (Pennycook et al., 2014). As we have argued above, both of these explanations focus attention on religious beliefs as propositional claims about reality. Clearly, this is part of what drives this association. However, we argue that the association between cognitive style and religiosity only makes sense as part of a larger dynamic that fundamentally includes social context.

To summarize our argument, religious beliefs are not simply straightforward beliefs about objective things (although they may function that way in many circumstances; see Dawkins, 2006). Rather, they are instances of *motivated cognition* that serve, among other things, as strategic social heuristics. Credible evidence that a person sincerely holds a given religious belief therefore indicates that he will tend to unreflectively abide by the moral norms of his religious community (although of course this expectation is only probabilistic). In general, sincere affirmation of religious belief is therefore a reliable social signal indicating that a person is not likely to critically or opportunistically re-evaluate moral expectations or obligations. Such re-evaluation would constitute the overriding of a heuristic response, and it takes analytical cognition to override heuristics and de-emphasize social trade-offs. In other words, religiosity is intimately tied to social density in a way that depends on intuitive cognitive processes, and this dynamic is the foundation for the relationship between cognitive style and religious belief.

Notes

1 Confusingly, conservatives in the United States often call themselves "individualists," which is somewhat misleading. Moral psychologists have consistently found that social conservatives across cultures exhibit more loyalty to in-groups and acceptance of group-level authority than liberals or progressives do (e.g., Haidt, 2013; Jenson, 1998). Social conservatives are thus "collectivistic" in a cultural psychological sense, not a Marxian one.

2 However, within some cultural contexts, such as the contemporary United States, broad theories grounded in objective facts, such as evolution and climate change, can also come to function as indices of group membership (see Kahan, 2016).
3 This decision to forego analytical reflection may be particularly effective for signaling commitment when the religious belief contradicts a dominant culture's ontological claims (Sosis & Alcorta, 2003). How insulated beliefs are from critical analysis is thus a function of: (1) how sacred an individual considers such beliefs to be (Ginges & Atran, 2009), which likely depends on ritual participation (e.g., Sheikh, Ginges, Coman, & Atran, 2012); and (2) the tightness or looseness of her social context (Gelfand et al., 2011). Individual differences also play a crucial role.

References

Aarnio, K., & Lindeman, M. (2005). Paranormal beliefs, education, and thinking styles. *Personality and Individual Differences*, 39(7), 1227–1236.

Aarnio, K., & Lindeman, M. (2007). Religious people and paranormal believers: Alike or different? *Journal of Individual Differences*, 28(1), 1–9. doi:10.1027/1614-0001.28.1.1

Ahmed, A. M. (2009). Are religious people more prosocial? A quasi-experimental study with Madrasah pupils in a rural community in India. *Journal for the Scientific Study of Religion*, 48(2), 368–374. doi:10.1111/j.1468-5906.2009.01452.x

Atran, S. (2011). *Talking to the Enemy: Religion, Brotherhood, and the (Un)Making of Terrorists*. New York: Ecco.

Atran, S., & Ginges, J. (2012). Religious and sacred imperatives in human conflict. *Science*, 336(6083), 855–857. doi:10.1126/science.1216902

Atran, S., & Henrich, J. (2010). The evolution of religion: How cognitive by-products, adaptive learning heuristics, ritual displays, and group competition generate deep commitments to prosocial religions. *Biological Theory*, 5(1), 18–30. doi:10.1162/BIOT_a_00018

Bainbridge, W. S. (2005). Atheism. *Interdisciplinary Journal of Research on Religion*, 1: 2.

Banerjee, K., & Bloom, P. (2013). Would Tarzan believe in God? Conditions for the emergence of religious belief. *Trends in Cognitive Sciences*, 17(1), 7–8. doi:10.1016/j.tics.2012.11.005

Baron-Cohen, S., Wheelwright, S., Spong, A., Scahill, V., & Lawson, J. (2001). Are intuitive physics and intuitive psychology independent? A test with children with Asperger Syndrome. *Journal of Developmental and Learning Disorders*, 5(1), 47–78.

Baumard, N., & Boyer, P. (2013). Religious beliefs as reflective elaborations on intuitions: A modified dual-process model. *Current Directions in Psychological Science*, 22(4), 1–6. doi:10.1177/0963721413478610

Bear, A., & Rand, D. G. (2016). Intuition, deliberation, and the evolution of cooperation. *Proceedings of the National Academy of Sciences*, 113(4), 936–941. doi:10.1073/pnas.1517780113

Berger, P. L. (1967). *The Sacred Canopy: Elements of a Sociological Theory of Religion*. New York: Doubleday.

Bering, J. (2011). *The Belief Instinct: The Psychology of Souls, Destiny, and the Meaning of Life*. New York: W. W. Norton & Company.

Browne, M., Pennycook, G., Goodwin, B., & McHenry, M. (2014). Reflective minds and open hearts: Cognitive style and personality predict religiosity and spiritual thinking in a community sample. *European Journal of Social Psychology*, 44(7), 736–742. doi:10.1002/ejsp.2059

Bulbulia, J. (2008). Meme infection or religious niche construction? An adaptationist alternative to the cultural maladaptationist hypothesis. *Method & Theory in the Study of Religion*, 20(1), 67–107. doi:10.1163/157006808X260241

Bulbulia, J., & Sosis, R. (2011). Signalling theory and the evolution of religious cooperation. *Religion*, 41(3), 363–388.

Caldwell-Harris, C. L. (2012). Understanding atheism/non-belief as an expected individual-differences variable. *Religion, Brain & Behavior*, 2(1), 4–23. doi:10.1080/2153599X.2012.668395

Chen, D. (2010). Club goods and group identity: Evidence from Islamic resurgence during the Indonesian financial crisis, earlier version with model. *Journal of Political Economy*, 118(2), 300–354.

Colzato, L. S., Hommel, B., & Shapiro, K. L. (2010a). Religion and the attentional blink: Depth of faith predicts depth of the blink. *Frontiers in Psychology*, 1: 147. doi:10.3389/fpsyg.2010.00147

Colzato, L. S., van Beest, I., van den Wildenberg, W. P. M., Scorolli, C., Dorchin, S., Meiran, N., … Hommel, B. (2010b). God: Do I have your attention? *Cognition*, 117(1), 87–94. doi:10.1016/j.cognition.2010.07.003

Colzato, L. S., van den Wildenberg, W. P. M., & Hommel, B. (2008). Losing the big picture: How religion may control visual attention. *PLOS ONE*, 3(11): e3679. doi:10.1371/journal.pone.0003679

Corgnet, B., Espín, A. M., & Hernán-González, R. (2015). The cognitive basis of social behavior: Cognitive reflection overrides antisocial but not always prosocial motives. *Frontiers in Behavioral Neuroscience*, 9: 287. doi:10.3389/fnbeh.2015.00287

Dawkins, R. (2006). *The God Delusion*. Boston: Houghton Mifflin.

De Neys, W., & Glumicic, T. (2008). Conflict monitoring in dual process theories of thinking. *Cognition*, 106(3), 1248–1299. doi:10.1016/j.cognition.2007.06.002

Deppe, K. D., Gonzalez, F. J., Neiman, J. L., Jacobs, C., Pahlke, J., Smith, K. B., & Hibbing, J. R. (2015). Reflective liberals and intuitive conservatives: A look at the Cognitive Reflection Test and ideology. *Judgment and Decision Making*, 10(4), 314–331.

Ditto, P. H., Pizarro, D. A., & Tannenbaum, D. (2009). Motivated moral reasoning. In B. H. Ross (Ed.), *Psychology of Learning and Motivation* (Vol. 50, pp. 307–338). Amsterdam: Academic Press.

Douglas, M. (1970). *Natural Symbols: Explorations in Cosmology*. London: Barrie & Rockliff.

Durkheim, É. (1912/2008). *The Elementary Forms of Religious Life* (Ed. M. S. Cladis, Trans. C. Cosman). Oxford, UK: Oxford University Press.

Evans, J. St. B. T., & Stanovich, K. E. (2013). Dual-process theories of higher cognition: Advancing the debate. *Perspectives on Psychological Science*, 8(3), 223–241. doi:10.1177/1745691612460685

Finley, A. J., Tang, D., & Schmeichel, B. J. (2015). Revisiting the relationship between individual differences in analytic thinking and religious belief: Evidence that measurement order moderates their inverse correlation. *PLOS ONE*, 10(9): e0138922. doi:10.1371/journal.pone.0138922

Frederick, S. (2005). Cognitive reflection and decision making. *Journal of Economic Perspectives*, 19(4), 25–42. doi:10.1257/089533005775196732

Geertz, C. (1993). Religion as a cultural system. In *The Interpretation of Cultures: Selected Essays* (pp. 87–125). London: Fontana Press.

Gelfand, M. J., Raver, J. L., Nishii, L., Leslie, L. M., Lun, J., Lim, B. C., … Yamaguchi, S. (2011). Differences between tight and loose cultures: A 33-nation study. *Science*, 332(6033), 1100–1104. doi:10.1126/science.1197754

Gervais, W. M. (2013). Perceiving minds and gods: How mind perception enables, constrains, and is triggered by belief in gods. *Perspectives on Psychological Science*, 8(4), 380–394. doi:10.1177/1745691613489836

Gervais, W. M., & Norenzayan, A. (2012). Analytic thinking promotes religious disbelief. *Science*, 336(6080), 493–496. doi:10.1126/science.1215647

Ginges, J., & Atran, S. (2009). Noninstrumental reasoning over sacred values: An Indonesian case study. In B. H. Ross (Ed.), *Psychology of Learning and Motivation* (Vol. 50, pp. 193–206). Cambridge, MA: Academic Press.

Haidt, J. (2013). *The righteous mind: Why good people are divided by politics and religion*. New York: Vintage Books.

Haidt, J., & Kesebir, S. (2010). Morality. In S. Fiske, D. Gilbert, & G. Lindzey (Eds.), *Handbook of Social Psychology*, 5th Edition (pp. 797–832). Hoboken, NJ: John Wiley & Sons, Inc.

Hall, D. L., Cohen, A. B., Meyer, K. K., Varley, A. H., & Brewer, G. A. (2015). Costly signaling increases trust, even across religious affiliations. *Psychological Science*, 26(9), 1368–1376. doi:10.1177/0956797615576473

Henrich, J. (2009). The evolution of costly displays, cooperation and religion. *Evolution and Human Behavior*, 30(4), 244–260. doi:10.1016/j.evolhumbehav.2009.03.005

Henrich, J., Heine, S. J., & Norenzayan, A. (2010). The weirdest people in the world? *The Behavioral and Brain Sciences*, 33(2–3), 61–83; discussion 83–135. doi:10.1017/S0140525X0999152X

Hommel, B., & Colzato, L. S. (2010). Religion as a control guide: On the impact of religion on cognition. *Zygon®*, 45(3), 596–604. doi:10.1111/j.1467-9744.2010.01116.x

Hommel, B., Colzato, L. S., Scorolli, C., Borghi, A. M., & van den Wildenberg, W. P. M. (2011). Religion and action control: Faith-specific modulation of the Simon effect but not Stop-Signal performance. *Cognition*, 120(2), 177–185. doi:10.1016/j.cognition.2011.04.003

Iannaccone, L. R. (1994). Why strict churches are strong. *American Journal of Sociology*, 99(5), 1180–1211. doi:10.1086/230409

Irons, W. (2001). Religion as a hard-to-fake sign of commitment. In R. Nesse (Ed.), *Evolution and the Capacity for Commitment* (pp. 292–309). New York: Russell Sage Foundation.

Iyer, R., Koleva, S., Graham, J., Ditto, P., & Haidt, J. (2012). Understanding libertarian morality: The psychological dispositions of self-identified libertarians. *PLOS ONE*, 7(8): e42366. doi:10.1371/journal.pone.0042366

Jack, A. I., Dawson, A. J., Begany, K. L., Leckie, R. L., Barry, K. P., Ciccia, A. H., & Snyder, A. Z. (2013). fMRI reveals reciprocal inhibition between social and physical cognitive domains. *NeuroImage*, 66, 385–401. doi:10.1016/j.neuroimage.2012.10.061

Jack, A. I., Friedman, J. P., Boyatzis, R. E., & Taylor, S. N. (2016). Why do you believe in God? Relationships between religious belief, analytic thinking, mentalizing and moral concern. *PLOS ONE*, 11(3): e0149989. doi:10.1371/journal.pone.0149989

Jack, A. I., Robbins, P., Friedman, J. P., & Meyers, C. D. (2014). More than a feeling: Counterintuitive effects of compassion on moral judgment. In J. Systma (Ed.), *Advances in Experimental Philosophy of Mind* (pp. 125–180). New York: Bloomsbury.

Jenson, J. (1998). *Mapping Social Cohesion: The State of Canadian Research*. Ottawa: Renouf Publishing. Retrieved from www.cccg.umontreal.ca/pdf/CPRN/CPRN_F03.pdf

Ji, L.-J., Zhang, Z., & Nisbett, R. E. (2004). Is it culture or is it language? Examination of language effects in cross-cultural research on categorization. *Journal of Personality and Social Psychology*, 87(1), 57–65. doi:10.1037/0022-3514.87.1.57

Kahan, D. M. (2016). "Ordinary science intelligence": A science-comprehension measure for study of risk and science communication, with notes on evolution and climate change. *Journal of Risk Research*, 20(8), 995–1016. doi:10.1080/13669877.2016.1148067

Kelemen, D. (2004). Are children "intuitive theists"? Reasoning about purpose and design in nature. *Psychological Science*, 15(5), 295–301. doi:10.1111/j.0956-7976.2004.00672.x

Layman, G. C., & Carmines, E. G. (1997). Cultural conflict in American politics: Religious traditionalism, postmaterialism, and U.S. political behavior. *The Journal of Politics*, 59(3), 751–777. doi:10.2307/2998636

Lewis, J. D., & Weigert, A. (1985). Trust as a social reality. *Social Forces*, 63(4), 967–985. doi:10.1093/sf/63.4.967

Lindeman, M., Svedholm-Häkkinen, A. M., & Lipsanen, J. (2015). Ontological confusions but not mentalizing abilities predict religious belief, paranormal belief, and belief in supernatural purpose. *Cognition*, 134, 63–76. doi:10.1016/j.cognition.2014.09.008

Liu, C.-C. (2010). The relationship between personal religious orientation and emotional intelligence. *Social Behavior and Personality*, 38(4), 461–468. doi:10.2224/sbp.2010.38.4.461

Ma-Kellams, C., & Lerner, J. (2016). Trust your gut or think carefully? Examining whether an intuitive, versus a systematic, mode of thought produces greater empathic accuracy. *Journal of Personality and Social Psychology*, 111(5), 674–685. doi:10.1037/pspi0000063

Markovits, H., & Nantel, G. (1989). The belief-bias effect in the production and evaluation of logical conclusions. *Memory & Cognition*, 17(1), 11–17. doi:10.3758/BF03199552

Mayer, R. C., Davis, J. H., & Schoorman, F. D. (1995). An integrative model of organizational trust. *Academy of Management Review*, 20(3), 709–734. doi:10.5465/AMR.1995.9508080335

McCauley, R. N. (2011). *Why Religion is Natural and Science is Not*. New York: Oxford University Press.

Morgan, J. (2016). Religion and dual-process cognition: A continuum of styles or distinct types? *Religion, Brain & Behavior*, 6(2), 112–129. doi:10.1080/2153599X.2014.966315

Nisbett, R. E., Peng, K., Choi, I., & Norenzayan, A. (2001). Culture and systems of thought: Holistic versus analytic cognition. *Psychological Review*, 108(2), 291–310.

Norenzayan, A., Gervais, W. M., & Trzesniewski, K. H. (2012). Mentalizing deficits constrain belief in a personal God. *PLOS ONE*, 7(5): e36880. doi:10.1371/journal.pone.0036880

Norenzayan, A., Shariff, A. F., Gervais, W. M., Willard, A. K., McNamara, R. A., Slingerland, E., & Henrich, J. (2016). The cultural evolution of prosocial religions. *Behavioral and Brain Sciences*, 39: e1. doi:10.1017/S0140525X14001356

Norris, P., & Inglehart, R. (2011). *Sacred and Secular: Religion and Politics Worldwide*. Cambridge: Cambridge University Press.

Oviedo, L. (2013). Religious cognition as a dual-process: Developing the model. *Method & Theory in the Study of Religion*, 27(1), 31–58. doi:10.1163/15700682-12341288

Pacini, R., & Epstein, S. (1999). The relation of rational and experiential information processing styles to personality, basic beliefs, and the ratio-bias phenomenon. *Journal of Personality and Social Psychology*, 76(6), 972–987. doi:10.1037/0022-3514.76.6.972

Paglieri, F., Borghi, A. M., Colzato, L. S., Hommel, B., & Scorolli, C. (2013). Heaven can wait: How religion modulates temporal discounting. *Psychological Research*, 77(6), 738–747.

Pennycook, G. (2014). Evidence that analytic cognitive style influences religious belief: Comment on Razmyar and Reeve (2014). *Intelligence*, 43, 21–26.

Pennycook, G., Cheyne, J. A., Barr, N., Koehler, D. J., & Fugelsang, J. A. (2014). Cognitive style and religiosity: The role of conflict detection. *Memory & Cognition*, 42(1), 1–10.

Pennycook, G., Cheyne, J. A., Koehler, D. J., & Fugelsang, J. A. (2013). Belief bias during reasoning among religious believers and skeptics. *Psychonomic Bulletin & Review*, 20(4), 806–811. doi:10.3758/s13423-013-0394-3

Pennycook, G., Cheyne, J. A., Seli, P., Koehler, D. J., & Fugelsang, J. A. (2012). Analytic cognitive style predicts religious and paranormal belief. *Cognition*, 123(3), 335–346. doi:10.1016/j.cognition.2012.03.003

Pennycook, G., Fugelsang, J. A., & Koehler, D. J. (2015). Everyday consequences of analytic thinking. *Current Directions in Psychological Science*, 24(6), 425–432. doi:10.1177/0963721415604610

Pennycook, G., Ross, R. M., Koehler, D. J., & Fugelsang, J. A. (2016). Atheists and agnostics are more reflective than religious believers: Four empirical studies and a meta-analysis. *PLOS ONE*, 11(4): e0153039. doi:10.1371/journal.pone.0153039

Rand, D. G. (2016). Cooperation, fast and slow: Meta-analytic evidence for a theory of social heuristics and self-interested deliberation. *Psychological Science*, 27(9), 1–15. doi:10.1177/0956797616654455

Rappaport, R. A. (1999). *Ritual and Religion in the Making of Humanity*. Cambridge; New York: Cambridge University Press.

Razmyar, S., & Reeve, C. L. (2013). Individual differences in religiosity as a function of cognitive ability and cognitive style. *Intelligence*, 41(5), 667–673. doi:10.1016/j.intell.2013.09.003

Seligman, A. B., Weller, R. P., Puett, M. J., & Simon, B. (2008). *Ritual and Its Consequences: An Essay on the Limits of Sincerity*. Oxford; New York: Oxford University Press.

Shamay-Tsoory, S. G., Aharon-Peretz, J., & Perry, D. (2009). Two systems for empathy: A double dissociation between emotional and cognitive empathy in inferior frontal gyrus versus ventromedial prefrontal lesions. *Brain: A Journal of Neurology*, 132(3), 617–627. doi:10.1093/brain/awn279

Shaver, J., & Bulbulia, J. (2016). Signaling theory and religion. In N. Clements (Ed.), *Religion: Mental Religion* (pp. 101–117). Farmington Hills: Macmillan Interdisciplinary Handbooks.

Sheikh, H., Ginges, J., Coman, A., & Atran, S. (2012). Religion, group threat and sacred values. *Judgment and Decision Making*, 7(2), 110–118.

Shenhav, A., Rand, D. G., & Greene, J. D. (2012). Divine intuition: Cognitive style influences belief in God. *Journal of Experimental Psychology. General*, 141(3), 423–428. doi:10.1037/a0025391

Sibley, C. G., & Bulbulia, J. (2012). Faith after an earthquake: A longitudinal study of religion and perceived health before and after the 2011 Christchurch New Zealand earthquake. *PLOS ONE*, 7(12): e49648. doi:10.1371/journal.pone.0049648

Sosis, R., & Alcorta, C. (2003). Signaling, solidarity, and the sacred: The evolution of religious behavior. *Evolutionary Anthropology*, 12(6), 264–274.

Sosis, R., & Bressler, E. R. (2003). Cooperation and commune longevity: A test of the costly signaling theory of religion. *Cross-Cultural Research*, 37(2), 211–239.

Stanovich, K. E., & West, R. F. (2008). On the relative independence of thinking biases and cognitive ability. *Journal of Personality and Social Psychology*, 94(4), 672–695. doi:10.1037/0022-3514.94.4.672

Steadman, L. B., & Palmer, C. T. (2010). *Supernatural and Natural Selection: Religion and Evolutionary Success*. London: Routledge.

Talhelm, T., Haidt, J., Oishi, S., Zhang, X., Miao, F. F., & Chen, S. (2015). Liberals think more analytically (more "WEIRD") than conservatives. *Personality and Social Psychology Bulletin*, 41(2), 250–267. doi:10.1177/0146167214563672

Talhelm, T., Zhang, X., Oishi, S., Shimin, C., Duan, D., Lan, X., & Kitayama, S. (2014). Large-scale psychological differences within China explained by rice versus wheat agriculture. *Science*, 344(6184), 603–608. doi:10.1126/science.1246850

Triandis, H. C., & Suh, E. M. (2002). Cultural influences on personality. *Annual Review of Psychology*, 53, 133–160. doi:10.1146/annurev.psych.53.100901.135200

Twenge, J. M., Exline, J. J., Grubbs, J. B., Sastry, R., & Campbell, W. K. (2015). Generational and time period differences in American adolescents' religious orientation, 1966–2014. *PLOS ONE*, 10(5): e0121454. doi:10.1371/journal.pone.0121454

Van Leeuwen, N. (2014). Religious credence is not factual belief. *Cognition*, 133(3), 698–715. doi:10.1016/j.cognition.2014.08.015

Varnum, M. E. W., Grossmann, I., Kitayama, S., & Nisbett, R. E. (2010). The origin of cultural differences in cognition: Evidence for the social orientation hypothesis. *Current Directions in Psychological Science*, 19(1), 9–13. doi:10.1177/0963721409359301

Waytz, A., Cacioppo, J., & Epley, N. (2014). Who sees human? The stability and importance of individual differences in anthropomorphism. *Perspectives on Psychological Science: A Journal of the Association for Psychological Science*, 5(3), 219–232. doi:10.1177/1745691610369336

Witkin, H. A., & Goodenough, D. R. (1977). Field dependence and interpersonal behavior. *Psychological Bulletin*, 84(4), 661–689. doi:10.1037/0033-2909.84.4.661

Wood, C., & Morgan, J. (2017). *Not by Faith Alone: Religious Ritual Influences Cognitive Style More than Propositional Beliefs*. Unpublished manuscript.

Xygalatas, D. (2013). What is natural and unnatural about religion and science? *Religion, Brain & Behavior*, 3(2), 161–164. doi:10.1080/2153599X.2013.767043

Yilmaz, O., Karadöller, D. Z., & Sofuoglu, G. (2016). Analytic thinking, religion, and prejudice: An experimental test of the dual-process model of mind. *The International Journal for the Psychology of Religion*, 26(4), 360–369. doi:10.1080/10508619.2016.1151117

Yonker, J. E., Edman, L. R. O., Cresswell, J., & Barrett, J. L. (2016). Primed analytic thought and religiosity: The importance of individual characteristics. *Psychology of Religion and Spirituality*, 8(4), 298–308. doi:10.1037/rel0000095

Zuckerman, M., Silberman, J., & Hall, J. A. (2013). The relation between intelligence and religiosity: A meta-analysis and some proposed explanations. *Personality and Social Psychology Review*, 17(4), 325–354. doi:10.1177/1088868313497266

3
TOWARDS UNDERSTANDING INTUITION AND REASON IN PARANORMAL BELIEFS

Marjaana Lindeman

Introduction

When the British anthropologist Sir James Frazer (1854–1941) set out to study the cult of Diana of Aricia, the Roman goddess of the hunt, he eventually ended up with a continuum theory of thinking. He supposed that ways of thinking had developed from magic, through religion, to science over the course of human history. He also wondered whether this kind of development would continue in the future and concluded that "we cannot tell" (Frazer, 1922/1963, p. 827).

Now, after a century, we know the answer. Scientific education has not eliminated supernatural beliefs. In the country with the world's best universities, the United States, there are far more astrologers than astronomers (Gilovich, 1991). In Finland, whose education system has been rated as one of the best in the world, nearly half of the population thinks that angels exist and that death may not be final (The Church Research Institute, 2016). The question of why well-educated individuals still believe in the supernatural is intriguing. Why does the supernatural still captivate even though an exciting and more realistic scientific worldview is available?

Many scientists have been interested in paranormal beliefs, and their multifaceted manifestations, explanations and correlates have received much research attention. Good reviews of the studies in this area are available to the interested reader (e.g., Bering, 2011; Hood, 2009; Irwin, 2009; Vyse, 2014). Books for a wider audience are also worthy of attention (e.g., Hutson, 2012; Shermer, 2011). These works discuss several issues that are not addressed in the present review, including biological and demographic variables and the impact of threat, personality, education and social environment on beliefs.

The focus of the present chapter is in themes that have not been explored in depth in previous work. Due to the advancements in dual-process theories of higher cognition and domain-specific cognition, the focus of the research has expanded to analytical and intuitive thinking and to the content of beliefs. Because the number of such studies has rapidly increased in recent years and has offered new insight, my aim here is to review and discuss paranormal beliefs in terms of these lines of research.

For purposes of simplicity, I will sometimes speak here about believers vs. skeptics, although believing is obviously a non-dichotomic phenomenon. Several concepts have been in use to describe the same type of beliefs. Despite their different etymologies, the concepts 'paranormal,' 'magical,' 'superstitious' and 'supernatural' have been shown to mean the same thing (Lindeman & Svedholm, 2012), so I will use the terms interchangeably. The concept of 'religious' is slightly different. Although belief in the supernatural is the key defining attribute of religiosity, religions also bring with them non-supernatural doctrines, rituals, art and politics, as well as social, moral and emotional aspects, whereas nothing comparable exists with other supernatural beliefs.

I begin negligently, without defining the beliefs, because it has turned out to be a difficult task. Initially, superstitious, paranormal, supernatural and magical beliefs were seen simply as mistakes. This definition is unusable because, in that case, the belief that New York is a city in Texas should be classified as a superstition. Defining beliefs as that which violate the fundamental and scientifically founded principles of nature does not help either. The belief that color is an attribute of a material object contradicts the laws of physics, but it is not a paranormal belief (color is an interpretation that our brain makes about light energy).

Although defining paranormal beliefs has been difficult, the difference between them and other beliefs is intuitively easy to detect. For some reason, everyone knows that believing in ghosts is quite different from an incorrect conception of color. Some scholars even defined the paranormal as phenomena that most members of society would recognize as falling into this category (Campbell, 1996). However, the reason why identification is easy did not attract attention.

Paranormal beliefs and dual-process theories of reasoning

The idea that human thinking is not a singular system is not new. The notion of diverse thinking systems has gone through different variations over the centuries, including the ancient Greek philosophers' distinctions between the rational soul and other souls and the French scientist Blaise Pascal's (1623–1662) timeless quote: "The heart has its reasons, which reason does not know." Perhaps closest to the present perspective was the English philosopher William of Ockham (1287–1347), who distinguished reason from faith and stated radically that scientific explanations should be made without references to the supernatural because the supernatural is simply a question of faith.

Kahneman and Tversky's Nobel Prize-winning work on heuristic decision-making (Kahneman, 2011; Tversky & Kahneman, 1974) and increased knowledge about the human mind and its evolutionary origins overall have greatly advanced our understanding of dual processing in higher cognition. In recent times, dual-process theories have been proposed in several fields of psychology, including social, developmental, personality and cognitive psychology as well as cognitive neuroscience (Evans, 2008; Evans & Stanovich, 2009). Two dual-process theories in particular have been applied to research on paranormal beliefs. Here I refer to them as the Epsteinian approach and the process approach.

The Epsteinian approach

Cognitive-experiential self-theory

One of the most popular theories of the two ways of knowing is Epstein's cognitive-experiential self-theory (CEST), a combined theory of cognition and personality (Epstein, 2010; Epstein & Pacini, 1999; Pacini & Epstein, 1999). According to CEST, humans operate with two information-processing systems that have different operating rules: the experiential system, also known as the intuitive system, and the rational system, also known as the analytical system. The experiential and the rational systems are proposed to operate synchronously under most circumstances, with people only aware of what appears to them to be a single process. However, under other circumstances, as in conflicts between 'reason' and 'the heart,' the different qualities of the two thinking systems become apparent.

The experiential system is assumed to be an evolutionarily old, primarily nonverbal, and automatically operating cognitive system. According to CEST, experiential/ intuitive information processing is holistic, associative and concrete. It is based primarily on experiences: namely, experiences – either direct or vicarious – are the only reality in the system. The experiential system encompasses all phenomena that are based on non-analytical information processing; for instance, irrational fears and superstitions, and especially all kinds of intuitions. In CEST, an intuition is aptly defined as a sense of knowing without knowing how one knows.

Rational/analytical processes, in turn, are described as evolutionarily recent, mostly conscious, and affect-free verbal processes that result in explicit, deliberative knowledge. Concepts of truth and reality are based on logical considerations and evidence rather than personal experiences. Whereas intuitive processes help us to learn from experience and to behave automatically and effectively with minimal cognitive effort, analytical processes can operate at higher levels of abstraction and can correct intuitive biases as well as enable the transmitting of information and the progression of knowledge.

CEST helps us to understand paranormal beliefs in two ways. First, early empirical findings on paranormal believers' ways of thinking and the coexistence of two conflicting beliefs, all thus far conducted along separate lines of research, can be incorporated into one framework. Second, several studies on paranormal beliefs have used the Rational-Experiential Inventory (REI) and have provided important information about believers' and skeptics' thinking styles.

Early empirical work

According to CEST, superstitious thinking has the same attributes as intuitive thinking in general (Epstein, 2010). Of these attributes, associative and holistic thinking in particular have received much research attention, and the findings have been unambiguous. Although not based on CEST, a host of studies have shown that more than nonbelievers, believers connect two or more things liberally together in their minds, resulting in impressions of causality, contagion and covariation (reviews: Rozin & Nemeroff, 2002; Wiseman & Watt, 2006). For example, believers rate randomly paired words (e.g., elephant-banana) as being more closely and meaningfully related than do skeptics (Mohr, Graves, Gianotti, Pizzagalli, & Brugger, 2001).

Moreover, many scholars have mentioned that a special sense of holism – an extreme form of outspread associations – characterizes superstitious and magical thinking. This feeling has been described as a sense of global totality, an undivided unity, an interconnected cosmos and a fundamental relation between a human being and the universe (Malinowski, 1948/1992; Piaget, 1929/1951). In support of these ideas, one study showed that whereas other participants accepted the existence of chance and randomness in the universe, members of a New Age (spiritualist) community believed in a fully determined universe and the unity between self and events in the outside world: "It's not outside, it's all the same," as one interviewee said (see also Farias, Claridge, & Lalljee, 2005; Lesser & Marilyn, 1985, p. 68).

CEST also emphasizes the conflict between intuitive and rational beliefs, an observation that has a long history in studies on paranormal beliefs. Decades ago, Mauss (1902/1972) wrote that in magic the individual does not reason, or if he does, this reasoning is unconscious. Tylor (1871/1974) argued that magic is felt and lived rather than thought. In the report on his ethnographic studies on the Trobriand Islands in New Guinea, Malinowski (1948/1992) described his bafflement upon finding that people can have two so completely contradictory beliefs about one thing. He found, for example, that the Trobrianders believed that the spirit of the dead, Baloma, impregnates women if they bathe in a lagoon and that becoming pregnant in other ways is not possible. At the same time, however, the Trobrianders knew that a man and a woman have to be together to make conception possible.

A similar co-existence of supernatural and rational beliefs has been observed in contemporary studies; for example, in beliefs about the nature of death (Astuti & Harris, 2008), illness (Legare & Gelman, 2008) and biological processes (Lindeman & Saher, 2007). Subbotsky has obtained relevant evidence in many experiments. In one of his studies, adult participants believed in scientific explanations rather than in the experimenter's magic spells when asked verbally what had caused a piece of plastic to be badly scratched after it had been put in a box. When the participants were asked to put their hands in the box, however, they felt more anxious and requested the experimenter not to repeat the magic spell (Subbotsky, 2001).

Many things develop in the same way, by adding new material alongside old content. Our nervous system is hierarchically built, layered like a cake (Peters,

2013), and our body hair stands up when we are cold although we nowadays have more efficient shields against low temperatures. Similarly, studies on learning show that in many cases, science education does not replace intuitive misconceptions and that the misconceptions can coincide with rational knowledge (e.g., Reiner, Slotta, Chi, & Resnick, 2000; Shtulman & Harrington, 2015).

Nonetheless, paranormal beliefs are more paradoxical than many other beliefs: people often know that their beliefs are irrational and unreasonable and that the superstitious rituals they engage in do not work (Epstein & Pacini, 1999; Risen, 2016; Rozin & Nemeroff, 2002). Paranormal beliefs are thus unlike any other incorrect beliefs, as people typically do not believe in the things they consider unbelievable or use expedients they consider to be unworkable.

Rational-Experiential Inventory

One of the main arguments of CEST is that individuals differ in the degree to which they rely on experiential and rational information processing. Because assessment methods for individual differences had been lacking, Epstein, Pacini, Denes-Raj, and Heier (1996) developed the REI. Nowadays, the original REI (Epstein et al., 1996) or its newer versions (Norris & Epstein, 2011; Pacini & Epstein, 1999) constitute one of the most common methods in studies on the relationship between intuitive and analytical thinking and paranormal beliefs.

The REI has two subscales. The Rationality subscale is based on the Need for Cognition scale (NfC; Cacioppo, Petty, Feinstein, & Jarvis, 1996), which assesses engagement in and enjoyment of effortful cognitive activity. The scale includes statements such as 'I enjoy problems that require hard thinking' and 'I prefer complex to simple problems.' The concept of rationality in the name of the subscale is misleading because, as several scholars have mentioned, enjoying thinking does not imply rationality (Petty, Briñol, Loersch, & McCaslin, 2009; Svedholm & Lindeman, 2013; Yates & Chandler, 2000). One can enjoy contemplating nonsense, after all. Therefore here I will use the original and well-established scale name, Need for Cognition.

Items in the other subscale, Faith in Intuition (FI), were generated by Epstein and his colleagues to assess the extent to which individuals depend on gut feelings when making decisions and follow their heart as a guide for actions. Example items include 'I like to rely on my intuitive impressions' and 'I trust my initial feelings about people.' According to CEST, intuitive and analytical thinking styles are not opposites on one continuum but, rather, two independent dimensions. A person can thus be high or low in one or both styles. In support of this argument, several studies have shown a lack of correlation between NfC and FI scores (e.g., Barr, Pennycook, Stolz, & Fugelsang, 2015; Pennycook, Cheyne, Koehler, & Fugelsang, 2016; Pretz & Totz, 2007).

Epstein et al. (1996) were the first to show that when superstitions increase, need for cognition decreases and faith in intuition increases. Most subsequent studies have replicated these findings. The positive relationship between faith in intuition and paranormal beliefs has typically been strong, with correlations usually ranging from 0.35 to 0.50. The association between need for cognition and paranormal beliefs is negative but weaker, with correlations seldom reaching a value higher than −0.25 (e.g., Aarnio & Lindeman, 2007; Epstein et al., 1996; Lindeman & Svedholm-Häkkinen, 2016; Lobato, Mendoza, Sims, & Chin, 2014; Svedholm & Lindeman, 2013).

As a whole, the studies demonstrate quite clearly that people who believe in supernatural phenomena do not enjoy intellectual challenges and prefer to follow their instincts and rely on their intuition. Cognitive motivation to analyze one's thinking and the available information, as measured by the Need for Cognition scale, seems to decrease the beliefs but the correlation is not very strong.

The process approach

'Process approach' refers here to Evans and Stanovich's model of Type 1 and Type 2 processes, previously called System 1 and System 2 (Evans & Stanovich, 2013; Stanovich, West, & Toplak, 2010). Evans and Stanovich are dual-process scholars who first developed their theories independently but have recently integrated their work. This line of research differs from the Epsteinian approach in important respects. Evans (2009) has argued that researchers often confuse these two approaches. He wrote that the two types of cognitive processes simply cannot be equated with such personality characteristics as intuitive and analytical thinking styles, and continued: "I fail to understand how systems and styles can be combined ... in this way" (p. 36). Although we have fallen into this confusion in our research group as well, it is easy to concur with this remark.

According to this approach, Type 1 and Type 2 processes have only a few defining attributes. Type 1 processes are autonomous processes which do not require working memory or controlled attention, whereas Type 2 processes rely heavily on working memory. Other attributes, such as those described by the Epsteinian approach, are regarded only as correlates of the two processes. Examples of Type 1 processes include the behavioral regulation of emotions, evolutionary modules for solving adaptive problems, implicit learning processes and overlearned associations. Type 1 processes yield default responses unless higher-order, Type 2 reasoning processes do not intervene with these judgments and improve or correct them. Type 2 thinking enables uniquely human facilities, such as hypothetical thinking, mental simulation and consequential decision-making.

Applying the process model to paranormal belief

To understand the relationship between analytical thinking and paranormal beliefs, Stanovich's tripartite model of mind is particularly useful. The model divides Type 2 processes further into algorithmic and reflective processes (Stanovich, 2009, 2012; Stanovich & West, 1997). Algorithmic-level processes refer to variations in cognitive abilities, that is, in optimal and maximal performance which is typically assessed with intelligence tests or other cognitive aptitude tests. As we do not constantly use our full intellectual resources and do not try to reach our highest potential in everyday life, examining typical reasoning is at least as important as examining maximum performance. In the tripartite model, typical reasoning processes are known as 'reflective processes.' They are thinking styles, or thinking dispositions, which reflect one's epistemic values and attitudes towards knowledge and the acquisition of information.

Reflective processes

Reflective processes correspond with Epsteinian-type thinking styles but with one essential qualification. In Stanovich's model, individual differences in intuitive and analytic thinking styles are driven by Type 2 processes (i.e., intuitive people are simply non-analytic), whereas in the Epsteinian approach, the intuitive thinking style is usually discussed together with automatic and unconscious Type 1 processes. Stanovich's model thus makes it clear that when we ask people whether they prefer to rely on their intuition and trust their hunches, we are examining Type 2 epistemic styles, not intuitive processes per se. Although the concepts related to epistemic styles and Type 1 and Type 2 processes are often misused, most scholars, I believe, understand the difference and have interpreted their empirical findings properly.

Epstein's and Stanovich's models differ also in the number of thinking styles they deal with. Whereas the Epsteinian approach has examined two independent thinking styles, faith in intuition and need for cognition, Stanovich has focused on reflective thinking, a style close to need for cognition.

Stanovich (2012) described people with strong reflective thinking as individuals who collect information before making up their minds, seek various points of view before drawing conclusions, think extensively about problems before responding and calibrate the degree of strength of their opinions to the degree of evidence available. To assess reflective processes, Stanovich and his colleagues have developed two tests that have been used in research on paranormal belief, the Argument Evaluation Test (AET; Stanovich & West, 1997) and the Actively Open-minded Thinking scale (AOT; Sá, West, & Stanovich, 1999).

AET assesses a person's ability to evaluate the objective quality of several arguments (e.g., whether the welfare system should be drastically cut back in size). The test has several phases and the quality of the arguments has to be determined by expert judges, so only a few researchers have used AET in studies on paranormal beliefs. Stanovich and West (1997) found that those with a high reliance on argument quality displayed significantly lower scores on a superstitious thinking scale than other participants. Similarly, Gray and Gallo (2016) found that skeptics were better than believers at evaluating the quality of the arguments presented. Also, in our study, those who were good at evaluating arguments believed less in astrology, telepathy and other paranormal phenomena than other participants (Svedholm & Lindeman, 2013).

In studies on paranormal beliefs and analytical thinking style, the strongest associations have been observed for actively open-minded thinking. The AOT scale includes 41 statements; for example, 'Changing your mind is a sign of weakness' (reverse coded), 'There are basically two kinds of people in this world, good and bad,' and 'No one can talk me out of something I know is right.' Overall, actively open-minded thinking indicates openness to new ideas, spending a great deal of time on problems before giving up, and willingness to change one's beliefs and to switch perspectives (Sá et al., 1999). The correlations between AOT and adults' disbelief in superstitions have been as strong as approximately 0.50 (Sá, Kelley, Ho, & Stanovich, 2005; Svedholm & Lindeman, 2013) and between 0.30 and 0.40 among children (Kokis, Macpherson, Toplak, West, & Stanovich, 2002; Toplak, West, & Stanovich, 2014). Thus it seems that actively open-minded thinking captures something essential to paranormal beliefs and taps critical thinking better than the Need for Cognition scale.

Overall, the above findings support the idea that reflective thinking hinders paranormal beliefs or, more generally, that Type 2 processes override intuitive judgments if an error is detected. However, recall that people often know that their paranormal beliefs are irrational and that their superstitious rituals do not work. In other words, people can detect an error but choose nevertheless not to correct it – a process Risen (2016) referred to as acquiescence. These findings cannot be easily explained by the original process approach. As Risen has argued, dual-process models have an unstated assumption that when people detect an error, they will correct it (but see Pennycook, Fugelsang, & Koehler, 2015). However, the superstition and magical thinking literature evinces that this assumption does not always hold. To resolve this contradiction, Risen argued that the *detection* and *correction* of error must be decoupled (see also De Neys, 2014). Analyzing the processes underlying acquiescence in future studies can shed new explanatory light on paranormal beliefs.

Algorithmic processes: intellectual abilities

Research on the relationship between paranormal beliefs and algorithmic processes, more commonly known as cognitive abilities, has a longer history than research on thinking styles. Nevertheless, the results have been more contradictory than those obtained concerning reflective processes.

To illustrate, some studies show that believers have slightly lower intelligence than skeptics (Hergovich & Arendasy, 2005; Killen, Wildman, & Wildman II, 1974; Sá et al., 2005). However, other studies suggest that paranormal beliefs are not strongly related to fluid intelligence (Stuart-Hamilton, Nayak, & Priest, 2006), verbal intelligence (Pennycook, Cheyne, Seli, Koehler, & Fugelsang, 2012) or memory tasks (a review: Gray & Gallo, 2016). Similarly, some studies indicate that believers make more probability errors than skeptics (Pennycook et al., 2012; Rogers, 2014), while other studies refute these findings (Blackmore, 1997; Musch & Ehrenberg, 2002). Finally, some studies show that deductive reasoning errors increase as paranormal beliefs increase (Lawrence & Peters, 2004; Wierzbicki, 1985). Again, opposite findings show that having paranormal beliefs does not predict failure in logical reasoning tasks (Gray & Gallo, 2016; Lesser & Marilyn, 1985).

When considering paranormal beliefs and intellectual abilities, the Cognitive Reflection Test (CRT; Frederick, 2005) should also be mentioned as it is a much-used test in research on paranormal and religious beliefs. The CRT is a good measure of both cognitive ability and reflective thinking style (Toplak, West, & Stanovich, 2011). It assesses the tendency of individuals to suppress an intuitive and spontaneous response and to reflect on the question further to find the correct response. An example is as follows: "A bat and a ball cost $1.10 in total. The bat costs $1.00 more than the ball. How much does the ball cost?" Research results quite consistently show that when paranormal beliefs increase, correct responses decrease (Bouvet & Bonnefon, 2015; Cheyne & Pennycook, 2013; Lindeman & Svedholm-Häkkinen, 2016; Pennycook et al., 2012; but see Toplak et al., 2011). The associations have not been very strong, however, possibly because doing well on the test strongly depends on cognitive abilities.

Algorithmic processes: cognitive inhibition

It is also possible that unintentional cognitive inhibition may play an important role in establishing and maintaining paranormal beliefs. Cognitive inhibition refers to the stopping or overriding of a mental process; for example, suppressing unwanted or irrelevant thoughts and gating irrelevant information from working memory. It is like a guardian in the intuitive mind – in the jungle where a variety of cognitive processes and competences are likely at any moment to collide, clash and compete (Houdé, 2000; Kipp Harnishfeger, 1995). Cognitive inhibition is one of the main features of executive functions, the key computational function of the algorithmic mind (Stanovich, 2009).

Although cognitive inhibition has received little research attention in the field of paranormal beliefs, it is noteworthy how similar the correlates of paranormal beliefs are to the correlates of decreased cognitive inhibition. Like paranormal beliefs, weak cognitive inhibition is associated with anxiety and neuroticism (a review: Nigg, 2000), feelings of threat (Linville, 1996), loose associations (White & Shah, 2006) and intuitive thinking (Moutier & Houdé, 2003). Moreover, severe breakdowns in cognitive inhibition occur in diseases that are also associated with supernatural beliefs; for example, in schizophrenia (Nigg, 2000).

Although empirical evidence is limited, some studies suggest that believers in the supernatural have weaker cognitive inhibition than disbelievers. First, paranormal believers have performed more poorly than skeptics on each subscale of the Wisconsin Card Sorting Test, including on perseverative errors (Lindeman, Riekki, & Hood, 2011), the subscale most often connected with inhibitory problems. In addition, a functional magnetic resonance imaging (fMRI) study showed that when participants were viewing pictures inducing supernatural explanations for the stories they had read, brain regions indicating cognitive inhibition were activated more strongly in skeptics than in supernatural believers (Lindeman, Svedholm, Riekki, Raij, & Hari, 2013).

Summary

The main findings from the two dual-process approaches can now be summarized as follows. The results concerning cognitive abilities are the most equivocal. On the one hand, if differences in intellectual abilities exist, the direction is usually the same in that believers show lower cognitive competence than disbelievers. On the other hand, the difference is small. Moreover, decreased unintentional cognitive inhibition can also predict paranormal beliefs, but the evidence is still preliminary.

Results on variations in Type 2 reflective processes are more robust: compared with skeptics, the thinking style of paranormal believers is more intuitive and less analytical. Although the association between beliefs and analytical thinking style has sometimes been weak, the tendency of believers to score low on the AOT has been exceptionally strong, implying believers' epistemological absolutism, cognitive rigidity, dogmatism, categorical thinking and resistance to belief change. However, only a few studies on paranormal beliefs have used the AOT, so future studies are needed to confirm the findings.

Caveats and questions

Most of the above-cited results were based on bivariate correlations or comparisons between believer and skeptic groups. These results can give false impressions; for example, that paranormal beliefs increase linearly with increasing faith in intuition and decreasing need for cognition, actively open-minded thinking and correct Cognitive Reflection Test responses. That is not necessarily the case, however.

First, all believers may not be intuitive thinkers and all skeptics may not be analytical thinkers. Among religious believers and nonbelievers (Lindeman & Lipsanen, 2016), as well as among religious, paranormal and spiritual believers (Schofield, Baker, Staples, & Sheffield, 2016), there might be different subgroups which cannot be detected with variable-centered analyses such as correlations and analyses of variance. One study has indeed revealed such unexpected groups as analytically thinking paranormal believers and skeptics who trust their intuitions (Napola, 2015). In this study, the majority of skeptics (84%) had higher need for cognition than faith in intuition, but 16% of them had the opposite. Of believers, in turn, 56% had higher faith in intuition than need for cognition, 30% had higher need for cognition than faith in intuition, and among 14% of the participants, need for cognition and faith in intuition were both high. Although the previously found trend concerning beliefs and thinking styles was hence primarily confirmed, the results remind us of the possibility that believers and skeptics are not homogeneous groups, but can represent subgroups which differ in their cognitive characteristics. This is plausible as many other factors affect paranormal beliefs, such as education, social environment and personality.

Second, it would be important to know whether the various thinking styles are independent from each other or whether they overlap and, if they do, which of the methods predict paranormal beliefs best. To address this question, I analyzed the contributions of faith in intuition, need for cognition, actively open-minded thinking and correct CRT responses by performing a regression analysis of our data (N = 2,789 Finnish individuals; for more details about the data, see Lindeman, Svedholm-Häkkinen, & Lipsanen, 2015). The results showed that after controlling for age and sex, high faith in intuition was by far the strongest predictor of paranormal beliefs ($\beta = 0.37$, $p < 0.001$). Actively open-minded thinking ($\beta = -0.18$, $p < 0.001$) and correct CRT responses ($\beta = -0.08$, $p < 0.001$) also made a unique contribution to the beliefs. The only variable which had no relationship with the beliefs was need for cognition ($\beta = -0.01$, ns). In other words, faith in intuition, actively open-minded thinking and CRT performance all had independent effects on paranormal beliefs when the effects of the other thinking styles were eliminated. Although the results may imply that need for cognition is covered by the other scales, it is important to remember that such results are often unstable and depend heavily on the data.

The above results may highlight the possibility that actively open-minded thinking, the reflective processes measured by CRT, and need for cognition are lower-level constructs that underlie a more general master rationality motive (MRM). MRM is a concept coined by Stanovich (2008, 2011). It is a high-level control motivational state that resides in the reflective mind and drives the search for the cognitive critique of our beliefs and for the rational integration of inconsistent and incompatible beliefs and desires. Persons with a strong MRM want their beliefs to be true, want to act in accordance with reason and find a lack of rational integration aversive. Because MRM is proposed to be a more general cognitive disposition than actively open-minded thinking and related thinking styles, it is probable that people who are skeptical about paranormal beliefs will score high on the scale. So far, however, the scale has not been used in studies on paranormal beliefs.

Bringing all of the above-described results and arguments together, it is safe to conclude that strong intuitive thinking style and low analytical thinking style predict paranormal (supernatural, magical, superstitious) beliefs and that both intuitive and analytical thinking styles make independent contributions to these beliefs. These findings raise one central question: are intuitive and analytical thinking sufficient to explain paranormal beliefs? For example, how do the findings on paranormal believers' strong intuitive thinking fit with the fact that intuitions can also produce ingenious works? Michael S. Brown, who was awarded the Nobel Prize in medicine in 1985, has said that his research group went from one step to the next and that somehow they knew which was the right way to go: "And I can't really tell you how we knew that" (cited in Claxton, 2006, p. 58). Einstein said the same thing: "Words and language, whether written or spoken, do not seem to play any part in my thought processes" (Hadamard, 1954, p. 142). Of course, scientific thinking proceeds from intuitions to reflective thinking and verbalizable arguments because intuitive thinking in scientific work means a stage of thinking, not a permanent thinking style. Nonetheless, the intuitive thinking style influences a host of affairs ranging from job type to food choice in everyday life (e.g., Akinci & Sadler-Smith, 2013; Ares, Mawad, Giménez, & Maiche, 2014). In other words, intuitive and analytical thinking styles can apply to all thought irrespective of its content, and yet it is their peculiar content that sets paranormal beliefs apart from other unfounded beliefs. In our studies, we have explored the possibility that core knowledge confusions underlie all paranormal beliefs and that it is these intuitive confusions that intuitive thinkers count on whereas analytical thinkers do not.

Paranormal beliefs and core knowledge confusions

The term 'core knowledge' refers to knowledge about evolutionarily important entities and processes in the world. It is knowledge that children universally learn, almost without explicit instruction and irrespective of culture, roughly at the same age early in life (Carey, 1985; Spelke & Kinzler, 2007; Wellman & Gelman, 1998).

Although the exact nature of core knowledge remains to be determined, increasing evidence suggests that what is critical when considering paranormal beliefs are the main properties that differentiate the mental from the physical – and within the physical domain, animate from inanimate and living from lifeless. The differences can be summarized as follows: Physical phenomena are material and objective but mental phenomena (beliefs, desires and emotions) are subjective and immaterial. Animate beings can commit intentional, purposeful acts, but inanimate entities cannot. Physical objects have an independent existence in space, while mental states do not, and they can move other objects by physical force, whereas mental states also cannot. Living organisms grow and die; lifeless ones do not. And finally, access to the physical world is necessary for perception, which informs beliefs and knowledge, but desires and emotions can arise mentally without biological senses.

The vast majority of core knowledge develops by preschool age, but the differences between the domains are not at once entirely clear. Jean Piaget was among the first to demonstrate the varieties of mental-physical confusions among children. For example, when he interviewed a 7-year-old girl about the nature of a thought, the girl explained that a thought is in the head, that it is white and round, and that one cannot see it because it is too far back in the mouth (Piaget, 1929/1951).

Our own research on paranormal beliefs has been inspired by how analogous children's confusions are to those found in adults' paranormal beliefs. A few examples which illustrate the similarity are given below.

> *Children*: Children do not appreciate that biological senses, such as vision and hearing, are necessary conditions for informational access, but see knowledge as arising purely mentally within the individual, like desires (Wimmer, Hogrefe, & Perner, 1988). For example, young children might believe that a person can know which toy is hidden in a container although the person has never seen the toy (Pillow & Weed, 1997).
> *Adults*: Belief in telepathy, clairvoyance and precognition.
> *Children*: Developing understanding of intentional behavior and the human manufacture of artifacts induces small children to see all kinds of things in terms of purpose and intentional design. They may think that mountains

are made for climbing, that clouds are for raining and that the sun is for warmth (Kelemen, 1999; Piaget, 1929/1951).

Adults: Belief in creationism and the purpose of events.

Children: As long as knowledge of biological processes as the prerequisites of life is undeveloped, understanding the finality of death is not possible (Carey, 1985). Although young children may understand that the dead cannot eat or drink, they tend to believe that psychological states, especially beliefs, emotions and desires, can continue after death (Bering & Bjorklund, 2004).

Adults: Belief in an afterlife.

Children: Young children have difficulties in understanding the representational nature of symbols, and they tend to equate symbolic contents with the objects they represent. In interviews, many children thought that the sun had always had its name, that the name of the sun was in the sun, and that we could see the name if we looked at the sun (Piaget, 1929/1951). The responses reveal that the children had not yet grasped the idea that symbols have no realistic connection to their referents, any more than saying the word 'rain' can cause it to actually rain.

Adults: Belief in tarot cards and astrology.

Children: Before the mental-physical distinction is fully developed, children tend to believe that reality can be modified by thoughts and desires. In Vikan and Clausen's (1993) study, almost all 4- to 6-year-olds believed that a child who is in school could influence her mother at home just by making a wish. In another study, 3-year-olds believed that an object could appear inside a box if they first thought about the object (Woolley & Wellman, 1993).

Adults: Belief in psychokinesis and telekinesis; that is, the capacity of thoughts to influence physical objects.

In the above examples, children and adults make category mistakes: they borrow properties of one category (e.g., physical objects) to characterize an entity in another ontological category (e.g., mental phenomena). Category mistakes are different from ordinate mistakes. If we say that "the thunderstorm is broken," we are making a category mistake because a thunderstorm is an event, not a material object which can break (Chi & Hausmann, 2003). However, if we think that the planet Venus has electromagnetic effects on the Earth, we are making an ordinate mistake. If we think that the symbolic attributes of harmony and solidarity, which astrologers have assigned to Venus, influence the Earth, we are making a category mistake.

We have earlier demonstrated that paranormal, superstitious, magical and supernatural beliefs can be best defined as core knowledge confusions (Lindeman & Svedholm, 2012). This definition has many advantages. It can integrate several constructs that have been used in separate lines of research into beliefs (e.g., animism, anthropomorphism, promiscuous teleological reasoning, spirituality and mind-body dualism). The definition also helps us to outline which beliefs should be categorized as paranormal and which should not. For example, belief in graphology may be unfounded, but it is not superstitious because it does not include any category mistakes (for details, see Lindeman & Svedholm, 2012).

Ontological violations in supernatural beliefs are also discussed in the field of cognitive science of religion. The main tenet is that religious concepts violate a few but never many ontological assumptions about persons, animals, plants, artifacts or natural, nonliving objects. Thus, an admiring horse or a flying cow is a supernatural concept but a chattering, climbing pig is not (Atran & Norenzayan, 2005; Upala, Gonce, Tweney, & Slone, 2007). We, in contrast, have suggested that mixing the core attributes of the higher-order categories of mental and physical, animate and inanimate, and living and lifeless, rather than the number of violations, is essential. Hence, according to our framework, none of those examples are good examples of supernatural beliefs because the ability to differentiate between flying and non-flying animals, or animate beings with complex emotions and animate beings without, is not core knowledge. Moreover, I would argue that the reason why people find it easy to differentiate supernatural beliefs from other unfounded beliefs is expressly the mix-up of the basic properties of mental and physical, animate and inanimate, and living and lifeless. That is why an incorporeal spirit feels more descriptive of the supernatural than a flying cow.

Much evidence shows that people who believe in paranormal phenomena make more ontological mistakes in core knowledge than do skeptics (Barber, 2014; Lindeman & Aarnio, 2007; Lindeman, Blomqvist, & Takada, 2012; Lindeman et al., 2008; Lobato et al., 2014; Pennycook, Cheyne, Barr, Koehler, & Fugelsang, 2015; Svedholm, Lindeman, & Lipsanen, 2010). Most of these studies have used a sentence-rating task. In this task, participants are presented with statements which mix the core attributes of lifeless and living (e.g., 'Stars live in the sky'), lifeless and animate (e.g., 'Earth wants water'), and inanimate and animate organisms (e.g., 'The house knows its history') as well as mental phenomena and physical objects (e.g., 'Grief moves in the stomach').

That core knowledge confusions in particular are typical of believers is implied by findings showing that believers rate these sentences as more literally true than skeptics do. However, believers do not differ from skeptics when rating the literal truth of clearly literal sentences (e.g., 'Mozart was a composer') or clearly metaphorical ones (e.g., 'The surprising piece of news is a bomb'). We have also found, as might be expected, that analytical thinkers have less ontological confusions than intuitive thinkers (Lindeman, 2011; Lindeman & Aarnio, 2007; Svedholm & Lindeman, 2013). Furthermore, confusions between mental and non-mental phenomena have even been observed in perceptual processes: more so than skeptics, paranormal believers detect illusory agents and illusory faces (Van Elk, 2013; Riekki, Lindeman, Aleneff, Halme, & Nuortimo, 2013) and attribute intentions to random movement (Riekki, Lindeman, & Raij, 2014).

An intriguing possibility is that ontological violations are side effects of human mental design and that they retain their autonomous power from childhood throughout life and explain supernatural beliefs among adults. This is what several scholars in the cognitive science of religion have suggested (e.g., Barrett, 2000; Bering, 2006; Guthrie, 1993; Hood, 2009; Kelemen, 2004). For example, according to Guthrie (1993), seeing intentional agents is an evolutionarily based, involuntary, mostly unconscious process which produces false positives: because detecting intentional agents has been adaptive in our evolutionary past, people may notice intentional beings even in inanimate nature. In the same way, there are no false negatives in nonreligious paranormal beliefs, only false positives; for example, thoughts are assumed to be over-powerful and the mind, over-sovereign. Thus, universal cognitive architecture may be responsible for the existence of paranormal beliefs, whereas culture is responsible for the specific forms the beliefs might take.

At first sight, the fact that millions of people all over the world do not believe in the supernatural seems to challenge the above argument. And we have already seen that disbelievers do not endorse ontological confusions but take them metaphorically. However, most of the studies concerned were based on self-reports, and they leave open the possibility that implicit ontological confusions can also be endorsed implicitly.

We recall that skeptics may, in general, have stronger cognitive inhibition than believers. Inhibition can also be temporarily compromised by asking study participants to respond very quickly. Speeded responding increases cognitive load and causes inhibitory failures, making judgments more reflective of intuitive processes. Preliminary evidence does indeed suggest that when forced to think intuitively, ontological confusions can be found not only among paranormal believers but among other people as well.

Kelemen and her colleagues (Kelemen & Rosset, 2009; Kelemen, Rottman, & Seston, 2013) have conducted several experimental studies on the role of inhibition in endorsing unwarranted intentional explanations. They showed that if asked to respond quickly, university students and even physical scientists explained natural phenomena, such as sunlight, by reference to a purpose and design in nature. In our study as well, the number of ontological confusions increased across all participants when asked to respond quickly (Svedholm & Lindeman, 2013). Importantly, the confusions lost their relationship to paranormal beliefs under speeded responding, which possibly indicates that even individuals who do not believe in paranormal phenomena make similar confusions under demanding conditions. It may thus be the case that ontological confusions can be implicit and that, consequently, they are most discernible when thinking is dominated by intuitive processing.

Why people believe

As a summary, we can now delineate an overall, albeit tentative, view of intuition and reason in the formation and maintenance of paranormal beliefs.

Paranormal beliefs are best understood as culturally and historically variable beliefs that are based on ontological confusions of core knowledge about physical, psychological and biological phenomena. These confusions are typical of the early phases of children's cognitive development, and it is possible, although not yet rigorously proven, that the misconceptions do not disappear when growing up. In adulthood, the confusions can be unintentionally inhibited, or they can suddenly come to mind as intuitions that can either be trusted or intentionally rejected as irrelevant.

Particularly, individuals with an intuitive thinking style tend to consider ontologically impossible phenomena to be feasible, making the adoption of culturally available supernatural ideas possible. Belief in ghosts and other spirits is possible only if one accepts, in one way or another, that a mind can live without a biological body. The intuitive thinking style also entails a broad spectrum of heuristics and biases which further make culturally prevailing paranormal conceptions easy to digest. Associative and experiential thought processes can predispose an individual to assume that the co-occurrence of a full moon and a strange experience reflects causation, or that one's personal experience of a flash of light, and the interpretation associated with it, proves the existence of angels.

Concurrently with ontological confusions and paranormal beliefs, intuitive thinkers may have rational and well-founded knowledge about the same things. Conflicting beliefs can be held in parallel because they are processed differently, one more analytically and the other more unconsciously. That intuition speaks in favor of the supernatural although reason can find no rational foundations for the beliefs is sometimes frankly admitted. As a Finnish vicar has said: "I allow myself a belief in the virgin birth although I understand that according to modern biology it is impossible."

Some people, in turn, try to explain the conflict away. However, it is easier to believe in astrology than to convincingly explain how it works, and it is easier to believe in God than to justify his existence. The conflict breeds foggy metaphors and ambiguous rationalizations: we try to explain verbally something which cannot be verbalized. This sits well with the view of Epstein and Pacini (1999), Stanovich (2004) and Evans (2010) that confabulation is one of the functions of the reflective mind: "We make up stories to maintain the illusion that we are the chief executive who is really in control" (Evans, 2010, p. 6).

Although intuitions are compelling as well as resistant to change, and deep-rooted culturally shared supernatural beliefs can be difficult to resist, they both can be abandoned after critical evaluation. Cognitive abilities may be one underlying factor, but an analytical thinking style is more important. A critical attitude towards ontological confusions and the supernatural is particularly characteristic of individuals who prefer actively open-minded thinking; that is, those who aim at flexible and objective reasoning and who avoid absolutism, dichotomies and dogmatism.

Analytical thinkers are also able to avoid general cognitive biases. Among other things, they are better at detecting conflicts; for example, between reality and supernatural beliefs (Pennycook, Cheyne, Barr, Koehler, & Fugelsang, 2014). Furthermore, for analytical thinkers, the personal experience of a psychic's ability to accurately predict a specific event does not suffice: clairvoyance cannot be rationally explained, and psychics have so far not managed to demonstrate their abilities under objective conditions. Because reflective thinkers seek various points of view before making a conclusion, they have also noticed, for instance, what was wrong when astrologers claimed that the murder of Swedish politician Anna Lindh in 2003 could be forecasted from her astrological chart. All of the forecasts were given after the murder.

To conclude, I quote the philosopher Bertrand Russell (1921/1949, p. 231), who wrote that belief is the central problem in the analysis of mind: "Believing seems the most mental thing we do. ... The whole intellectual life consists of beliefs, and of the passages from one belief to another." By carefully scrutinizing what we believe and why, not only may critical thinking increase, but eternal questions such as 'what is the purpose of life?' might also be approached from a new point of view. That is, not as a difficult question to which the correct answer is hard to find, but as a question that is wrongly posed.

References

Aarnio, K., & Lindeman, M. (2007). Religious people and paranormal believers: Alike or different? *Journal of Individual Differences*, 28(1), 1–9. doi:00A0;10.1027/1614-0001.28.1.1

Akinci, C., & Sadler-Smith, E. (2013). Assessing individual differences in experiential (intuitive) and rational (analytical) cognitive styles. *International Journal of Selection and Assessment*, 21(2), 211–221. doi:00A0;10.1111/ijsa.12030

Ares, G., Mawad, F., Giménez, A., & Maiche, A. (2014). Influence of rational and intuitive thinking styles on food choice: Preliminary evidence from an eye-tracking study with yogurt labels. *Food Quality and Preference*, 31, 28–37. doi:00A0;10.1016/j.foodqual.2013.07.005

Astuti, R., & Harris, P. L. (2008). Understanding mortality and the life of the ancestors in rural Madagascar. *Cognitive Science*, 32(4), 713–740. doi:00A0;10.1080/03640210802066907

Atran, S., & Norenzayan, A. (2005). Religion's evolutionary landscape: Counterintuition, commitment, compassion, communion. *Behavioral and Brain Sciences*, 27(6), 713–730. doi:00A0;10.1017/S0140525X04000172

Barber, J. (2014). Believing in a purpose of events: Cross-cultural evidence of confusions in core knowledge. *Applied Cognitive Psychology*, 28(3), 432–437. doi:00A0;10.1002/acp.3003

Barr, N., Pennycook, G., Stolz, J. A., & Fugelsang, J. A. (2015). Reasoned connections: A dual-process perspective on creative thought. *Thinking & Reasoning*, 21(1), 61–75. doi:00A0;10.1080/13546783.2014.895915

Barrett, J. L. (2000). Exploring the natural foundations of religion. *Trends in Cognitive Sciences*, 4(1), 29–34. doi:00A0;10.1016/S1364-6613(99)01419-01419

Bering, J. M. (2006). The folk psychology of souls. *Behavioral and Brain Sciences*, 29(5), 453–462. doi:00A0;10.1017/S0140525X06009101

Bering, J. M. (2011). *The belief instinct*. New York: Norton.

Bering, J. M., & Bjorklund, D. F. (2004). The natural emergence of reasoning about the afterlife as a developmental regularity. *Developmental Psychology*, 40(2), 217–233. doi:00A0;10.1037/0012-1649.40.2.217

Blackmore, S. (1997). Probability misjudgment and belief in the paranormal: A newspaper survey. *British Journal of Psychology*, 88(4), 683–690. doi:00A0;10.1111/j.2044-8295.1997.tb02665.x

Bouvet, R., & Bonnefon, J.-F. (2015). Non-reflective thinkers are predisposed to attribute supernatural causation to uncanny experiences. *Personality and Social Psychology Bulletin*, 41(7), 955–961. doi:00A0;10.1177/0146167215585728

Cacioppo, J. T., Petty, R. E., Feinstein, J. A., & Jarvis, W. B. G. (1996). Dispositional differences in cognitive motivation: The life and times of individuals varying in need for cognition. *Psychological Bulletin*, 119(2), 197–253. doi:00A0;10.1037/0033-2909.119.2.197

Campbell, C. (1996). Half-belief and the paradox of ritual instrumental activism: A theory of modern superstition. *British Journal of Sociology*, 47(1), 151–166. Retrieved from www.jstor.org/stable/591121.

Carey, S. (1985). *Conceptual change in childhood*. London: MIT Press.

Cheyne, J. A., & Pennycook, G. (2013). Sleep paralysis postepisode distress modeling potential effects of episode characteristics, general psychological distress, beliefs, and cognitive style. *Clinical Psychological Science*, 1(2), 135–148. doi:00A0;10.1177/2167702612466656

Chi, M. T. H., & Hausmann, R. G. M. (2003). Do radical discoveries require ontological shifts? In L. V. Shavinina (Ed.), *International handbook on innovation* (Vol. 3, pp. 430–444). Dordrech: Elsevier.

Claxton, G. (2006). Beyond cleverness: How to be smart without thinking. In J. Henry (Ed.), *Creative management and development* (pp. 47–63). London: Sage.

De Neys, W. (2014). Conflict detection, dual processes, and logical intuitions: Some clarifications. *Thinking & Reasoning*, 20(2), 169–187. doi:00A0;10.1080/13546783.2013.854725

Epstein, S. (2010). Demystifying intuition: What it is, what it does, and how it does it. *Psychological Inquiry*, 21(4), 295–312. doi:00A0;10.1080/1047840X.2010.523875

Epstein, S., & Pacini, R. (1999). Some basic issues regarding dual-process theories from the perspective of cognitive-experiential self-theory. In S. Chaiken & Y. Trope (Eds.), *Dual-process theories in social psychology* (pp. 462–482). New York: Guilford Press.

Epstein, S., Pacini, R., Denes-Raj, V., & Heier, H. (1996). Individual differences in intuitive-experiential and analytical-rational thinking styles. *Journal of Personality and Social Psychology*, 71(2), 390–405. doi:00A0;10.1037/0022-3514.71.2.390

Evans, J. St. B. T. (2008). Dual-processing accounts of reasoning, judgment and social cognition. *Annual Review of Psychology*, 59, 255–278. doi:00A0;10.1146/annurev.psych.59.103006.093629

Evans, J. St. B. T. (2009). How many dual-process theories do we need? One, two, or many? In J. St. B. T. Evans (Ed.), *In two minds: Dual processes and beyond* (pp. 33–54). New York: Oxford University Press.

Evans, J. St. B. T. (2010). *Thinking twice*. Oxford: Oxford University Press.

Evans, J. St. B. T., & Stanovich, K. E. (Eds.). (2009). *In two mind: Dual processes and beyond*. Oxford: Oxford University Press.

Evans, J. St. B. T., & Stanovich, K. E. (2013). Dual-process theories of higher cognition: Advancing the debate. *Perspectives on Psychological Science*, 8(3), 223–241. doi:00A0;10.1177/1745691612460685

Farias, M., Claridge, G., & Lalljee, M. (2005). Personality and cognitive predictors of New Age practices and beliefs. *Personality and Individual Differences*, 39(5), 979–989.

Frazer, J. G. (1922/1963). *The golden bough: A study in magic and religion*. New York: Macmillan.

Frederick, S. (2005). Cognitive reflection and decision making. *The Journal of Economic Perspectives*, 19(4), 25–42. doi:00A0;10.1257/089533005775196732

Gilovich, T. (1991). *How we know what isn't so: The fallibility of human reason in everyday*. New York: The Free Press.

Gray, S. J., & Gallo, D. A. (2016). Paranormal psychic believers and skeptics: A large-scale test of the cognitive differences hypothesis. *Memory & Cognition*, 44(2), 242–261. doi:00A0;10.3758/s13421-13015-0563-x

Guthrie, S. (1993). *Faces in the clouds*. New York: Oxford University Press.

Hadamard, J. (1954). *An essay on the psychology of invention in the mathematical field*. New York: Dover.

Hergovich, A., & Arendasy, M. (2005). Critical thinking ability and belief in the paranormal. *Personality and Individual Differences*, 38(8), 1805–1812. doi:00A0;10.1016/j.paid.2004.11.008

Hood, B. M. (2009). *SuperSense: From superstition to religion – the brain science of belief.* London: Constable and Robinson.

Houdé, O. (2000). Inhibition and cognitive development: Object, number, categorization, and reasoning. *Cognitive Development*, 15(1), 63–73. doi:00A0;10.1016/S0885-2014(00)00015-0

Hutson, M. (2012). *The laws of magical thinking: How irrationality makes us happy, healthy and sane.* Oxford: Oneworld Publications.

Irwin, H. J. (2009). *The psychology of paranormal: A researcher's handbook.* Hertfordshire: University of Hertfordshire Press.

Kahneman, D. (2011). *Thinking, fast and slow.* New York: Farrar, Straus & Giroux.

Kelemen, D. (1999). The scope of teleological thinking in preschool children. *Cognition*, 70(3), 241–272. doi:00A0;10.1016/S0010-0277(99)00010-00014

Kelemen, D. (2004). Are children "intuitive theists"? *Psychological Science*, 15(5), 295–301. doi:00A0;10.1111/j.0956-7976.2004.00672.x

Kelemen, D., & Rosset, E. (2009). The human function compunction: Teleological explanation in adults. *Cognition*, 111(1), 138–143. doi:00A0;10.1016/j.cognition.2009.01.001

Kelemen, D., Rottman, J., & Seston, R. (2013). Professional physical scientists display tenacious teleological tendencies: Purpose-based reasoning as a cognitive default. *Journal of Experimental Psychology: General*, 142(4), 1074–1083. doi:00A0;10.1037/a0030399

Killen, P., Wildman, R. W., & Wildman II, R. W. (1974). Superstitiousness and intelligence. *Psychological Reports*, 34(3 suppl.), 1158. doi:00A0;10.2466/pr0.1974.34.3c.1158

Kipp Harnishfeger, K. (1995). The development of cognitive inhibition. In F. N. Dempster & C. J. Brainerd (Eds.), *Interference and inhibition in cognition* (pp. 175–204). San Diego: Academic Press.

Kokis, J. V., Macpherson, R., Toplak, M. E., West, R. F., & Stanovich, K. E. (2002). Heuristic and analytic processing: Age trends and associations with cognitive ability and cognitive styles. *Journal of Experimental Child Psychology*, 83(1), 26–52. doi:00A0;10.1016/S0022-0965(02)00121-00122

Lawrence, E., & Peters, E. (2004). Reasoning in believers in the paranormal. *Journal of Nervous and Mental Disease*, 192(11), 727–733. Retrieved from http://journals.lww.com/jonmd/Abstract/2004/11000. doi:00A0;10.1097/01.nmd.0000144691.22135.d0

Legare, C. H., & Gelman, S. A. (2008). Bewitchment, biology, or both: The co-existence of natural and supernatural explanatory frameworks across development. *Cognitive Science*, 32(4), 607–642. doi:00A0;10.1080/03640210802066766

Lesser, R., & Marilyn, P. (1985). Magical thinking in formal operational adults. *Human Development*, 28, 57–70. doi:00A0;10.1159/000272942

Lindeman, M. (2011). Biases in intuitive reasoning and belief in complementary and alternative medicine. *Psychology & Health*, 26(3), 371–382. doi:00A0;10.1080/08870440903440707

Lindeman, M., & Aarnio, K. (2007). Superstitious, magical, and paranormal beliefs: An integrative model. *Journal of Research in Personality*, 41(4), 731–744. doi:00A0;10.1016/j.jrp.2006.06.009

Lindeman, M., Blomqvist, S., & Takada, M. (2012). Distinguishing spirituality from other constructs: Not a matter of well-being but of belief in supernatural spirits. *Journal of Nervous and Mental Disease*, 200(2), 167–173. doi:00A0;10.1097/NMD.0b013e3182439719

Lindeman, M., Cederström, S., Simola, P., Simula, A., Ollikainen, S., & Riekki, T. (2008). Sentences with core knowledge violations increase the size of N400 among paranormal believers. *Cortex*, 44(10), 1307–1315. doi:00A0;10.1016/j.cortex.2007.07.010

Lindeman, M., & Lipsanen, J. (2016). Diverse cognitive profiles of religious believers and non-believers. *International Journal for the Psychology of Religion*, 26(3), 185–192. doi:00A0;10.1080/10508619.2015.1091695

Lindeman, M., Riekki, T., & Hood, B. M. (2011). Is weaker inhibition associated with supernatural beliefs? *Journal of Cognition and Culture*, 11(1–2), 231–239. doi:00A0;10.1163/156853711X570038

Lindeman, M., & Saher, M. (2007). Vitalism, purpose and superstition. *British Journal of Psychology*, 98(1), 33–44. doi:00A0;10.1348/000712606X101808

Lindeman, M., & Svedholm, A. M. (2012). What's in a term? Paranormal, superstitious, magical and supernatural beliefs by any other name would mean the same. *Review of General Psychology*, 16(3), 241–255. doi:00A0;10.1037/a0027158

Lindeman, M., Svedholm, A. M., Riekki, T., Raij, T., & Hari, R. (2013). Is it just a brick wall or a sign from the universe? An fMRI study of supernatural believers and skeptics. *Social Cognitive and Affective Neuroscience*, 8(8), 943–949. doi:00A0;10.1093/scan/nss096

Lindeman, M., & Svedholm-Häkkinen, A. M. (2016). Does poor understanding of physical world predict religious and paranormal beliefs? *Applied Cognitive Psychology*, 30(5), 736–742. doi:00A0;10.1002/acp.3248

Lindeman, M., Svedholm-Häkkinen, A. M., & Lipsanen, J. (2015). Ontological confusions but not mentalizing abilities predict religious belief, paranormal belief, and belief in supernatural purpose. *Cognition*, 134, 63–76. doi:00A0;10.1016/j.cognition.2014.09.008

Linville, P. (1996). Attention inhibition: Does it underlie ruminative thought? In R. S. J. Wyer (Ed.), *Ruminative thoughts: Advances in social cognition* (Vol. 9, pp. 121–134). Mahwah, NJ: Erlbaum.

Lobato, E., Mendoza, J., Sims, V., & Chin, M. (2014). Examining the relationship between conspiracy theories, paranormal beliefs, and pseudoscience acceptance among a university population. *Applied Cognitive Psychology*, 28(5), 617–625. doi:00A0;10.1002/acp.3042

Malinowski, B. (1948/1992). *Magic, science and religion*. Prospect Heights, IL: Waveland Press.

Mauss, M. (1902/1972). *A general theory of magic*. London: Routledge & Kegan Paul.

Mohr, C., Graves, R. E., Gianotti, L. R. R., Pizzagalli, D., & Brugger, P. (2001). Loose but normal: A semantic association study. *Journal of Psycholinguistic Research*, 30(5), 475–483. doi:00A0;10.1023/A:1010461429079

Moutier, S., & Houdé, O. (2003). Judgement under uncertainty and conjunction fallacy inhibition training. *Thinking & Reasoning*, 9(3), 185–201. doi:00A0;10.1080/13546780343000213

Musch, J., & Ehrenberg, K. (2002). Probability misjudgment, cognitive ability, and belief in the paranormal. *British Journal of Psychology*, 93(2), 169–178. doi:00A0;10.1348/000712602162517

Napola, J. (2015). *Cognitive biases, cognitive miserliness, and belief inflexibility: Comparing paranormal and religious believers and sceptics in terms of analytical and intuitive thinking* (Master's thesis). Available at https://helda.helsinki.fi/handle/10138/159872.

Nigg, J. (2000). On inhibition/disinhibition in developmental psychopathology: Views from cognitive and personality psychology and a working inhibition taxonomy. *Psychological Bulletin*, 126(2), 220–246. doi:00A0;10.1037/0033-2909.126.2.220

Norris, P., & Epstein, S. (2011). An experiential thinking style: Its facets and relations with objective and subjective criterion measures. *Journal of Personality*, 79(5), 1043–1080. doi:00A0;10.1111/j.1467-6494.2011.00718.x

Pacini, R., & Epstein, S. (1999). The relation of rational and experiential information processing styles to personality, basic beliefs, and the ratio-bias phenomenon. *Journal of Personality and Social Psychology*, 76(6), 972–987. doi:00A0;10.1037/0022-3514.76.6.972

Pennycook, G., Cheyne, J. A., Barr, N., Koehler, D. J., & Fugelsang, J. A. (2014). Cognitive style and religiosity: The role of conflict detection. *Memory & Cognition*, 42(1), 1–10. doi:00A0;10.3758/s13421-13013-0340-0347

Pennycook, G., Cheyne, J. A., Barr, N., Koehler, D. J., & Fugelsang, J. A. (2015). On the reception and detection of pseudo-profound bullshit. *Judgment and Decision Making*, 10(6), 549–563.

Pennycook, G., Cheyne, J. A., Koehler, D. J., & Fugelsang, J. A. (2016). Is the cognitive reflection test a measure of both reflection and intuition? *Behavior Research Methods*, 48(1), 341–348. doi:00A0;10.3758/s13428-13015-0576-0571

Pennycook, G., Cheyne, J. A., Seli, P., Koehler, D. J., & Fugelsang, J. A. (2012). Analytic cognitive style predicts religious and paranormal belief. *Cognition*, 123(3), 335–346. doi:00A0;10.1016/j.cognition.2012.03.003

Pennycook, G., Fugelsang, J. A., & Koehler, D. J. (2015). Everyday consequences of analytic thinking. *Current Directions in Psychological Science*, 24(6), 425–432. doi:00A0;10.1177/0963721415604610

Peters, B. M. (2013). Evolutionary psychology: Neglecting neurobiology in defining the mind. *Theory & Psychology*, 23(3), 305–322. doi:00A0;10.1177/0959354313480269

Petty, R. E., Briñol, P., Loersch, C., & McCaslin, M. J. (2009). The need for cognition. In M. R. Leary & R. H. Hoyle (Eds.), *Handbook of individual differences in social behavior* (pp. 318–329). New York: Guilford Press.

Piaget, J. (1929/1951). *The child's conception of the world*. London: Routledge & Kegan Paul.

Pillow, B. H., & Weed, S. T. (1997). Preschool children's use of information about age and perceptual access to infer another person's knowledge. *The Journal of Genetic Psychology*, 158(3), 365–376. doi:00A0;10.1080/00221329709596675

Pretz, J. E., & Totz, K. S. (2007). Measuring individual differences in affective, heuristic, and holistic intuition. *Personality and Individual Differences*, 43(5), 1247–1257. doi:00A0;10.1016/j.paid.2007.03.015

Reiner, M., Slotta, J. D., Chi, M. T. H., & Resnick, L. B. (2000). Naive physics reasoning: A commitment to substance-based conceptions. *Cognition and Instruction*, 18(1), 1–34. doi:00A0;10.1207/S1532690XCI1801_01

Riekki, T., Lindeman, M., Aleneff, M., Halme, A., & Nuortimo, A. (2013). Paranormal and religious believers are more prone to illusory face perception than skeptics and non-believers. *Applied Cognitive Psychology*, 27(2), 150–155. doi:00A0;10.1002/acp.2874

Riekki, T., Lindeman, M., & Raij, T. (2014). Supernatural believers attribute more intentions to random movement than skeptics: An fMRI study. *Social Neuroscience*, 9(4), 400–411.

Risen, J. L. (2016). Believing what we do not believe: Acquiescence to superstitious beliefs and other powerful intuitions. *Psychological Review*, 123(2), 182–207. doi:00A0;10.1037/rev0000017

Rogers, P. (2014). Paranormal believers' proneness to probability reasoning biases: A review of the empirical literature. In N. Galbraith (Ed.), *Aberrant beliefs and thinking: Current issues in thinking and reasoning* (pp. 114–131). Hove, UK: Psychology Press.

Rozin, P., & Nemeroff, C. J. (2002). Sympathetic magical thinking: The contagion and similarity "heuristics." In T. Gilovich, D. Griffin, & D. Kahneman (Eds.), *Heuristics and biases: The psychology of intuitive judgment* (pp. 201–216). Cambridge: Cambridge University Press.

Russell, B. (1921/1949). *The analysis of mind*. London: George Allen & Unwin.

Sá, W. C., Kelley, C. N., Ho, C., & Stanovich, K. E. (2005). Thinking about personal theories: Individual differences in the coordination of theory and evidence. *Personality and Individual Differences*, 38(5), 1149–1161. doi:00A0;10.1016/j.paid.2004.07.012

Sá, W. C., West, R. F., & Stanovich, K. E. (1999). The domain specificity and generality of belief bias: Searching for a generalizable critical thinking skill. *Journal of Educational Psychology*, 91(3), 497–510. doi:00A0;10.1037/0022-0663.91.3.497

Schofield, M. B., Baker, I. S., Staples, P., & Sheffield, D. (2016). Mental representations of the supernatural: A cluster analysis of religiosity, spirituality and paranormal belief. *Personality and Individual Differences*, 101, 419–424. doi:00A0;10.1016/j.paid.2016.06.020

Shermer, M. (2011). *The believing brain: From ghosts and gods to politics and conspiracies – how we construct beliefs and reinforce them as truths.* New York: Times Books.

Shtulman, A., & Harrington, K. (2015). Tensions between science and intuition across the lifespan. *Topics in Cognitive Science*, 8(1), 118–137. doi:00A0;10.1111/tops.12174

Spelke, E., & Kinzler, K. (2007). Core knowledge. *Developmental Science*, 10(1), 89–96. doi:00A0;10.1111/j.1467-7687.2007.00569.x

Stanovich, K. E. (2004). *The robot's rebellion: Finding meaning in the age of Darwin.* London: University of Chicago Press.

Stanovich, K. E. (2008). Higher-order preferences and the master rationality motive. *Thinking & Reasoning*, 14(1), 111–127. doi:00A0;10.1080/13546780701384621

Stanovich, K. E. (2009). Distinguishing the reflective, algorithmic, and autonomous minds: Is it time for a tri-process theory? In J. St. B. T. Evans & K. Frankish (Eds.), *In two minds: Dual processes and beyond* (pp. 55–88). Oxford: Oxford University Press.

Stanovich, K. E. (2011). *Rationality and the reflective mind.* New York: Oxford University Press.

Stanovich, K. E. (2012). On the distinction between rationality and intelligence: Implications for understanding individual differences in reasoning. In K. J. Holyoak & R. G. Morrison (Eds.), *The Oxford handbook of thinking and reasoning* (pp. 343–365). New York: Oxford University Press.

Stanovich, K. E., & West, R. F. (1997). Reasoning independently of prior belief and individual differences in actively open-minded thinking. *Journal of Educational Psychology*, 89(2), 342–357. doi:00A0;10.1037/0022-0663.89.2.342

Stanovich, K. E., West, R. F., & Toplak, M. E. (2010). Individual differences as essential components of heuristics and biases research. In K. Manktelow, D. Over, & S. Elqayam (Eds.), *The science of reason: A festschrift for Jonathan St. B. T. Evans* (pp. 335–396). Hove, UK: Psychology Press.

Stuart-Hamilton, I., Nayak, L., & Priest, L. (2006). Intelligence, belief in the paranormal, knowledge of probability and aging. *Educational Gerontology*, 32(3), 173–184. doi:00A0;10.1080/03601270500476847

Subbotsky, E. (2001). Causal explanations of events by children and adults: Can alternative causal modes coexist in one mind? *British Journal of Developmental Psychology*, 19(1), 23–45. doi:00A0;10.1348/026151001165949

Svedholm, A. M., & Lindeman, M. (2013). The separate roles of the reflective mind and involuntary inhibitory control in gatekeeping paranormal beliefs and the underlying intuitive confusions. *British Journal of Psychology*, 104(3), 303–319. doi:00A0;10.1111/j.2044-8295.2012.02118.x

Svedholm, A. M., Lindeman, M., & Lipsanen, J. (2010). Believing in the purpose of events – why does it occur, and is it supernatural? *Applied Cognitive Psychology*, 24(2), 252–265. doi:00A0;10.1002/acp.1560

The Church Research Institute (2016). *Osallistuva luterilaisuus. Suomen evankelis-luterilainen kirkko vuosina 2012–2015* [Partaking Lutheranism. The Finnish Evangelical-Lutheran Church of Finland in 2012–2015]. Kuopio: Grano.

Toplak, M. E., West, R. F., & Stanovich, K. E. (2011). The Cognitive Reflection Test as a predictor of performance on heuristics-and-biases tasks. *Memory & Cognition*, 39(7), 1275–1289. doi:00A0;10.3758/s13421-13011-0104-0101

Toplak, M. E., West, R. F., & Stanovich, K. E. (2014). Rational thinking and cognitive sophistication: Development, cognitive abilities, and thinking dispositions. *Developmental Psychology*, 50(4), 1037–1048. doi:00A0;10.1037/a0034910

Tversky, A., & Kahneman, D. (1974). Judgment under uncertainty: Heuristics and biases. *Science*, 185(4157), 1124–1131. doi:00A0;10.1126/science.185.4157.1124

Tylor, E. B. (1871/1974). *Primitive culture: Research into the development of mythology, philosophy, religion, art, and custom.* New York: Gordon Press.

Upala, M. A., Gonce, L. O., Tweney, R. D., & Slone, D. J. (2007). Contextualizing counterintuitiveness: How context affects comprehension and memorability of counterintuitive concepts. *Cognitive Science*, 31(3), 415–439. doi:00A0;10.1080/15326900701326568

Van Elk, M. (2013). Paranormal believers are more prone to illusory agency detection than skeptics. *Consciousness and Cognition*, 22(3), 1041–1046. doi:00A0;10.1016/j.concog.2013.07.004

Vikan, A., & Clausen, S. (1993). Freud, Piaget, or neither? Beliefs in controlling others by wishful thinking and magical behavior in young children. *Journal of Genetic Psychology*, 154(3), 297–314. doi:00A0;10.1080/00221325.1993.10532183

Vyse, S. A. (2014). *Believing in magic: The psychology of superstition.* New York: Oxford University Press.

Wellman, H. M., & Gelman, S. A. (1998). Knowledge acquisition in foundational domains. In W. Damon (Ed.), *Handbook of child psychology: Cognition, perception, and language* (Vol. 2, pp. 523–573). New York: Wiley.

White, H. A., & Shah, P. (2006). Uninhibited imaginations: Creativity in adults with attention-deficit/hyperactivity disorder. *Personality and Individual Differences*, 40(6), 1121–1131. doi:00A0;10.1016/j.paid.2005.11.007

Wierzbicki, M. (1985). Reasoning errors and belief in paranormal. *Journal of Social Psychology*, 125(4), 489–494. doi:00A0;10.1080/00224545.1985.9713529

Wimmer, H., Hogrefe, G. J., & Perner, J. (1988). Children's understanding of informational access as source of knowledge. *Child Development*, 59(2), 386–396. Retrieved from www.jstor.org/pss/1130318. doi:00A0;10.2307/1130318.

Wiseman, R., & Watt, C. (2006). Belief in psychic ability and the misattribution hypothesis: A qualitative review. *British Journal of Psychology*, 97(3), 323–338. doi:00A0;10.1348/000712605X72523

Woolley, J. D., & Wellman, H. M. (1993). Origin and truth: Young children's understanding of imaginary mental representations. *Child Development*, 64(1), 1–17. doi:00A0;10.2307/1131434

Yates, G. C., & Chandler, M. (2000). Where have all the skeptics gone? Patterns of new age beliefs and anti-scientific attitudes in preservice primary teachers. *Research in Science Education*, 30(4), 377–387. doi:00A0;10.1007/BF02461557

4

THE EARTH IS FLAT! OR IS IT?

How thinking analytically might just convince you the Earth isn't flat

Viren Swami

Introduction

In early 2016, the American rapper Bobby Ray Simmons Jr., better known as B.o.B, began posting dozens of tweets in which he claimed that the Earth is flat. "A lot of people are turned off by the phrase 'flat earth'… but there's no way u can see all the evidence and not know… grow up", he tweeted, before presenting a range of arguments as to why science must be wrong. As an example, he argued that if the Earth were indeed curved, evidence of that curvature would be apparent when looking at the horizon in the distance: "No matter how high in elevation you are… the horizon is always eye level… sorry cadets… I didn't wanna believe it either". When cosmologist and astrophysicist Neil deGrasse Tyson pointed out the inaccuracies in B.o.B's argument, the rapper took to releasing a 'diss' track in which he said that Tyson needed "to loosen up his vest" and in which he called science a "cult" (Brait, 2016).

It is difficult to know how many people actually believe the Earth is flat, but what is clear is that flat-Earthdom occupies a similar space to other conspiracy theories. A conspiracy theory refers to a subset of false beliefs or narratives in which an omnipresent and omnipotent group of actors is said to be working together in pursuit of malevolent goals (Swami & Furnham, 2014). For flat-Earthers, that group is sometimes claimed to be Jewish people, other times to be Freemasons (in his tweets, for example, B.o.B included an image that appeared to suggest that the heliocentric globe model was a Freemason conspiracy), or even a cult of scientists. In all cases the conspiracy theorist believes that their views are being suppressed and silenced for nefarious ends. What's more, even before B.o.B came out in favour of the flat Earth theory, it was apparent that belief in conspiracy theories (broadly speaking) is a widespread and stable aspect of public opinion (Freeman & Bentall, 2017).

For example, in a 2011 nationally representative survey of almost two thousand U.S. adults, Oliver and Wood (2014) reported that 55% of respondents agreed with at least one of seven conspiracy theories they were presented with. The most widely endorsed conspiracy theory – endorsed by 25% of respondents – was the belief that the financial crisis at the time was orchestrated by a select few Wall Street bankers to extend the power of the Federal Reserve and further their control over the world economy. Similarly, the Obama 'birther' conspiracy theory – the claim that President Barack Obama was not born in the U.S. and does not have an authentic Hawai'ian passport – was endorsed by 24% of respondents. Moreover, there were no linear trends in general belief in conspiracy theories across sociopolitical spectra. As Oliver and Wood (2014, p. 959) concluded, "conspiratorial reasoning is not simply a style of one political group but is evident across the ideological spectrum and manifests itself in a variety of distinguishable forms".

But what does it really matter that some people believe in conspiracy theories? Should it concern us that B.o.B thinks the Earth is flat? Certainly, some scholars argue that such beliefs might even be a good thing (for reviews, see Fenster, 1999; Swami & Coles, 2010) as they may help reveal anomalies in mainstream accounts of events or even foster social change by mapping trajectories, and the effects, of power. By most accounts, however, widespread belief in conspiracy theories is worrying because such beliefs are known to be associated with negative outcomes in a range of everyday domains (for a review, see Douglas, Sutton, Jolley, & Wood, 2016). As examples, belief in conspiracy theories has been found to be associated with reduced intention to engage in politics and environmentally friendly behaviour (Jolley & Douglas, 2014a), lower intention to vaccinate (2014b), riskier sexual attitudes and behaviours (e.g., Ford, Wallace, Newman, Lee, & Cunningham, 2013; Hutchinson et al., 2007), less egalitarian human rights attitudes (Swami et al., 2012), more racist and prejudiced attitudes (Swami, 2012; Swami, Barron, Weis, & Furnham, 2017), decreased trust in governance (Einstein & Glick, 2015), and lower acceptance of scientific evidence (Lewandowsky, Gignac, & Oberauer, 2013; van der Linden, 2015).

In view of these negative associations, it is perhaps not surprising that attempts to understand the psychosocial origins of belief in conspiracy theories and, by extension, to reduce conspiracist ideation have re-emerged as important topics of research in the past several years. In brief, this field of research can be divided into four basic elements postulating that belief in conspiracy theories is: (a) the outcome of latent psychopathology; (b) a rational, sense-making response to stressful events; (c) the outcome of a complex constellation of individual difference traits; and (d) a function of cognitive biases and thinking styles. In this chapter, I (very) briefly summarise the first three of these elements before focusing more fully on the fourth. I go on to argue that if scholars and practitioners are serious in their intention to reduce conspiracist ideation, then focusing on thinking styles in particular may offer an effective means of doing so.

The paranoid style

The suggestion that a conspiratorial mindset might be the outcome of latent psychopathology can be traced back to the publication of Hofstadter's (1964) seminal paper, "The Paranoid Style in American Politics". Although Hofstadter (1964) was attempting to describe a particular trend in American politics at the time – one that evoked "the sense of heated exaggeration, suspiciousness, and a conspiratorial fantasy" (p. 80) – the notion of a 'paranoid style' of political engagement was picked up by later scholars. By the close of the century, conspiracist ideation had come to be seen as the outcome of collective (Groh, 1987) or, more often, individual psychopathology (Robins & Post, 1997). This trend toward viewing belief in conspiracy theories in psychopathological terms has experienced something of a resurgence more recently, with scholars arguing that – at least in part – a conspiracist worldview may reflect underlying paranoia or delusional thinking (Swami et al., 2011).

In support of this perspective, a number of studies have focused specifically on associations between belief in conspiracy theories and schizotypy, a set of cognitive, perceptual, and affective traits ranging from normal, imaginative dissociative states to extreme states related to psychosis, particularly schizophrenia. These studies have reported significant and positive associations between belief in conspiracy theories and schizotypal domains (e.g., Barron et al., 2018; Barron, Morgan, Towell, Altemeyer, & Swami, 2014; Dagnall, Drinkwater, Parker, Denovan, & Parton, 2015; Darwin, Neave, & Holmes, 2011; Swami et al., 2013). In explanation, it has been suggested that traits of suspiciousness seen in high schizotypal individuals may result in them disbelieving official or mainstream sources of information. Corroborating evidence for this perspective comes from a study indicating that maladaptive, non-schizotypal suspiciousness was predictive of belief in conspiracy theories (Swami, Weis, Lay, Barron, & Furnham, 2016). Additionally, characteristics associated with paranoid ideation seen in schizotypy may result in distorted ideation, such as hyperactive agency detection, that result in conspiracist ideation (Darwin et al., 2011; van der Tempel & Alcock, 2015).

Other relevant work has reported significant associations between belief in conspiracy theories and belief in superstition, magical ideation, and the paranormal (Brotherton, French, & Pickering, 2013; Bruder, Haffke, Neave, Nouripanah, & Imhoff, 2013; Darwin et al., 2011; Stieger, Gumhalter, Tran, Voracek, & Swami, 2013; Swami et al., 2013). One explanation that lends itself here is that endorsement of one set of anomalous beliefs (e.g., a belief in the paranormal) may make acceptance of other anomalous beliefs (e.g., conspiracy theories) more likely (Ramsay, 2006). In both cases, however, an underlying psychopathological tendency may be the determining factor that makes the assimilation and maintenance of anomalous beliefs more likely (Drinkwater, Dagnall, & Parker, 2012). In short, it is possible that a belief in conspiracy theories – along with other anomalous beliefs – is underpinned by latent psychopathology.

A rational explanation

While the lens of psychopathology is certainly a plausible one vis-à-vis belief in conspiracy theories, most scholars believe that it cannot provide a complete account simply because of the widespread nature of such beliefs (Swami & Furnham, 2014). Instead, some scholars have returned to Hofstadter (1964), who also argued that some events (e.g., a political assassination) are difficult to comprehend because they are typically unimaginable, confusing, or stressful. By reducing and simplifying such phenomena and by linking together a disparate series of events (e.g., a political assassination and a terrorist attack), conspiracy theories offer what appear to be coherent explanations, particularly for individuals or groups who feel powerless, disadvantaged, or voiceless (Parish & Parker, 2001; Sunstein & Vermeule, 2009; Swami & Coles, 2010; van Prooijen & Douglas, 2017). In this view, conspiracy theories can be conceptualised as relatively neutral, rational narratives of the world that help restore agency, control, and understanding (Nefes, 2015).

There is some evidence to support this perspective, particularly among individuals who occupy marginalised positions in society (Thorburn & Bogart, 2005). For example, experiences that are known to be distressing (e.g., a perceived lack of control and subjective uncertainty) heighten the tendency to perceive patterns in unrelated stimuli (Whitson & Galinsky, 2008; Whitson, Galinsky, & Kay, 2015) and to make personified inferences about others (Sullivan, Landau, & Rothschild, 2010), which in turn promote belief in conspiracy theories (van Prooijen & Jostmann, 2013). In addition, at least one cross-sectional study has reported that more stressful life events are associated with stronger belief in conspiracy theories (Swami, Weiss et al., 2016). In explanation, it was suggested that individuals who experience more stressful life events engage in sense-making processes aimed at restoring individual agency and a belief that the world is orderly and predictable (cf. van Prooijen & Acker, 2015). Attributing blame for tragedies or disasters to small groups of actors may also inadvertently provide support for the status quo when its legitimacy is under threat and, thereby, increase individual feelings of social safety (Jolley, Douglas, & Sutton, 2017).

Another way of looking at this perspective is to suggest that a conspiratorial worldview is no different from other meta-explanatory frameworks (e.g., political or religious beliefs) that offer an explanation of the world. To the extent that each of these frameworks provides an illusion of control, they may have features in common and help individuals deal with feelings of powerlessness (Pratt, 2003). That is, they offer individuals a seemingly rational explanation of traumatic or stressful events, which in turn promotes sense-making (van Prooijen, Krouwel, & Pollet, 2015). Of course, not all conspiracy theories emerge as a result of traumatic experiences – flat-Earthdom being a good example – which in turn suggests that a more nuanced understanding may be required. Nevertheless, the basic point is that some conspiracist beliefs may emerge in response to situational or contextual cues as individuals seek to understand, and make judgements about, the world around them (Radnitz & Underwood, 2017).

A conspiracist profile

Drawing on the sense-making perspective, but also attempting to move the discussion forward, psychologists working from an individual differences perspective have documented a number of reliable antecedents of belief in conspiracy theories in non-clinical respondents. Perhaps the most robust of these findings is that a belief in one conspiracy theory makes the assimilation of other conspiracy theories more likely (Swami, Chamorro-Premuzic, & Furnham, 2010; Swami et al., 2011; Swami & Furnham, 2012; Wood, Douglas, & Sutton, 2012). For example, one study reported that individuals who more strongly endorsed a ranged of conspiracy theories were more likely to accept an entirely fictional conspiracy theory (Swami et al., 2011). In Goertzel's (1994) view, conspiracy theories form part of what he termed a "monological belief system": once a conspiratorial mindset has been adopted, individuals begin to see patterns in unrelated phenomena, even if those patterns are internally contradictory (Wood et al., 2012).

Other studies have attempted to operationalise those factors that Hofstadter identified as being pertinent to the conspiratorial mindset. For example, some scholars have found significant associations between stronger belief in conspiracy theories and higher anomie, distrust in authority, political cynicism, and feelings of powerlessness as well as lower self-esteem (Abalakina-Paap, Stephan, Craig, & Gregory, 1999; Brotherton et al., 2013; Bruder et al., 2013; Chichoka, Marchlewska, & de Zavala, 2016; Goertzel, 1994; Swami, 2012; Swami et al., 2010, 2011, 2013; Swami & Furnham, 2012). Some early work also linked belief in conspiracy theories with higher authoritarianism (Abalakina-Paap et al., 1999; McHoskey, 1995), suggesting that conspiracy theorists may have a greater propensity to blame out-groups, but more recent and larger-scale work has reported null effects (Oliver & Wood, 2014). Yet another differential trait that may shape belief in conspiracy theories is self-attributed need for uniqueness, which suggests that some people may endorse conspiracy theories as a means of attaining uniqueness (Imhoff & Lamberty, 2017).

Other work from a differential perspective has focused on the Big Five personality traits. For instance, some studies have reported a significant association between belief in conspiracy theories and the Big Five trait of Openness to Experience (Swami et al., 2010, 2011). It has been suggested that more open individuals may show a greater willingness to accept unique or unusual ideas, although it is also possible this association is an artefact of shared conceptual space between Openness to Experience and personality pathology (Swami, Furnham et al., 2016). Moreover, associations between the Big Five traits and belief in conspiracy theories have tended to be relatively weak and equivocal (Brotherton et al., 2013; Bruder et al., 2013; Imhoff & Bruder, 2013; Stieger et al., 2013; Swami & Furnham, 2012), and it is unclear at present whether it is possible to reliably develop personality profiles of conspiracy theorists.

Cognitive aspects

In addition to the perspectives described above, some scholars have focused on cognitive aspects of conspiracist ideation. In early work, McHoskey (1995) attempted to explain the spread of conspiracy theories based on biased assimilation of information and attitude polarisation. Using the John F. Kennedy assassination as an example, he argued that proponents of the official government explanation (that Lee Harvey Oswald acted alone) and the conspiracy theory (that multiple actors were involved in the assassination and cover-up of that fact) both uncritically accept evidence that is supportive of their own argument. This biased assimilation of information leads, in turn, to attitude polarisation rather than a moderation of existing attitudes, which makes competing explanations essentially immutable. A recent study of Facebook interactions supported this general perspective, finding that polarised users of conspiracy news were more focused on posts by their own community as opposed to scientific news (Bessi et al., 2015).

Similarly, Clarke (2002) suggested that conspiracy theories are easily accepted because of the fundamental attribution error, a general tendency to overvalue dispositional over situational explanations for observed events or behaviours. More specifically, he argued that conspiracy theorists are more likely to blame easily personified actors or networks of actors, thereby making a dispositional inference even when reasonable situational explanations are available. The tendency to form dispositional inferences may be heightened for events that trigger strong affective responses (Sunstein & Vermeule, 2009) because such events are more likely to focus attention away from affect-neutral, situational explanations. In addition, accepting an affect-laden conspiracy theory may also help to justify the affective states produced by an event. One study demonstrated this by showing that exposure to Oliver Stone's film *JFK* (in which it was alleged that the Kennedy assassination was a conspiracy) made viewers feel angry and, in turn, altered their beliefs toward greater acceptance of the conspiracy theory (Butler, Koopman, & Zimbardo, 1995).

More recently, Brotherton and French (2014) suggested that belief in conspiracy theories may be associated with susceptibility to the conjunction fallacy, an error of probabilistic reasoning where individuals overestimate the likelihood of co-occuring events. In support of this hypothesis, they reported that participants who more strongly endorsed conspiracy theories also made more conjunction errors than participants with weaker conspiracist ideation. Other work has supported the association between the conjunction fallacy and belief in conspiracy theories, but also reported that conjunction-framing manipulations produced only small variations in relationship strength (Dagnall, Denovan, Drinkwater, Parker, & Clough, 2017). Other relevant work has suggested that belief in conspiracy theories is a product of a representativeness bias such that individuals accept explanations that are proportional to the consequences of an event (Leman & Cinnirella, 2007), although it should also be noted that such beliefs do not appear to be associated with a nothing-happens-by-accident heuristic (i.e., a biased perception of randomness; Dieguez, Wagner-Egger, & Gauvrit, 2015).

Taken together, these studies suggest that reasoning biases may underscore a propensity to believe in conspiracy theories (Brotherton & French, 2014). However, it is also possible that these findings are underpinned by general cognitive ability. Performance on tasks of heuristics and biases is significantly correlated with cognitive ability (e.g., Stanovich & West, 1999, 2000), and it is, therefore, possible that the latter is the more distal antecedent that leads to both heuristic biases and belief in conspiracy theories. Indeed, two studies have reported that stronger belief in conspiracy theories is significantly, albeit weakly, associated with lower objective (crystalised) intelligence (Swami et al., 2011) and self-reported intelligence (Swami & Furnham, 2012). More generally, it is possible that the associations between scores on tests of heuristics and biases and conspiracist ideation reflect inter-individual differences in thinking dispositions that shape how we seek, interpret, and assimilate evidence (Leman, 2007).

Thinking styles

To test the hypothesis that thinking dispositions may underpin conspiracist ideation, my colleagues and I conducted a series of interrelated studies (Swami, Voracek, Stieger, Tran, & Furnham, 2014). In the first, cross-sectional study with 990 British respondents, we examined associations between belief in conspiracy theories, intuitive and analytic thinking styles, open-minded thinking, need for cognition, and need for closure. Our results indicated that greater belief in conspiracy theories was significantly associated with lower analytic thinking ($\beta = -0.22$), greater intuitive thinking ($\beta = 0.12$), and lower open-minded thinking ($\beta = -0.07$). Broadly speaking, these findings indicated that a lower tendency to rely on deliberative, analytic processing of information and a higher tendency to rely on frugal, intuitive information processing was associated with stronger belief in conspiracy theories.

We followed this up with three studies that examined the effects of priming analytic thinking on belief in conspiracy theories. Priming effects involve stimulation of respondents' mental representations that then influences subsequent non-conscious (but not fully automatic) evaluations, judgements, or actions (Molden, 2014). Here, the influence of the prime is assumed to occur outside of either awareness of this influence or intention to utilise the activated representation in subsequent judgement or action (Loersch & Payne, 2014). Our decision to focus on the effects of priming emerged from earlier work showing that relatively simple primes are successful in inducing analytic thinking (e.g., Rusou, Zakay, & Usher, 2013; Song & Schwarz, 2008; Uhlmann, Poehlman, Tannenbaum, & Bargh, 2011).

Thus, in a second study, we asked 112 British undergraduates to first complete a measure of belief in conspiracy theories. Five weeks later, they returned to the laboratory where they completed a scrambled-sentence verbal fluency test that has been shown to prime analytic thinking (Gervais & Norenzayan, 2012) before completing the same measure of belief in conspiracy theories as before. We found that participants who had completed the analytic prime compared to a control prime had significantly lower belief in conspiracy theories during the second testing session. In a third study, we asked British undergraduates ($N = 189$) to complete a measure of belief in conspiracy theories. When they returned four weeks later, they were asked to complete the same measure in the same easy-to-read font or a disfluent, difficult-to-read font that has been shown to prime analytic thinking (Song & Schwarz, 2008; but see Meyer et al., 2015). We found a reduction in belief in conspiracy theories across testing sessions, but only in the group that had completed the questionnaire in the disfluent font. In a final study with a British community sample ($N = 140$), we found that participants who completed measures of generic conspiracist ideation and belief in a specific conspiracy theory (the 7/7 London bombings) in the disfluent font had significantly lower scores than those who had completed the questionnaire in the easy-to-read font.

Taken together, we argued that our results showed that greater analytic thinking was associated with lower belief in conspiracy theories, which is consistent with other work showing that analytic thinking measured at the individual difference level or induced by experimental manipulation is a strong predictor of greater scepticism toward epistemically suspect beliefs (for a review, see Pennycook, Fugelsang, & Koehler, 2015). More fully, we argued that careful and critical processing of information may cripple the epistemological assumptions that underlie conspiracist ideation, particularly beliefs that are erroneous (e.g., that the Earth is flat), tenuous (e.g., that there is a cult of scientists working to suppress the idea that the Earth is flat), or require a leap of faith (e.g., that NASA exists to promote the 'myth' of a round Earth). Conversely, a propensity to think intuitively may promote acceptance of ideas that require little cognitive effort (i.e., that there is an omnipresent conspiracy to suppress flat-Earthdom).

Thinking critically

Although the results of Swami et al. (2014) suggest that analytic thinking is associated with lower conspiracist ideation, it is important to stress that our findings require independent verification and are limited in a number of ways. For one thing, there has been much discussion about the robustness of priming effects in social psychology broadly (see Molden, 2014) and with the replicability of analytic thinking priming specifically (Deppe et al., 2015). Moreover, the notion that disfluent fonts prime analytic thinking has also been disputed (Meyer et al., 2015), leading to the possibility that our findings were artefactual, influenced by experimenter bias, or shaped by hypothesis-guessing on the part of participants. Alternative methods of testing that do not involve priming (e.g., through developing critical thinking skills) may be a useful way of driving the field forward. Importantly, Swami et al. (2014) also did not control for cognitive ability, which has been identified as an important omission in studies of analytic thinking (Pennycook et al., 2015).

Nevertheless, there are some additional reasons to think that greater analytic thinking may be associated with lower conspiracist ideation. First, the cross-sectional association between greater analytic thinking and lower conspiracist beliefs has now been replicated in a number of distinct samples (Ballová Mikušková, 2017; Barron et al., 2018; van Prooijen, 2017; see also Stojanov, 2015), which suggests that the association is robust. Importantly, recent work has reported that analytic thinking may act as a mediator between belief in conspiracy theories and other, more proximate factors. For example, there is evidence that education is associated with reduced conspiracist beliefs (Douglas, Sutton, Callan, Dawtry, & Harvey, 2016), and one mechanism that has been highlighted is that higher education promotes greater analytic thinking, which in turn reduces a need for simple solutions for complex problems (van Prooijen, 2017). Likewise, Barron et al. (2018) have reported that higher schizotypy is associated with lower analytic thinking, which in turn is associated with greater conspiracist belief.

Second, relevant work has examined the effects of informational framing on belief in the moon landing conspiracy theory (i.e., that the Apollo moon landing did not occur and that NASA intentionally deceived the public into thinking that astronauts had set foot on the moon; Swami et al., 2013). This study found that when photographs of the moon landing were accompanied by text supportive of the conspiracy theory, it resulted in increased belief in the conspiracy theory. However, when the same photographs were presented with information critical of the conspiracy theory, it attenuated belief in the conspiracy. The authors argued that message bias has an influence on acceptance of conspiracy theories, but also that informational sets that prompt analytic, cognitively focused consideration of the message may help reduce belief in conspiracy theories (see also Banas & Miller, 2013; Jolley & Douglas, 2017).

Reducing conspiracist ideation

The question that this chapter has been leading to is whether it might be possible to reduce conspiracist ideation. I say 'reduce' and not 'completely eliminate' because the latter seems very unlikely. To the extent that conspiracy theories emerge as a rational response to stressful, difficult-to-comprehend events, it seems likely that such narratives will remain an aspect of contemporary societies. Even where it is possible to engage in dialogue with conspiracy theorists – recall the exchange between B.o.B and Neil deGrasse Tyson – conspiracy theorists may choose to isolate themselves informationally simply because the dialogue partner is perceived as part of the conspiracy. Engaging in dialogue in these instances may merely serve to entrench existing attitudes, rather than dispel them (McHoskey, 1995; Sunstein & Vermeule, 2009). For example, in one study of Californian parents, it was found that refuting claims of an autism-vaccination link reduced misperceptions about vaccines, but also further entrenched the intent not to vaccinate (Nyhan, Reifler, Richey, & Freed, 2014).

But reducing conspiracist ideation in general terms may be a different question (Grimes, 2016), and the good news is that moving from a position of staunch conspiracism to more informed understanding is possible (Narayan & Preljevic, 2017). Let me return briefly to the data from Oliver and Wood (2014), who reported that 25% of American respondents endorsed the belief that the financial crisis was orchestrated by a group of Wall Street bankers. For the same item, 37% disagreed or strongly disagreed and – more importantly – 38% neither agreed nor disagreed. I would argue that the crucial battle is over the latter group, those who have not made their minds up one way or the other. And it is with this group that promoting analytic thinking may have the biggest impact. Assisting individuals to develop analytic thinking skills and providing them with the tools with which to critically evaluate evidence may be crucial in turning these neutrals into conspiracy theory deniers. Indeed, Blair (2012) made a similar point when he wrote that the ability to think critically may be the key to assisting individuals to recognise, understand, and avoid conspiracist messages.

Of course, suggesting that we need to promote analytic thinking is hardly new. Hundreds of papers have been published and countless debates have taken place about how best to promote critical-analytic thinking skills, particularly in educational settings. In my view, the problem is not that researchers, practitioners, and stakeholders are indifferent to these issues, but rather that there is insufficient knowledge about how to practically and effectively alleviate deficits in analytic thinking. According to one meta-analysis, pedagogical approaches that value knowledge-seeking, in concert with lived-through experience, have real potential to bring real advances in critical-analytic thinking (Murphy, Wilkinson, Soter, Hennessey, & Alexander, 2009). In a world where celebrities are tweeting about conspiracy theories and in which conspiracist accounts are widely available and easily accessible (Guidry, Carlyle, Messner, & Jin, 2015), such efforts are to be welcomed. But I fear they may be too late for B.o.B.

References

Abalakina-Paap, M., Stephan, W. G., Craig, T., & Gregory, W. L. (1999). Beliefs in conspiracies. *Political Psychology*, 20(3), 637–647.

Ballová Mikušková, E. (2017). Conspiracy beliefs of future teachers. *Current Psychology*. doi:00A0;10.1007/s12144-017-9561-4

Banas, J. A., & Miller, G. (2013). Inducing resistance to conspiracy theory propaganda: Testing inoculation and metainoculation strategies. *Human Communication Research*, 39(2), 184–207.

Barron, D., Furnham, A., Weis, L., Morgan, K. D., Towell, T., & Swami, V. (2018). The relationship between schizotypal facets and conspiracist beliefs: Examining the mediating effects of cognitive processes. *Psychiatry Research*, 259, 15–20. doi:00A0;10.1016/j.psychres.2017.10.001

Barron, D., Morgan, K., Towell, T., Altemeyer, B., & Swami, V. (2014). Associations between schizotypy and belief in conspiracist ideation. *Personality and Individual Differences*, 70, 156–158.

Bessi, A., Coletto, M., Davidescu, G. A., Scala, A., Caldarelli, G., & Quattrociocchi, W. (2015). Science vs conspiracy: Collective narratives in the age of misinformation. *PLoS ONE*, 10: e0118093.

Blair, J. A. (2012). The Keegstra affair: A test case for critical thinking. In C. W. Tindale (Ed.), *Groundwork in the theory of argumentation: Selected papers of J. Anthony Blair* (pp. 13–22). New York: Springer.

Brait, E. (2016, January 26). Flat earth rapper BoB releases Neil deGrasse Tyson diss track. *Guardian*. Retrieved from: www.theguardian.com/music/2016/jan/26/flat-earth-rapper-bob-neil-degrasse-tyson-diss-track

Brotherton, R., & French, C. C. (2014). Belief in conspiracy theories and susceptibility to the conjunction fallacy. *Applied Cognitive Psychology*, 28(2), 238–248.

Brotherton, R., French, C. C., & Pickering, A. D. (2013). Measuring belief in conspiracy theories: The Generic Conspiracist Beliefs Scale. *Frontiers in Psychology*, 4: 279.

Bruder, M., Haffke, P., Neave, N., Nouripanah, N., & Imhoff, T. (2013). Measuring individual differences in generic beliefs in conspiracy theories across cultures: Conspiracy Mentality Questionnaire. *Frontiers in Psychology*, 4: 225.

Butler, L. D., Koopman, C., & Zimbardo, P. G. (1995). The psychological impact of the film "JFK". *Political Psychology*, 16(2), 237–257.

Chichoka, A., Marchlewska, M., & de Zavala, A. G. (2016). Does self-love or self-hate predict conspiracy beliefs? Narcissism, self-esteem, and the endorsement of conspiracy theories. *Social Psychological and Personality Science*, 7(2), 157–166.

Clarke, S. (2002). Conspiracy theories and conspiracy theorizing. *Philosophy of the Social Sciences*, 32(2), 131–150.

Dagnall, N., Denovan, A., Drinkwater, K., Parker, A., & Clough, P. (2017). Statistical bias and endorsement of conspiracy theories. *Applied Cognitive Psychology*, 31(4), 368–378.

Dagnall, N., Drinkwater, K., Parker, A., Denovan, A., & Parton, M. (2015). Conspiracy theory and cognitive style: A worldview. *Frontiers in Psychology*, 6: 206. doi:00A0;10.3389/fpsyg.2015.00206

Darwin, H., Neave, N., & Holmes, J. (2011). Belief in conspiracy theories: The role of paranormal belief, paranoid ideation and schizotypy. *Personality and Individual Differences*, 50(8), 1289–1293.

Deppe, K. D., Gonzalez, F. J., Neiman, J. L., Jacobs, C., Pahlke, J., Smith, K. B., & Hibbing, J. R. (2015). Reflective liberals and intuitive conservatives: A look at the Cognitive Reflection Test and ideology. *Judgement and Decision Making*, 10(4), 314–331.

Dieguez, S., Wagner-Egger, P., & Gauvrit, N. (2015). Nothing happens by accident, or does it? A low prior for randomness does not explain belief in conspiracy theories. *Psychological Science*, 26(11), 1762–1770.

Douglas, K. M., Sutton, R. M., Callan, M. J., Dawtry, R. J., & Harvey, A. J. (2016). Someone is pulling the strings: Hypersensitive agency detection and belief in conspiracy theories. *Thinking and Reasoning*, 22(1), 57–77.

Douglas, K. M., Sutton, R. M., Jolley, D., & Wood, M. J. (2016). The social, political, environmental, and health-related consequences of conspiracy theories. In M. Bilewicz, A. Cichocka, & W. Soral (Eds.), *The psychology of conspiracy* (pp. 183–203). Hove, UK: Routledge.

Drinkwater, K., Dagnall, N., & Parker, A. (2012). Reality testing, conspiracy theories, and paranormal beliefs. *Journal of Parapsychology*, 76(1), 57–77.

Einstein, K. L., & Glick, D. M. (2015). Do I think BLS data are BS? The consequences of conspiracy theories. *Political Behavior*, 37(3), 679–701.

Fenster, M. (1999). *Conspiracy theories: Secrecy and power in American culture*. Minneapolis, MN: University of Minnesota Press.

Ford, C. L., Wallace, S. P., Newman, S. P., Lee, S.-J., & Cunningham, W. E. (2013). Belief in AIDS-related conspiracy theories and mistrust in the government: Relationship with HIV testing among at-risk older adults. *The Gerontologist*, 53(6), 973–984.

Freeman, D., & Bentall, R. P. (2017). The concomitants of conspiracy concerns. *Social Psychiatry and Psychiatric Epidemiology*, 52(5), 595–604.

Gervais, W. M., & Norenzayan, A. (2012). Analytical thinking promotes religious disbelief. *Science*, 336(6080), 493–496.

Goertzel, T. (1994). Belief in conspiracy theories. *Political Psychology*, 15(4), 731–742.

Grimes, D. R. (2016). On the viability of conspiratorial beliefs. *PLoS ONE*, 11: e0147905.

Groh, D. (1987). The temptation of conspiracy theory, or: Why do bad things happen to good people? In C. F. Graumann & S. Moscovici (Eds.), *Changing conceptions of conspiracy* (pp. 1–37). New York: Springer-Verlag.

Guidry, J. P. D., Carlyle, K., Messner, M., & Jin, Y. (2015). On pins and needles: How vaccines are portrayed on Pinterest. *Vaccine*, 33(39), 5051–5056.

Hofstadter, R. (1964, November). The paranoid style in American politics. *Harper's Magazine*, 77–86.

Hutchinson, A. B., Begley, E. B., Sullivan, P., Clark, H. A., Boyett, B. C., & Kellerman, S. E. (2007). Conspiracy beliefs and trust in information about HIV/AIDS among minority men who have sex with men. *Journal of Acquired Immune Deficiency Syndromes*, 45(5), 603–605.

Imhoff, R., & Bruder, M. (2013). Speaking (un-)truth to power: Conspiracy mentality as a generalised political attitude. *European Journal of Personality*, 28(1), 25–43.

Imhoff, R., & Lamberty, P. K. (2017). Too special to be duped: Need for uniqueness motivates conspiracy beliefs. *European Journal of Social Psychology*, 47(6), 724–734.

Jolley, D., & Douglas, K. M. (2014a). The social consequences of conspiracism: Exposure to conspiracy theories decreases intentions to engage in politics and to reduce one's carbon footprint. *British Journal of Psychology*, 105(1), 35–56.

Jolley, D., & Douglas, K. M. (2014b). The effects of anti-vaccine conspiracy theories on vaccination intentions. *PLoS ONE*, 9(2): e89177.

Jolley, D., & Douglas, K. M. (2017). Prevention is better than cure: Addressing anti-vaccine conspiracy theories. *Journal of Applied Social Psychology*, 47(8), 459–469.

Jolley, D., Douglas, K. M., & Sutton, R. M. (2017). Blaming a few bad apples to save the threatened barrel: The system-justifying function of conspiracy theories. *Political Psychology*, in press. doi:00A0;10.1111/pops.12404

Leman, P. J. (2007). The born conspiracy. *New Scientist*, 195(2612), 35–38.

Leman, P. J., & Cinnirella, M. (2007). A major event has a major cause. *Social Psychological Review*, 9(2), 18–28.

Lewandowsky, S., Gignac, G. E., & Oberauer, K. (2013). The role of conspiracist ideation and worldviews in predicting rejection of science. *PLoS ONE*, 10(8): e75637.

Loersch, C., & Payne, B. K. (2014). Situated inference and the what, who, and where of priming. *Social Cognition*, 32, 137–151.

McHoskey, J. W. (1995). Case closed? On the John F. Kennedy assassination: Biased assimilation of evidence and attitude polarization. *Basic and Applied Social Psychology*, 17(3), 395–409.

Meyer, A., Frederick, S., Burnham, T. C., Guevara Pinto, J. D., Boyer, T. W., Linden, J., ... & Schuldt, J. P. (2015). Disfluent fonts don't help people solve math problems. *Journal of Experimental Psychology: General*, 144(2), e16–e30.

Molden, D. C. (2014). Understanding priming effects in social psychology: What is "social priming" and how does it occur? *Social Cognition*, 32, 1–11.

Murphy, P. K., Wilkinson, I. A. G., Soter, A. O., Hennessey, M. N., & Alexander, J. F. (2009). Examining the effects of classroom discussion on students' high-level comprehension of text: A meta-analysis. *Journal of Educational Psychology*, 101(3), 740–764.

Narayan, B., & Preljevic, M. (2017). An information behaviour approach to conspiracy theories: Listening in on voices from within the vaccination debate. *Information Research*, 22(1), 1–16.

Nefes, T. S. (2015). Scrutinizing impacts of conspiracy theories on readers' political views: A rational choice perspective on anti-Semitic rhetoric in Turkey. *British Journal of Sociology*, 66(3), 557–575.

Nyhan, B., Reifler, J., Richey, S., & Freed, G. L. (2014). Effective messages in vaccine promotion: A randomized trial. *Pediatrics*, 133(4), 835–842.

Oliver, J. E., & Wood, T. J. (2014). Conspiracy theories and the paranoid style(s) of mass opinion. *American Journal of Political Science*, 58(4), 952–966.

Parish, J., & Parker, M. (2001). *The age of anxiety: Conspiracy theory and the human sciences*. New York: Wiley-Blackwell.

Pennycook, G., Fugelsang, J. A., & Koehler, D. J. (2015). Everyday consequences of analytic thinking. *Current Directions in Psychological Science*, 24, 425–432.

Pratt, R. (2003). Theorizing conspiracy. *Theory and Society*, 32(2), 255–271.

Radnitz, S., & Underwood, P. (2017). Is belief in conspiracy theories pathological? A survey experiment on the cognitive roots of extreme suspicion. *British Journal of Political Science*, 47(1), 113–129.

Ramsay, R. (2006). *Conspiracy theories*. Harpenden, UK: Pocket Essentials.

Robins, R. S., & Post, J. M. (1997). *Political paranoia*. New Haven, CT: Yale University Press.

Rusou, Z., Zakay, D., & Usher, M. (2013). Pitting intuitive and analytical thinking against each other: The case of transitivity. *Psychonomic Bulletin and Review*, 20(3), 608–614.

Song, H., & Schwarz, N. (2008). If it's hard to read, it's hard to do: Processing fluency affects effort prediction and motivation. *Psychological Science*, 19(10), 986–988.

Stanovich, K. E., & West, R. F. (1999). Discrepancies between normative and descriptive models of decision making and the understanding/acceptance principle. *Cognitive Psychology*, 38(3), 349–385.

Stanovich, K. E., & West, R. F. (2000). Individual differences in reasoning: Implications for the rationality debate? *Behavioral and Brain Sciences*, 23(5), 645–665.

Stieger, S., Gumhalter, N., Tran, U. S., Voracek, M., & Swami, V. (2013). Girl in the cellar: A repeated cross-sectional investigation of belief in conspiracy theories about the kidnapping of Natascha Kampusch. *Frontiers in Psychology*, 4: 297.

Stojanov, A. (2015). Reducing conspiracy theory beliefs. *Psihologija*, 48, 251–266.

Sullivan, D., Landau, M. J., & Rothschild, Z. K. (2010). An existential function of enemyship: Evidence that people attribute influence to personal and political enemies to compensate for threats to control. *Journal of Personality and Social Psychology*, 98(3), 434–449.

Sunstein, C. R., & Vermeule, A. (2009). Conspiracy theories: Causes and cures. *Journal of Political Philosophy*, 17(2), 202–227.

Swami, V. (2012). Social psychological origins of conspiracy theories: The case of the Jewish conspiracy theory in Malaysia. *Frontiers in Psychology*, 3: 280.

Swami, V., Barron, D., Weis, L., & Furnham, A. (2017). To Brexit or not to Brexit: The roles of Islamophobia, conspiracist beliefs, and integrated threat in voting intentions for the United Kingdom European Union membership referendum. *British Journal of Psychology*, in press. doi:00A0;10.1111/bjop.12252

Swami, V., Chamorro-Premuzic, T., & Furnham, A. (2010). Unanswered questions: A preliminary investigation of personality and individual difference predictors of 9/11 conspiracist beliefs. *Applied Cognitive Psychology*, 24(6), 749–761.

Swami, V., & Coles, R. (2010). The truth is out there: Belief in conspiracy theories. *The Psychologist*, 23(7), 560–563.

Swami, V., Coles, R., Stieger, S., Pietschnig, J., Furnham, A., Rehim, S., & Voracek, M. (2011). Conspiracist ideation in Britain and Austria: Evidence of a monological belief system and associations between individual psychological differences and real-world and fictitious conspiracy theories. *British Journal of Psychology*, 102(3), 443–463.

Swami, V., & Furnham, A. (2012). Examining conspiracist beliefs about the disappearance of Amelia Earhart. *The Journal of General Psychology*, 139(4), 244–259.

Swami, V., & Furnham, A. (2014). Political paranoia and conspiracy theories. In J.-P. Prooijen & P. A. M. van Lange (Eds.), *Power politics, and paranoia: Why people are suspicious of their leaders* (pp. 218–236). Cambridge: Cambridge University Press.

Swami, V., Furnham, A., Smyth, N., Weis, L., Lay, A., & Clow, A. (2016). Putting the stress on conspiracy theories: Examining associations between psychological stress, anxiety, and belief in conspiracy theories. *Personality and Individual Differences*, 99, 72–76.

Swami, V., Nader, I. W., Pietschnig, J., Stieger, S., Tran, U. S., & Voracek, M. (2012). Personality and individual difference correlates of attitudes toward human rights and civil liberties. *Personality and Individual Differences*, 53(4), 443–447.

Swami, V., Pietschnig, J., Tran, U. S., Nader, I. W., Stieger, S., & Voracek, M. (2013). Lunar lies: The impact of informational bias and individual differences in shaping conspiracist beliefs about the moon landings. *Applied Cognitive Psychology*, 27(1), 71–80.

Swami, V., Voracek, M., Stieger, S., Tran, U. S., & Furnham, A. (2014). Analytic thinking reduces belief in conspiracy theories. *Cognition*, 133(3), 572–585.

Swami, V., Weis, L., Lay, A., Barron, D., & Furnham, A. (2016). Associations between belief in conspiracy theories and the maladaptive personality traits of the Personality Inventory for DSM-5. *Psychiatry Research*, 236, 86–90.

Thorburn, S., & Bogart, L. M. (2005). Conspiracy beliefs about birth control: Barriers to pregnancy prevention among African Americans of reproductive age. *Health Education and Behavior*, 32(4), 474–489.

Uhlmann, E. L., Poehlman, T. A., Tannenbaum, D., & Bargh, J. A. (2011). Implicit puritanism in America moral cognition. *Journal of Experimental Social Psychology*, 47(2), 312–320.

van der Linden, S. (2015). The conspiracy-effect: Exposure to conspiracy theories (about global warming) decreases pro-social behavior and science acceptance. *Personality and Individual Differences*, 87, 171–173.

van der Tempel, J., & Alcock, J. (2015). Relationships between conspiracy mentality, hyperactive agency detection, and schizotypy: Supernatural forces at work? *Personality and Individual Differences*, 82, 136–141.

van Prooijen, J.-W. (2017). Why education predicts decreased belief in conspiracy theories. *Applied Cognitive Psychology*, 31(1), 50–58.

van Prooijen, J.-W., & Acker, M. (2015). The influence of control on belief in conspiracy theories: Conceptual and applied extensions. *Applied Cognitive Psychology*, 29(5), 753–761.

van Prooijen, J.-W., & Douglas, K. (2017). Conspiracy theories as part of history: The role of societal crisis situations. *Memory Studies*, 10(3), 323–333.

van Prooijen, J.-W., & Jostmann, N. B. (2013). Belief in conspiracy theories: The influence of uncertainty and perceived morality. *European Journal of Social Psychology*, 43(1), 109–115.

van Prooijen, J.-W., Krouwel, A. P. M., & Pollet, T. V. (2015). Political extremism predicts belief in conspiracy theories. *Social Psychological and Personality Science*, 6(5), 570–578.

Whitson, J. A., & Galinsky, A. D. (2008). Lacking control increases illusory pattern perception. *Science*, 322(5898), 115–117.

Whitson, J. A., Galinsky, A. D., & Kay, A. (2015). The emotional roots of conspiratorial perceptions, system justification, and belief in the paranormal. *Journal of Experimental Social Psychology*, 56, 89–95.

Wood, M. J., Douglas, K. M., & Sutton, R. M. (2012). Dead and alive: Beliefs in contradictory conspiracy theories. *Social Psychological and Personality Science*, 3(6), 767–773.

5

THE MORAL MYOPIA MODEL

Why and how reasoning matters in moral judgment

Justin F. Landy and Edward B. Royzman[1]

Introduction

Building on recent research, this chapter delineates a new theoretical perspective on moral reasoning, which we call the Moral Myopia Model (MMM). In short, the MMM states that deliberate thinking is associated with more complex representations of moral problem spaces and attention to multiple normative considerations, whereas a lack of deliberate thinking is associated with attending to only a single, salient concern. In the context of moral conflict, this means dogmatically adhering to a singular normative factor (such as respect for individual rights or maximization of utilitarian gains) rather than weighing multiple considerations. In the context of delineating the moral domain, it means treating violations of social convention as truly immoral, due to attending only to the salient conventional rule that they transgress. The MMM synthesizes the most up-to-date research in the area of moral reasoning and underscores the importance of deliberate thinking as a contributor to our moral judgments.

The study of moral reasoning is as old as the study of morality itself (Plato, 1987). Jean Piaget and Lawrence Kohlberg, widely viewed as the founding fathers of moral psychology, famously argued that moral development is constrained by cognitive development (Piaget, 1965) and that "the moral force in personality is cognitive" (Kohlberg, 1971, p. 230). Like Piaget, Kohlberg was a developmental psychologist. He proposed that as children's cognitive abilities mature, they progress from "pre-conventional" conceptions of morality (an egocentric focus on rewards and punishments for the self) to "conventional" moral reasoning (acceptance and application of moral rules and laws). He further argued that some adults advance to "post-conventional" moral reasoning – a willingness to disregard socio-conventional rules in the service of universal moral principles; that is, a mature understanding of the difference between what is normatively disallowed ("conventional") and what is "truly" immoral. Elliot Turiel (1983), and his collaborators, further explicated the difference between conventional and moral thinking, demonstrating that even children of 2 to 3 years of age can distinguish between conventional prohibitions and immorality proper, at least when target transgressions are plainly and accessibly specified. Turiel and others also argued that reasoning plays a crucial role in determining people's moral reactions to multifaceted considerations that arise in complex or morally dilemmatic situations (see Damon, 1975; Turiel, Hildebrandt, & Wainryb, 1991). The MMM is consistent with the general thrust of these perspectives; we argue that reasoning can be applied to resolve situations in which moral concerns clash and that it can promote differentiating between moral and conventional transgressions. We unite recent research supporting these contentions under a novel, straightforward theoretical model.

Outside of the moral domain, the MMM is in line with research showing that deliberate thinking is associated with consideration of multiple concerns in making judgments and enacting behaviors, whereas a lack of deliberate thinking is associated with myopic attention to immediately salient considerations. It thus builds on studies of the Alcohol Myopia Model (Steel & Josephs, 1990) and the Attentional Myopia Model (Mann & Ward, 2004, 2007), which have shown that intoxication and cognitive load produce a narrowing of attention such that people whose thinking is impaired attend to the most salient cues in their environment. For instance, dieters under cognitive load consumed more food than dieters not under load in a room where the food was the only salient stimulus in the environment, but consumed *less* food in a room with salient reminders of diet goals (a scale and diet books). Thus, when not under load, the dieters apparently attended to *both* their diet goals and their desire to consume, resulting in moderate consumption levels (which did not differ depending on the environment), but when under load, they focused more *singularly* on what was immediately salient (Mann & Ward, 2004).

Furthermore, individual differences in deliberate reasoning predict the complexity with which people represent problem spaces. Specifically, when presented with a choice between a certain gain or a risky gamble with a higher expected value, better thinkers were more likely to make the normatively correct choice and accept the gamble, and this effect was fully mediated by the sheer number of considerations that they thought about while making the decision (Cokely & Kelley, 2009). In other words, better thinkers considered more than just immediately salient aspects of the problem. Lastly, a new model of analytic thinking posits a key role for detecting conflict between multiple salient, intuitive responses (Pennycook, Fugelsang, & Koehler, 2015).

Based on this research, we propose that "moral myopia" consists of singularly attending to one salient aspect of a moral problem rather than thinking about multiple moral considerations (or "normative factors"; see Kagan, 1998) in a more complex, integrative way. Moral myopia should be more likely in the absence of deliberate thinking, whereas it should be less likely when the ability and inclination toward deliberate thinking are present, and the situation allows for it. We will examine this thesis in the context of the two most widely studied types of "moral encounters" (Monin, Pizarro, & Beer, 2007; Royzman, Goodwin, & Leeman, 2011): dilemmas pitting multiple moral considerations against one another; and responses to transgressions committed by others. Specifically, we show that good reasoning is associated with more complex, less dogmatic resolutions to moral dilemmas, and greater nuance and clarity in differentiating immorality from counter-normativity.

But what do we mean by reasoning and, in particular, "good" reasoning? For our purposes here, we conceive of reasoning as an effortful, deliberate cognitive process that requires mental resources to execute (e.g., Evans & Stanovich, 2013).[2] In particular, we will focus specifically on internal reasoning (i.e., thinking something through for oneself) rather than external reasoning (i.e., argumentation, discussion, and other sorts of collaborative thinking; Harman, Mason, & Sinnott-Armstrong, 2010). External reasoning is surely important in moral judgment; the role of internal reasoning has been more controversial of late, and so, in keeping with the general theme of this volume, that is where we will focus our attention.

We consider more reflective, more complex, and more careful thinking to be, *prima facie*, preferable to more intuitive, simple, and inattentive thinking, particularly in domains that are as important and valued as morality. We will examine various individual difference measures of reasoning, some of which are generally thought of as performance measures of the cognitive *ability* to reason in different domains (e.g., standardized IQ tests), some of which are self-report measures of cognitive *style* (i.e., one's willingness or propensity to engage in reasoning – e.g., the Rational-Experiential Inventory; Pacini & Epstein, 1999), and some of which are performance measures that likely depend on both cognitive ability and cognitive style (e.g., the Cognitive Reflection Test, also known as the CRT; Frederick, 2005; see Pennycook & Ross, 2016). When discussing this latter class of measure, we will refer to them as measures of "reasoning performance." In addition, we will examine the effects of experimental manipulations that should inhibit deliberate reasoning (e.g., cognitive load, sleep deprivation).

Therefore, throughout this chapter, the reader can consider "good reasoning" to be shorthand for "the cognitive abilities and styles, and situational factors, that allow one internally to think carefully about problems under consideration." We will show that individual differences in cognitive ability and cognitive style (as well as domain-general reasoning performance, which likely depends on both) and experimental manipulations that should interfere with deliberate reasoning all systematically predict moral judgment, and do so in ways that can be understood via the MMM.

Overview of alternative theoretical approaches

The MMM contrasts with the two most prominent theoretical perspectives on the role of reasoning in moral judgment. The first, Greene and colleagues' Dual-Process Model (DPM; Greene, Morelli, Lowenberg, Nystrom, & Cohen, 2008; Greene, Nystrom, Engell, Darley, & Cohen, 2004; Greene, Sommerville, Nystrom, Darley,

& Cohen, 2001; for a detailed review, see Cushman, Young, & Greene, 2010), proposes that moral judgment is often driven by automatic, unreasoned processes, but that more deliberate reasoning can overrule these processes. This distinction between two "systems" of thinking, one fast and intuitive, the other slow and deliberative, is not unique to this theory (e.g., Evans & Stanovich, 2013; Kahneman, 2011) – the theoretical innovation is the association of these two cognitive systems with two distinct systems of normative ethics. Specifically, intuition is said to promote moral judgments that adhere to deontological constraints, while reason is said to promote judgments that maximize utilitarian good. Thus, for instance, if one has the opportunity to kill one person to save several others, automatic processes would lead one to conclude that doing so is morally wrong (because it violates the deontological rule "do not kill"), whereas reasoning would lead one to conclude that it is morally right (because it maximizes the good, or at least minimizes the bad).

The second, Haidt's (2001) Social Intuitionist Model (SIM), proposes that moral judgments are nearly always caused by automatic, often emotional, "intuitions"[3] and that moral reasoning takes place only *after* a judgment is made, in order to justify it – "moral reasoning is rarely the direct cause of moral judgment" (Haidt, 2001, p. 815). The word "rarely" is important here – the SIM allows that moral reasoning may drive moral judgment under certain unusual circumstances or for certain unusual people (such as professional philosophers). Nonetheless, this model clearly predicts that most moral judgments will be driven by intuitions and that internal reasoning as such will play no role in producing them (see also Schnall, Haidt, Clore, & Jordan, 2008).[4]

Thus, both of these models make clear predictions about how reasoning should relate to the content of moral judgments. According to the DPM, better thinking should lead to more utilitarian, and less deontological, judgment outcomes. According to the SIM, better thinking should have no predictive relationship whatsoever with the *content* of one's moral judgments, because reasoning is used to marshal support for one's judgments, whatever they may be, after they have been formed. In contrast, the MMM says that reasoning is neither post hoc, nor does it bias toward any particular normative content, including utilitarianism. Rather, the MMM predicts that better thinking will be associated with more complex, integrative moral judgments that attend to multiple normative factors and do not merely consider simple, salient features of moral problems. In our view, this model better explains the most current findings in this area, as we detail below.

Reasoning and moral dilemmas

Suppose that you are standing near some train tracks. You notice a trolley that has lost control and is speeding down the tracks, hurtling toward five oblivious workmen, who will be killed if they are struck by the trolley. Next to you is a switch that you can flip to divert the trolley onto a side track, saving the five. However, there is one workman on the side track, who will be killed if you flip the switch. What should you do? Now, suppose instead that you are standing on a bridge overlooking the tracks and you see a trolley careening toward five workmen, but there is no side track and no switch. There is, however, a large man standing next to you on the bridge, and you realize that you could shove him off the bridge into the path of the trolley. His body will stop the trolley's momentum, saving the five but killing him. What should you do?

The moral dilemmas above are two versions of the famous "trolley problem" (Foot, 1967), often called the "switch" and "footbridge" dilemmas, respectively. A substantial amount of recent research on the role of reasoning in moral psychology has examined how reasoning is involved in resolving such difficult (if far-fetched) moral dilemmas all asking the same underlying question: is it right to sacrifice one in order to save many? Many of these dilemmas have been divided into "personal" and "impersonal" types, with personal dilemmas involving more direct and proximate harm to another person by one's own action, as in the footbridge dilemma, and impersonal dilemmas lacking this "up close and personal" quality, as in the switch dilemma. This distinction has been criticized (McGuire, Langdon, Coltheart, & Mackenzie, 2009), but it is relevant to much of the research we review below.

The DPM clearly predicts that deliberate reasoning should promote utilitarian moral judgments in these sorts of dilemmas, and there is considerable support for this prediction. Paxton, Ungar, and Greene (2012, Study 1) found that participants who had completed the Cognitive Reflection Test (CRT) – a series of mathematical puzzles requiring one to think carefully and overrule an intuitive response (Frederick, 2005) – rated utilitarian killing in three trolley-type dilemmas to be more morally acceptable than participants who had not. That is, completing the CRT apparently primed a reflective mindset in participants, which led to more utilitarian responding. However, this study showed no overall correlation between trait-level reasoning performance, as measured by the CRT, and acceptability ratings in these dilemmas.[5] Also consistent with the idea that deliberative thinking is associated with utilitarian responses in trolley-type dilemmas, research has shown that cognitive load (Conway & Gawronski, 2013, Study 2; Trémolière, De Neys, & Bonnefon, 2012, Study 2), time pressure (Suter & Hertwig, 2011), and stress (Starke, Ludwig, & Brand, 2012; Youssef et al., 2012), all of which should limit participants' ability to deliberate, can decrease utilitarian responding in trolley-type dilemmas. Cognitive load has also been found to increase the time taken to render utilitarian ("appropriate"), but not deontological ("inappropriate"), responses to these dilemmas, suggesting that interfering with deliberative thinking makes such responses more difficult (Greene et al., 2008). Similarly, self-reported individual differences in need for cognition (Conway & Gawronski, 2013, Study 1) and reliance on deliberation over intuition (Bartels, 2008) predict utilitarian responding.

However, there are also several findings that do not support a link between reasoned deliberation and utilitarian judgments. Baron, Scott, Fincher, and Metz (2015) failed to replicate the CRT-priming effect observed by Paxton et al. (2012). Moreover, cognitive load can *increase* the judged appropriateness of utilitarian killing in trolley-type dilemmas when participants have been primed to think abstractly (Körner & Volk, 2014), and sleep deprivation (53 hours of wakefulness), which should impair executive functioning, *increased* the likelihood of judging utilitarian killing to be "appropriate" in footbridge-like "personal" dilemmas, though only among participants with relatively low emotional intelligence (Killgore et al., 2007). Finally, blood alcohol content among bar patrons correlated positively with utilitarian responses to the footbridge problem (Duke and Bègue, 2015). Alcohol is known to impair executive functioning (Weissenborn & Duka, 2003), so the DPM should seemingly predict the opposite result.

Thus, there is quite a bit of evidence that good reasoning is associated with considering utilitarian harms to be "appropriate" or "acceptable" in trolley-type dilemmas, though some questions may be raised about the robustness of this association. However, even if we take this relationship to be robust, we do not think that it necessarily follows that good reasoning is associated with adherence to utilitarianism as a normative view, or even with truly utilitarian judgments.

The DPM predicts that good reasoning should be associated with applying one particular moral rule in these dilemmas – utility maximization. However, this prediction seems inconsistent with the observation that "do the most good" is a very simple rule and applying it should require little effortful thinking. As Baron et al. (2015) point out, it is cognitively quite easy (i.e., "intuitive") to extract a single cue in moral dilemmas, such as the number of lives that can be saved, and render a decision based on this cue. Kahane (2012, 2015) makes this point as well and argues that it is more likely that utilitarian responses in trolley-type dilemmas are associated with controlled reasoning, not because cognitive effort is spent determining which option maximizes utility (a trivially simple computation), but because it is spent *weighing competing moral considerations*.[6] Moreover, Białek and De Neys (2016) demonstrated that participants who give deontological responses in trolley-type dilemmas are aware of the conflicting moral principles at play. Thus, in concert with our general thesis, we propose that in the context of trolley-type dilemmas, more reflective thinking is associated with attending more to *both* deontological and utilitarian considerations – that is, with representing the decision space in a more complex way rather than focusing single-mindedly on one normative factor (whether utilitarian or deontological in nature), inconsistent with the DPM.

We demonstrated this directly in two studies in which participants responded to several trolley-type dilemmas (Royzman, Landy, & Leeman, 2015). Following the normative ethics literature, we asked participants whether the utility-maximizing harm was morally permissible and also whether it was morally required (Kamm, 2009; see also Lanteri, Chelini, & Rizzello, 2008; Sheskin & Baumard, 2016). Strict deontological ethics would treat killing another person as morally *prohibited*, and therefore as neither permissible nor required, while strict utilitarian ethics would treat maximizing utility as a moral *imperative*, and therefore as both permissible and required (see Kagan, 1998). Performance on the CRT predicted neither of these "dogmatic" response patterns and, in fact, was negatively associated with an overall measure of dogmatic responding (i.e., a combined measure of strict deontological and strict utilitarian responding). Instead, reasoning performance was positively associated with the belief that killing one to save many is permissible, but not required. We confirmed that, by this, our participants meant that either course of action was morally permissible – that is, reasoning performance predicted acceptance of *either* the deontological or utilitarian action rather than singular adherence to any simple, highly salient normative factor, be it deontological or utilitarian in nature.[7]

Additional evidence supports this assertion. For instance, Baron, Gürçay, Moore, and Starcke (2012) used a Rasch model to predict the propensity of individual participants to provide utilitarian responses in trolley-type dilemmas and the likelihood of utilitarian responses being given in each dilemma (i.e., the tendency of each *individual* to provide utilitarian responses and the tendency of each *item* to elicit utilitarian responses). They found that participants took the most time to render a response when the model predicted that they should be equally likely to give the deontological or the utilitarian response, and that response times did not differ as a function of which answer they eventually gave. If we take response time to be an indicator of the amount of deliberation or effort put into a response, then this suggests that participants are doing the most thinking when they are indifferent in terms of the deontological and utilitarian responses, but that more thinking does not predict one type of response over the other. The authors note that "we can view [response times] to moral dilemmas as typical of responses under conflict between two options, *with some considerations pulling one way, and some the other way.* When these considerations are balanced, the decision will be difficult and take longer" (Baron et al., 2012, p. 111, emphasis added; see also Koop, 2013), which is very consistent with our perspective here.

Furthermore, Tempesta et al. (2012) found that a night of sleep deprivation (approximately 26 hours spent continuously awake) produced faster response times to "impersonal," switch-like dilemmas, but did not affect the likelihood of judging utilitarian killing as "appropriate," which was approximately 50% in this study. Thus, sleep deprivation apparently disinhibited *both* utilitarian and deontological responding – that is, when participants' executive functioning was impaired, they were faster to provide both types of dogmatic response.

Finally, Moore, Clark, and Kane (2008) demonstrated directly that cognitive ability is associated with attention to more considerations when resolving moral dilemmas. Specifically, they manipulated (among other things) whether the person to be sacrificed in trolley-type dilemmas was already inevitably going to die – that is, whether sacrificing the person would end what would otherwise be expected to be a full life or would just slightly hasten an unavoidable death. Participants with high working memory capacity (WMC), a measure of cognitive resources, were influenced by this manipulation – they considered sacrificing a person who was going to die anyway to be more appropriate than sacrificing a person who was not. Participants low in WMC showed no sensitivity to this manipulation. This constitutes direct evidence that high-WMC participants attend to moral considerations that low-WMC participants may not.

Thus, recent evidence suggests that the oft-cited connection between deliberate reasoning and utilitarian judgment may not always be observed. Moreover, when it is, it may be due to more deliberative participants weighing multiple moral considerations and pronouncing utilitarian harms to be "acceptable" or "appropriate" because this is more closely in line with their actual normative judgment than is pronouncing them to be "unacceptable" or "inappropriate." When moral permissibility and obligation are probed separately, cognitive reflection is associated with treating *either* response to trolley-type dilemmas as permissible, and *neither* as obligatory. Moreover, slower responses are observed in cases where statistical models predict equal likelihoods of deontological and utilitarian responding, indicating that more thinking is associated with considering both "sides" of the moral dilemma, and sleep deprivation can disinhibit both utilitarian and deontological responses – when deliberative thinking is impaired, responses adhering to either simple, "dogmatic" stance become easier, presumably because attention is narrowed and people attend to only one normative factor or the other. Finally, higher working memory capacity is associated with attending to subtle features of dilemmas that could be considered meaningful normative factors. These findings converge on the conclusion that in the context of trolley-type dilemmas, better reasoning predicts concern with multiple, competing moral considerations, rather than simplistic adherence to any one normative factor, consistent with the MMM.

Morality, counter-normativity, and reasoning

Not only is reasoning involved in resolving moral dilemmas, it also plays a role in delineating the moral domain itself. Turiel (1983) found that people were more likely to treat directly harmful actions and violations of fairness as universally wrong, regardless of local norms or conventions, than other sorts of counter-normative actions – that is, to "fully moralize" harmful or unfair acts. This was repeatedly found in the context of the classic Moral-Conventional Distinction Task (MCDT). There is some variation in how this task is administered, but the basic design consists of two parts: one question probing how wrong or counter-normative a person's action is considered to be, and one or more questions testing for full moralization – a belief that the action would still be wrong under an alternate normative regime in which some element of the prohibition against the action has been counterfactually nullified. This nullification can take several forms – a decision handed down by a legitimate authority, a lack of rules or laws forbidding the act, or a consensus among members of a culture that the act is permissible. Paradigmatic transgressions of social conventions like dress codes and norms of address are typically not condemned in the context of normative systems that permit them. Paradigmatic moral violations like theft and assault, on the other hand, retain their condemnable status even in contexts where they are permitted (see Huebner, Lee, & Hauser, 2010; Turiel, 1983). Condemnation independent of normative context has long been considered a hallmark of a truly *moral* transgression. According to the MMM, good reasoning should be associated with better performance in distinguishing moral offenses from conventional offenses. For instance, people who are more reflective would be expected to be less condemning, and less moralizing, of dress code violations than their less reflective peers because they are better able to distinguish moral violations from conventional ones. This prediction stands in stark contrast to the predictions of the SIM, which says that reasoning performance should be unrelated to the content of moral judgments; better thinkers may be better able to *justify* condemning dress code violations, but should be no more or less likely to do so.

At first glance, the hypothesis that better thinking should be associated with less moralization of things like dress code violations might appear to be at odds with our discussion of dilemma resolution above in the sense that one who moralizes dress code violations might appear to be thinking about more moral concerns than one who does not. The key to resolving this apparent inconsistency is defining "moral" concerns. Turiel (1983) argues that paradigmatic moral violations intrinsically produce negative consequences for others – theft and assault, by their very nature, negatively affect people. Paradigmatic conventional violations, on the other hand, can also negatively affect others, whether by offending them or disrupting the social order, but the harm is not intrinsic to the act and would not be present under alternative normative systems. The MMM states that in the absence of deliberate thinking, people will myopically focus on a single, salient consideration when making moral judgments. One thing that should make a consideration salient is how well learned it is, and it seems reasonable that social conventions (and rules of all sorts) are quite well learned. Thus, our prediction can be rephrased as follows: in the context of moral judgment, better, more deliberative thinking will be associated with a more all-encompassing analysis of the problem, attending to whether something is intrinsically harmful *as well as* whether it violates some well-learned rule rather than only attending to the latter. Better thinking should thus predict less condemnation and less moralization of norm violations that are not intrinsically harmful, but there should be no relationship between thinking and judgments of intrinsically harmful acts, because attending to either the salient rule (e.g., "theft is bad") or the intrinsic harmfulness ("theft hurts the victim, no matter what") lead to the same resultant judgment. Conversely, in the absence of good reasoning, "immoral" should be treated as essentially synonymous with "counter-normative" in one's judgments. Quite a bit of research supports this prediction, though much of it was not originally intended to test it directly. We will first review evidence that better thinking is associated with less condemnation of nonmoral, counter-normative actions, taking condemnation as a reasonable proxy for moralization. We will then review evidence that directly demonstrates that good thinking predicts differentiation between morality and convention in the MCDT.

Much of the research on condemnation of actions that do not concern classically moral considerations of "justice, rights and welfare" (Turiel, 1983, p. 3) has focused on so-called "purity" violations – counter-normative but intrinsically harmless actions that involve sexual acts or disgusting content (e.g., Haidt & Graham, 2007; Horberg, Oveis, Keltner, & Cohen, 2009; Turiel et al., 1991). It is clear that some people strongly condemn actions like consensual, non-reproductive incest and unusual forms of masturbation (Haidt & Hersh, 2001; Haidt, Koller, & Dias, 1993), and recent research has investigated the role that reasoning plays in this condemnation. Individual differences in both cognitive ability and reasoning performance have been found to correlate negatively with condemnation of adult siblings who engage in reproductively inert, consensual sex, and of a man who privately has sexual intercourse with a dead chicken, though only the relationship with reasoning performance persisted when statistically accounting for religiosity, political beliefs, and explicit moral values (Pennycook, Cheyne, Barr, Koehler, & Fugelsang, 2014). Similarly, people who report relying on intuitive thinking on the Faith in Intuition Scale (one subscale of the Rational-Experiential Inventory; see Pacini & Epstein, 1999) were more condemning of disgusting actions such as incest (Björklund, 2004). Interestingly, no effect of rational thinking style was found in this study – in this case, it was unreasoned thought, rather than the absence of reasoned thought, that seems to be associated with condemning harmless actions.

Moreover, experimental research has provided evidence for a causal connection between deliberative thought and condemnation of harmless offenses. Prevention focus (i.e., a focus on maintaining the status quo and preventing unwanted outcomes) is known to produce more reasoned, analytic thinking, whereas promotion focus (i.e., a focus on surpassing the status quo and attaining "ideal" outcomes) produces associational, affective processing (Pham & Avnet, 2004, 2009). Quite consistent with the research reviewed above, priming prevention focus results in less condemnation of harmless incest, consumption of dog meat, and harmless cannibalism than does priming promotion focus (Cornwell & Higgins, 2016). That is, when they are in a state of mind that induces careful, analytic thinking, people treat harmless, disgusting acts less like moral wrongs.

More directly, Paxton et al. (2012) showed that reasoning can reduce condemnation of harmless incest, but only under conditions where deliberation is likely. Specifically, after reading a description of consensual, non-reproductive sibling incest, participants were randomly assigned to read a strong argument for why the act was not wrong (there is no chance of procreation, and therefore the evolutionary reason for revulsion at incest is not at play) or a weak argument (brothers and sisters love each other, and therefore it makes perfect sense for them to express their love sexually). Orthogonal to this manipulation, half of the participants were required to consider the argument they had read for two minutes before judging the acceptability of the siblings' actions, while the other half could respond immediately after reading the argument. Participants are more likely to think carefully and deliberatively when there is sufficient time to do so; that is, in the delayed condition. Consistent with this reasoning, participants who read strong arguments and reflected on them for two minutes rated the incestuous act as more morally acceptable than participants who read weak arguments and/or did not reflect. Reflecting on a good reason for not condemning (even if one did not generate the reason oneself) led to treating harmless offenses as less like moral wrongs.

These findings are consistent with our claim that better thinking should be associated with more clearly distinguishing intrinsically harmful moral violations from contingently harmful conventional violations, but do not demonstrate it directly. Fortunately, some additional research has directly evaluated the role of reasoning in responding to the MCDT. For instance, in a sample of incarcerated prisoners, IQ correlated highly with correctly classifying prototypical moral and conventional offenses, $r = 0.52$ (Aharoni, Sinnott-Armstrong, & Kiehl, 2011). That is, inmates with higher cognitive ability were more likely to classify moral violations (e.g., "after weeks of begging her, a man has sex with a woman against her wishes") as wrong "even if there were no rules, customs, or laws against them" (p. 488) and less likely to classify conventional violations (e.g., "at his mother's funeral, a man wears a t-shirt and shorts although everyone else is in formalwear") as such. This study was conducted using a variant of the MCDT designed to reduce strategic responding (a concern in research with incarcerated populations), and the predictive effect of IQ survived statistically accounting for trait-level psychopathy, and explained over 50% of the variance in responses.

We found quite similar results using a measure of reasoning performance (the CRT) and non-incarcerated participants (Royzman, Landy, & Goodwin, 2014). Specifically, we found that in a sample of online participants, performance on the CRT was negatively correlated with considering a conventional violation (wearing pajamas to work) and a harmless sexual violation (two adult siblings passionately kissing) to be wrong in a hypothetical country where there was widespread consensus that they were permissible (a measure of full moralization). Furthermore, there was no relationship between CRT and analogous judgments of moralization for intrinsically harmful actions (theft and exploitative deception). In other words, reasoning performance was not associated with being less moralizing of all offenses, but rather with specifically treating counter-normative actions that do not intrinsically cause harm as conventional, rather than moral, issues.

We have since extended this finding beyond this single dress code violation and sexual offense to a wide range of counter-normative actions that are sometimes moralized (Landy, 2016). Specifically, using Moral Foundations Theory (Graham, Haidt, & Nosek, 2009; Haidt & Graham, 2007) as a starting point, we presented participants with counter-normative actions representing five different types of violations: directly harmful actions, unfair actions, actions that are disrespectful or disobedient to authority, actions that are disloyal to an important in-group, and purity offenses of the sort described above. Across three studies, participants indicated how wrong they considered each violation to be, whether or not it would be wrong in a hypothetical country where it was approved by popular consensus, and whether it intrinsically produced negative consequences for others (all hallmarks of the moral domain). Reasoning performance, measured using the CRT and correct responding to belief-bias syllogisms (e.g., Baron et al., 2015; Markovits & Nantel, 1989), was negatively correlated with condemnation, moralization, and intrinsic harmfulness judgments of disobedient, disloyal, and impure actions. Judgments of harmful and unfair actions, which represent paradigmatically moral offenses, were largely unrelated to reasoning performance. These results generally support our proposed mechanism for why good thinking is associated with more clarity in distinguishing morality from convention: better thinkers appear to be better able to distinguish transgressive acts that have intrinsic negative consequences from those that have only contingent ones. Thus, research converges on the conclusion that deliberate thinking is associated with excluding harmless but counter-normative actions from the moral domain. Consistent with the MMM, better thinkers attend to the inherent harmfulness of an act, in addition to its mere compliance with well-learned norms, when defining the bounds of the moral.

Additional support for this idea comes from two studies of moral judgment using the Defining Issues Test (DIT; Rest, 1974; Rest, Narvaez, Thoma, & Bebeau, 1999). Rooted in Kohlberg's research, the DIT indexes the moral concerns that participants value in their judgments. The most important aspect of the test for our purposes is the Principled Morality score (later, Post-Conventional score) or "P-score," which measures the use of moral principles in resolving Kohlbergian moral dilemmas. The P-score can be thought of as a measure of how much a person relies on moral principles as opposed to knowledge of rules ("conventional" moral thinking, in Kohlberg's terms) when making moral judgments. A low P-score indicates treating immorality as more or less synonymous with counter-normativity, whereas a high P-score indicates reliance on higher-order normative considerations rather than conventional regularities to guide moral judgment. IQ was found to be the best predictor of P-scores among patients in a high-security psychiatric hospital, $r = 0.52$, and almost entirely accounted for associations between trait psychopathy and P-scores (O'Kane, Fawcett, & Blackburn, 1996). That is, psychopathy was somewhat unsurprisingly predictive of low P-scores, but this was almost entirely attributable to individual differences in IQ. Participants with higher cognitive ability were less likely to rely on rules in making moral judgments and more likely to rely on principles. Furthermore, partial sleep deprivation (approximately 2.5 hours of sleep per day for five days) produced markedly reduced P-scores among students at a military academy, compared to their baseline scores when rested (Olsen, Pallesen, & Eid, 2010) – impairment of cognitive resources led to more reliance on knowledge of what is against the rules in determining what is immoral.

All of this research converges on the conclusion that good thinking is associated with a reduced tendency to treat immorality as being defined by counter-normativity and with more attention to paradigmatically moral concerns, and some of it suggests that this relationship is causal. Whether an action violates a rule is generally important in people's moral judgments (Nichols & Mallon, 2006), but consistent with the MMM, better thinkers appear to think about considerations beyond well-learned rules and to have a more nuanced, more differentiated, and, one might say, richer moral domain. For them, what is against the rules is not necessarily immoral, as they attend to more than just norms when delineating the bounds of the moral.

Open questions and future directions

Current research on the role of reasoning in moral judgment is largely consistent with our thesis that good reasoning is associated with giving consideration to multiple normative factors, rather than exclusively attending to a single, salient consideration. We have primarily focused on two moral judgment research paradigms – resolution of trolley-type moral dilemmas and moralization of intrinsically harmless acts – arguing that the vast majority of extant research on both topics favors MMM over either DPM or SIM. Beyond these two research paradigms, there has been relatively little research on the role of reasoning in moral evaluation. However, this is a rapidly growing field that could not be fully explored in a single essay. Thus, we briefly review some of the more prominent additional research in this area, nearly all of which converges on an important role for internal reasoning in the etiology of moral judgments.

Reasoning appears to play a role in ascriptions of blame. Pizarro, Uhlmann, and Bloom (2003) examined blame judgments in the cases of "causally deviant" bad acts in which an actor intends a bad outcome, which they cause to happen, but not in the intended, prototypically criminal way. There appeared to be a fairly general tendency to reduce blame attributions in such cases, but more importantly for our purposes, this effect was moderated by deliberate reasoning – participants instructed to base their judgment on an "intuitive, gut feeling" attributed less blame in causally deviant cases, whereas participants instructed to give their "most rational, objective judgment" did not. Similarly, people appear to consider intentionality in their moral judgments to a lesser degree while under cognitive load (Buon, Jacob, Loissel, & Dupoux, 2013) – that is, while cognitive resources are otherwise occupied, people rely on a simple heuristic along the lines of: "if caused bad outcome, then bad." Consistent with the MMM, these results can be interpreted as intuitive thinking, leading to attending only to a very salient aspect of the moral problem (causation), and deliberative thinking, leading to attention to more complex, morally relevant considerations (intentions).

One of the most widely replicated effects in the study of moral judgment is the "side effect" effect (Knobe, 2003), in which foreseen negative side effects of intentional action are judged to be more intentional than foreseen positive side effects. Two recent studies have examined how reasoning relates to this peculiar asymmetry. One suggests that higher CRT performance predicts smaller differences in ascribed intentionality between positive and negative side effects (Pinillos, Smith, Nair, Marchetto, & Mun, 2011), while the other found no predictive effects of CRT performance or WMC when statistically accounting for individual differences in self-control and personality (Cokely & Feltz, 2009). It is thus unclear what role reasoning plays in this effect, and more research on this topic is clearly called for.

Bartels (2006) found that people who describe themselves as more rational than intuitive on the Rational-Experiential Inventory preferred policies that saved the most lives over policies that saved a larger proportion of one group (e.g., they preferred saving 230 people out of 920, rather than 225 out of 300). This could be interpreted as better thinkers preferring the utilitarian option, consistent with the DPM. However, we do not think that it is necessarily inconsistent with MMM. Our perspective says that better thinkers will attend to more moral considerations; however, unlike in the trolley-type dilemmas discussed above, it is not clear that there are any compelling normative factors in this scenario beyond saving the most lives possible. This result is therefore consistent with several accounts of moral judgment.

Cushman, Young, and Hauser (2006) took a unique approach to studying the role of conscious reasoning in moral judgment by examining whether people had introspective access to moral principles that guided their judgments. Specifically, they varied several aspects of trolley-type dilemmas within-subjects and asked participants to justify differences in their judgments caused by these manipulations. Participants readily articulated the difference between action and omission and endorsed it as morally relevant, suggesting that this principle (whether normatively correct or not) is available to conscious introspection and can guide moral judgments. Indeed, a re-analysis of this data showed that participants who could articulate this distinction were more likely to show the distinction in their judgments, suggesting a causal link between the expressed principle and the judgments themselves (Cushman et al., 2010). On the other hand, participants could not articulate the difference between intended harms and side effects, and though they could articulate the difference between harms achieved through physical contact and harms achieved through indirect means, they were hesitant to endorse this difference as morally relevant. These findings suggest that people have conscious access to at least some moral principles that can guide their judgments, consistent with some work on allocating scarce, life-saving medical resources, which finds that people are able to articulate several principles that do, empirically, affect these sorts of life-or-death moral decisions (Goodwin & Landy, 2014).

Lastly, reasoning appears to be related to the moral principles that people explicitly endorse. Related to the finding (reviewed above) that reasoning performance predicts condemnation and moralization of disobedient, disloyal, and impure actions (Landy, 2016), explicit beliefs that obedience to authority, in-group loyalty, and bodily and spiritual purity are important moral virtues are negatively associated with a preference for rational thinking (Garvey & Ford, 2014) and with cognitive ability (Pennycook et al., 2014) and reasoning performance (Landy, 2016; Pennycook et al., 2014). However, there is also some evidence that cognitive load can reduce endorsement of these values (Wright & Baril, 2011). At this time, it is not clear how to reconcile these results. Nonetheless, these findings converge on the conclusion that reasoning can shape not only one's moral judgments, but also one's moral values, and most evidence suggests that it does so in a manner consistent with our discussion of moralization above.

Overall, these various results point to a role for reasoning in moral judgment. They are generally consistent with our perspective here, though not uniquely so. However, they are largely inconsistent with the SIM's claim that internal reasoning typically plays no role in producing moral judgments. As research on these questions continues, it should become clearer what, if anything, these findings mean for the MMM. But, any theoretical perspective must ultimately be judged by the new testable predictions that it generates and the new questions that it raises rather than by how well it fits with existing data. To this end, we suggest several novel directions for future research based on our perspective here.

First, we would expect to observe direct evidence that better thinkers consider more information when resolving moral questions, a key claim of the MMM. Much of our theorizing here is owed to Cokely and Kelley (2009), who directly elicited from their participants reports of all that they had thought about while making decisions about risky gambles, finding that participants who scored higher on the CRT simply thought about more considerations than their low-CRT counterparts. We would expect a similar result in the moral domain: analysis of participants' self-reports of their thought processes and/or their online articulations of such processes in a think-aloud procedure (Ericsson & Simon, 1980) should reveal that better thinking is associated with attending to more considerations in moral judgment tasks. As of now, the only direct evidence for this comes from Moore et al. (2008), who found that high-WMC participants were sensitive to aspects of trolley-type dilemmas that low-WMC participants were not. Despite this lack of direct evidence that good thinking is associated with more complex representations of moral problem spaces, this theoretical claim makes sense of nearly all of the existing research in this area, and it is consistent with what is known about reasoning in other domains, as discussed above.

Second, we would expect our finding that good reasoning is associated with normative indifference to replicate in other types of moral dilemmas beyond trolley-type ones, as our original findings (Royzman, Landy, & Leeman, 2015) were meant to illustrate a fairly general phenomenon – any time two strong moral concerns are pitted against one another, better thinkers should be more likely to attend to both of them and to consider either action to be morally permissible. Studies replicating this effect outside of trolley-type dilemmas, and even outside of the conflict between deontological rules and utilitarian outcomes (e.g., scenarios like Kohlberg's [1971] Heinz dilemma, which pits two types of harms against one another, or Waytz, Dungan, and Young's [2013] whistleblowing dilemma, which pits fairness and loyalty, and perhaps self-interest, against one another) should support the generality of the perspective we have taken here.

On a related note, we think that it would generally be healthy for the field of moral judgment to move away from trolley-type dilemmas. Serious concerns have been raised about both the internal (Kahane & Shackel, 2008) and external (Bauman, McGraw, Bartels, & Warren, 2014) validity of these stimuli, and various other stimuli that pit utilitarian and deontological principles against one another have been developed but are not widely used (e.g., "broken promise scenarios," Royzman & Hagan, 2017; contextualized, pseudo-naturalistic dilemmas, Piazza & Landy, 2013; "rule dilemmas," Baron et al., 2015; vaccine failure dilemmas, Ritov & Baron, 1990). In the same vein, we think that more research should be done to understand how reasoning relates to lay conceptions of moral imperatives – very few studies in this area have included questions about moral requirements in addition to questions about permissibility (or "appropriateness" or "acceptability").

We would also like to make two more general recommendations for future research in this area. First, more experimental work establishing causal links between reasoning and moral judgments is sorely needed. There are several well-established ways to experimentally manipulate the amount of deliberate thinking that participants engage in (e.g., cognitive load, time pressure, priming, explicit instructions), but the majority of the research that we have reviewed (including our own) has focused on individual differences in cognitive style and/or ability. Such trait-level research is obviously important, but more experimental research would strengthen the claim that reasoning plays a causal role in producing moral judgments. Second, research is needed that examines what specific aspects of what we have called "good reasoning" reliably affect moral judgment. For simplicity's sake, we have treated many different psychological constructs (e.g., cognitive reflectivity, IQ, cognitive style, etc.) as measures of "good reasoning." But, in the wider literature, these are treated as at least somewhat distinct, which raises interesting questions about which aspects of cognition are related to which aspects of moral judgment. The finding by Pennycook et al. (2014) that cognitive reflectivity, but not cognitive ability, uniquely predicts condemnation of harmless purity offenses is a promising first step in this direction.

Our aim in this chapter has been to review the often disparate findings on the role of reasoning in moral judgment and to provide a coherent theoretical account of these findings. We have therefore deliberately not discussed the relationship between reasoning and moral *behavior*. At the present time, the literature that we have reviewed here and the literature on prosociality and cooperation have had surprisingly little influence on one another, but we see the potential for fruitful cross-pollination between them. In particular, we think that the Social Heuristics Hypothesis (Rand, 2016; Rand et al., 2014) has much to offer the study of moral judgment. On this view, cooperation with others is generally rewarded, and therefore becomes the default, intuitive response, while self-interested non-cooperative behavior relies on deliberate thinking. As we mentioned above (see Note 1), we think that moral judgments can be "intuitive" (i.e., fast and automatic) while still being rooted in reasoning. In the same way that cooperative behavioral strategies can become intuitive because they are typically the most advantageous strategies for the self in the long run, perhaps knowledge of moral rules and adherence to local conventions is generally rewarded and, thus, becomes similarly intuitive. Deliberation, then, is associated with incorporating other concerns into one's decision process when the situation calls for it.

Conclusion

In this chapter, we have reviewed a substantial amount of research on the role of reasoning in moral judgment and proposed a new theoretical view that synthesizes the disparate (and sometimes superficially conflicting) findings in this literature in a simple, coherent way. According to the Moral Myopia Model, all else being equal, better thinking is predictive of viewing moral problem spaces in more complex, differentiated ways, and taking more moral concerns into account during the judgment process rather than singularly attending to a single, salient concern, such as a deontological constraint, utility maximization, or a well-learned conventional norm. As we discussed, many of our own and others' recent findings in this area pose a challenge to the two dominant psychological theories of moral judgment: Greene's Dual-Process Model, which claims that reasoning tends to privilege a specific normative position (namely, act utilitarianism), and Haidt's Social Intuitionist Model, which claims that under typical circumstances, internal reasoning plays no role in producing moral judgments. At present, the MMM is only a theory of how reasoning matters for moral judgment – we readily acknowledge it does not constitute a comprehensive account of human moral cognition on the level of these theories, but we think that any such account must incorporate the theoretical perspective we have outlined here and acknowledge the critical role played by reasoning in the moral judgment process. As the title of this volume states, when it comes to moral judgment, reason matters.

Notes

1 We are grateful to Sydney Scott for her insightful comments on an earlier version of this chapter.
2 Two caveats must be made regarding this definition of reasoning. First, we do not mean to imply that all reasoning must be difficult or effortful. For example, when presented with the syllogism "Carla is Dave's daughter; Dave's daughters all have red hair; does Carla have red hair?" nearly everyone can surely arrive at the correct answer with little effort, but this would still qualify as reasoning (albeit reasoning applied to a very simple problem). However, the stimuli in the studies that we review, by design, constitute more difficult problems. They are intended to evoke more effortful reasoning, and so we adopt this definition for our purposes here. Second, we do not mean to imply that reasoned judgments about even difficult problems cannot become automatized over time – surely they can, like any repeated, intentional psychological process (see, e.g., Aarts & Custers, 2009; Kahneman & Klein, 2009). For example, if a person is presented with a novel moral question – say, whether euthanasia is morally permissible – they may reason through the problem more or less thoroughly (depending on their cognitive ability and style) and come to a conclusion. The next time they encounter this question, however, such reasoning may be less necessary because they have already arrived at the answer and now need only retrieve it from memory. Over time, this retrieval process may become automatic (i.e., "intuitive"), but this does not mean that the judgment is not rooted in reasoning. Unfortunately, very little research has investigated this possibility, so in this chapter, we mostly examine reasoning in the context of novel moral questions – most of the stimuli in the research we review involve highly unusual, rather fanciful moral problems that are likely new to most participants. We consider automatization to be an important topic for future research in the cognitive science of morality and a possible bridge between rationalist and intuitionist theories.
3 The conflation of automaticity with emotion is widespread in moral psychology, but it is clear that these are not necessarily the same thing; outside of the moral domain, at least, many automatic responses are devoid of emotion, and many emotional responses are arrived at only after considerable thought. Our focus here is on deliberate reasoning, not intuition, so for simplicity's sake, we will accept as a working assumption that automatic processes in moral judgment are often emotional in nature, and save opening this particular can of worms for another occasion.
4 Our purpose here is not to question the evidence for a role of intuitions in moral judgment, though we have done so in the past (Landy & Goodwin, 2015a, 2015b; Royzman, Kim, & Leeman, 2015; Royzman et al., 2011; Royzman, Leeman, & Baron, 2009). Rather, we wish to review recent evidence that overwhelmingly supports an important

role for reasoning in moral judgment, whatever the role of intuition may be. We will therefore largely avoid discussion of automatic processes in this chapter.

5 A follow-up study did show this correlation for a dilemma in which one person could be killed to save thousands, which suggests that this relationship may, importantly, depend on the parameters of the dilemma being considered. However, Trémolière and Bonnefon (2014) found that responses to dilemmas in which one person could be killed to save 500 showed no sensitivity to cognitive load or time pressure, both of which should reduce deliberative thinking. More research on the role of reasoning in resolving these sorts of catastrophic dilemmas is clearly warranted.

6 Kahane goes on to argue that controlled processing is associated more generally with counterintuitive responses to moral dilemmas, which can be utilitarian or deontological (in certain non-trolley-type dilemmas) and which he operationalizes as responses given by only small minorities of participants. Kahane and Greene, and their colleagues, have engaged in a lively debate over this claim, which remains unsettled (see Kahane et al., 2012; Paxton, Bruni, & Greene, 2014). For our part, we view deliberative thinking as being associated with neither utilitarianism nor counterintuitiveness per se, but with consideration of multiple normative concerns. Insofar as more or better thinking is required to attend to "counterintuitive" considerations that most people do not consider, this is consistent with Kahane's argument, but does not require it.

7 Which of these two normative factors is more salient to a given individual is likely to depend on their idiosyncratic moral values and their life history. For many people, deontological constraints against killing may be highly salient, while for others, a desire to do the most good possible may be more top-of-mind. Environmental cues can also impact the salience of competing normative factors (Broeders, van den Bos, Müller, & Ham, 2011). The point here is that reasoning performance is associated with neither of these normative positions in trolley-type dilemmas, but rather with attending to both simultaneously and yielding a more complex, integrative judgment.

References

Aarts, H., & Custers, R. (2009). Habit, action and consciousness. In W. P. Banks (Ed.), *Encyclopedia of consciousness* (Vol. 1, pp. 315–328). Oxford, UK: Elsevier.

Aharoni, E., Sinnott-Armstrong, W., & Kiehl, K. A. (2011). Can psychopathic offenders discern moral wrongs? A new look at the moral/conventional distinction. *Journal of Abnormal Psychology*, 121(2), 484–497.

Baron, J., Gürçay, B., Moore, A. B., & Starcke, K. (2012). Use of a Rasch model to predict response times to utilitarian moral dilemmas. *Synthese*, 189(Suppl 1), 107–117.

Baron, J., Scott, S., Fincher, K., & Metz, S. E. (2015). Why does the Cognitive Reflection Test (sometimes) predict utilitarian moral judgment (and other things)? *Journal of Applied Research in Memory and Cognition*, 4(3), 265–284.

Bartels, D. M. (2006). Proportion dominance: The generality and variability of favoring relative savings over absolute savings. *Organizational Behavior and Human Decision Processes*, 100(1), 76–95.

Bartels, D. M. (2008). Principled moral sentiment and the flexibility of moral judgment and decision making. *Cognition*, 108(2), 381–417.

Bauman, C. W., McGraw, A. P., Bartels, D. M., & Warren, C. (2014). Revisiting external validity: Concerns about trolley problems and other sacrificial dilemmas in moral psychology. *Social and Personality Psychology Compass*, 8/9, 536–554.

Białek, M., & De Neys, W. (2016). Conflict detection during moral decision-making: Evidence for deontic reasoners' utilitarian sensitivity. *Journal of Cognitive Psychology*, 28(5), 631–639.

Björklund, F. (2004). Just because it's disgusting does make it more wrong: Level of disgust affects moral judgment. *Lund Psychological Reports*, 5(3), 1–13.

Broeders, R., van den Bos, K., Müller, P. A., & Ham, J. (2011). Should I save or should I not kill? How people solve moral dilemmas depends on which rule is most accessible. *Journal of Experimental Social Psychology*, 47(5), 923–934.

Buon, M., Jacob, P., Loissel, E., & Dupoux, E. (2013). A non-mentalistic cause-based heuristic in human social evaluations. *Cognition*, 126(2), 149–155.

Cokely, E. T., & Feltz, A. (2009). Individual differences, judgment biases, and theory-of-mind: Deconstructing the intentional action side effect asymmetry. *Journal of Research in Personality*, 43(1), 18–24.

Cokely, E. T., & Kelley, C. M. (2009). Cognitive abilities and superior decision making under risk: A protocol analysis and process model evaluation. *Judgment and Decision Making*, 4(1), 20–23.

Conway, P., & Gawronski, B. (2013). Deontological and utilitarian inclinations in moral decision making: A process dissociation approach. *Journal of Personality and Social Psychology*, 104(2), 216–235.

Cornwell, J. F. M., & Higgins, E. T. (2016). Eager feelings and vigilant reasons: Regulatory focus differences in judging moral wrongs. *Journal of Experimental Psychology: General*, 145(3), 338–355.

Cushman, F., Young, L., & Greene, J. D. (2010). Multi-system moral psychology. In J. M. Doris & Moral Psychology Research Group (Eds.), *The moral psychology handbook* (pp. 47–71). Oxford, UK: Oxford University Press.

Cushman, F., Young, L., & Hauser, M. (2006). The role of conscious reasoning and intuition in moral judgment: Testing three principles of harm. *Psychological Science*, 17(12), 1082–1089.

Damon, W. (1975). Early conceptions of positive justice as related to the development of logical operations. *Child Development*, 46(2), 301–312.

Duke, A. A., & Bègue, L. (2015). The drunk utilitarian: Blood alcohol concentration predicts utilitarian responses in moral dilemmas. *Cognition*, 134, 121–127.

Ericsson, K. A., & Simon, H. A. (1980). Verbal reports as data. *Psychological Review*, 87(3), 215–251.

Evans, J. St. B. T., & Stanovich, K. E. (2013). Dual-process theories of higher cognition: Advancing the debate. *Perspectives on Psychological Science*, 8(3), 223–241.

Foot, P. (1967). The problem of abortion and the doctrine of the double effect. *Oxford Review*, 5, 5–15.

Frederick, S. (2005). Cognitive reflection and decision making. *Journal of Economic Perspectives*, 19(4), 25–42.

Garvey, K., & Ford, T. G. (2014). Rationality, political orientation, and the individualizing and binding moral foundations. *Letters on Evolutionary Behavioral Science*, 5(1), 9–12.

Goodwin, G. P., & Landy, J. F. (2014). Valuing different human lives. *Journal of Experimental Psychology: General*, 143(2), 778–803.

Graham, J., Haidt, J., & Nosek, B. A. (2009). Liberals and conservatives rely on different sets of moral foundations. *Journal of Personality and Social Psychology*, 96(5), 1029–1046.

Greene, J. D., Morelli, S. A., Lowenberg, K., Nystrom, L. E., & Cohen, J. D. (2008). Cognitive load selectively interferes with utilitarian moral judgment. *Cognition*, 107(3), 1144–1154.

Greene, J. D., Nystrom, L. E., Engell, A. D., Darley, J. M., & Cohen, J. D. (2004). The neural bases of cognitive conflict and control in moral judgment. *Neuron*, 44(2), 389–400.

Greene, J. D., Sommerville, R. B., Nystrom, L. E., Darley, J. M., & Cohen, J. D. (2001). An fMRI investigation of emotional engagement in moral judgment. *Science*, 293(5537), 2105–2108.

Haidt, J. (2001). The emotional dog and its rational tail: A social intuitionist approach to moral judgment. *Psychological Review*, 108(4), 814–834.

Haidt, J., & Graham, J. (2007). When morality opposes justice: Conservatives have moral intuitions that liberals may not recognize. *Social Justice Research*, 20(1), 98–116.

Haidt, J., & Hersh, M. A. (2001). Sexual morality: The cultures and emotions of conservatives and liberals. *Journal of Applied Social Psychology*, 31(1), 191–221.

Haidt, J., Koller, S. H., & Dias, M. G. (1993). Affect, culture, and morality, or, is it wrong to eat your dog? *Journal of Personality and Social Psychology*, 65(4), 613–628.

Harman, G., Mason, K., & Sinnott-Armstrong, W. (2010). Moral reasoning. In J. M. Doris & Moral Psychology Research Group (Eds.), *The moral psychology handbook* (pp. 206–245). Oxford, UK: Oxford University Press.

Horberg, E. J., Oveis, C., Keltner, D., & Cohen, A. B. (2009). Disgust and the moralization of purity. *Journal of Personality and Social Psychology*, 97(6), 963–976.

Huebner, B., Lee, J., & Hauser, M. D. (2010). The moral-conventional distinction in mature moral competence. *Journal of Cognition and Culture*, 10(1), 1–26.

Kagan, S. (1998). *Normative ethics*. Boulder, CO: Westview Press.

Kahane, G. (2012). On the wrong track: Process and content in moral psychology. *Mind and Language*, 27(5), 519–545.

Kahane, G. (2015). Sidetracked by trolleys: Why sacrificial moral dilemmas tell us little (or nothing) about utilitarian judgment. *Social Neuroscience*, 10(5), 551–560.

Kahane, G., & Shackel, N. (2008). Do abnormal responses show utilitarian bias? *Nature*, 452 (7185), e5–e6.

Kahane, G., Wiech, K., Shackel, N., Farias, M., Savulescu, J., & Tracey, I. (2012). The neural basis of intuitive and counterintuitive moral judgments. *Social Cognitive and Affective Neuroscience*, 7(4), 393–402.

Kahneman, D. (2011). *Thinking, fast and slow*. New York: Farrar, Strauss, and Giroux.

Kahneman, D., & Klein, G. (2009). Conditions for intuitive expertise: A failure to disagree. *American Psychologist*, 64(6), 515–526.

Kamm, F. M. (2009). Neuroscience and moral reasoning: A note on recent research. *Philosophy and Public Affairs*, 37(4), 330–345.

Killgore, W. D. S., Killgore, D. B., Day, L. M., Li, C., Kamimori, G. H., & Balkin, T. J. (2007). The effects of 53 hours of sleep deprivation on moral judgment. *Sleep*, 30(3), 345–352.

Knobe, J. (2003). Intentional action and side effects in ordinary language. *Analysis*, 63(279), 190–193.

Kohlberg, L. (1971). From is to ought: How to commit the naturalistic fallacy and get away with it in the study of moral development. In T. Mischel (Ed.), *Cognitive development and epistemology* (pp. 151–235). New York: Academic Press.

Koop, G. J. (2013). An assessment of the temporal dynamics of moral decisions. *Judgment and Decision Making*, 8(5), 527–539.

Körner, A., & Volk, S. (2014). Concrete and abstract ways to deontology: Cognitive capacity moderates construal level effects on moral judgments. *Journal of Experimental Social Psychology*, 55, 139–145.

Landy, J. F. (2016). Representations of moral violations: Category members and associated features. *Judgment and Decision Making*, 11(5), 496–508.

Landy, J. F., & Goodwin, G. P. (2015a). Does incidental disgust amplify moral judgment? A meta-analytic review of experimental evidence. *Perspectives on Psychological Science*, 10(4), 518–536.

Landy, J. F., & Goodwin, G. P. (2015b). Our conclusions were tentative, but appropriate: A reply to Schnall et al. (2015). *Perspectives on Psychological Science*, 10(4), 539–540.

Lanteri, A., Chelini, C., & Rizzello, S. (2008). An experimental investigation of emotions and reasoning in the trolley problem. *Journal of Business Ethics*, 83(4), 789–804.

Mann, T., & Ward, A. (2004). To eat or not to eat: Implications of the attentional myopia model for restrained eaters. *Journal of Abnormal Psychology*, 113(1), 90–98.

Mann, T., & Ward, A. (2007). Attention, self-control, and health behaviors. *Current Directions in Psychological Science*, 16(5), 280–283.

Markovits, H., & Nantel, G. (1989). The belief-bias effect in the production and evaluation of logical syllogisms. *Memory and Cognition*, 17(1), 11–17.

McGuire, J., Langdon, R., Coltheart, M., & Mackenzie, C. (2009). A reanalysis of the personal/impersonal distinction in moral psychology research. *Journal of Experimental Social Psychology*, 45(3), 577–580.

Monin, B., Pizarro, D. A., & Beer, J. S. (2007). Deciding versus reacting: Conceptions of moral judgment and the reason-affect debate. *Review of General Psychology*, 11(2), 99–111.

Moore, A. B., Clark, B. A., & Kane, M. J. (2008). Who shalt not kill? Individual differences in working memory capacity, executive control, and moral judgment. *Psychological Science*, 19(6), 549–557.

Nichols, S., & Mallon, R. (2006). Moral dilemmas and moral rules. *Cognition*, 100(3), 530–542.

O'Kane, A., Fawcett, D., & Blackburn, R. (1996). Psychopathy and moral reasoning: Comparison of two classifications. *Personality and Individual Differences*, 20(4), 505–514.

Olsen, O. K., Pallesen, S., & Eid, J. (2010). The impact of partial sleep deprivation on moral reasoning in military officers. *Sleep*, 33(8), 1086–1090.

Pacini, R., & Epstein, S. (1999). The relation of rational and experiential information processing styles to personality, basic beliefs, and the ratio-bias phenomenon. *Journal of Personality and Social Psychology*, 76(6), 972–987.

Paxton, J. M., Bruni, T., & Greene, J. D. (2014). Are "counter-intuitive" deontological judgments really counter-intuitive? An empirical reply to Kahane et al. (2012). *Social Cognitive and Affective Neuroscience*, 9(9), 1368–1371.

Paxton, J. M., Ungar, L., & Greene, J. D. (2012). Reflection and reasoning in moral judgment. *Cognitive Science*, 36(1), 163–177.

Pennycook, G., Cheyne, J. A., Barr, N., Koehler, D. J., & Fugelsang, J. A. (2014). The role of analytic thinking in moral judgements and values. *Thinking and Reasoning*, 20(2), 188–214.

Pennycook, G., Fugelsang, J. A., & Koehler, D. J. (2015). What makes us think? A three-stage dual-process model of analytic engagement. *Cognitive Psychology*, 80, 34–72.

Pennycook, G., & Ross, R. M. (2016). Commentary: Cognitive reflection vs. calculation in decision making. *Frontiers in Psychology*, 7: 9. doi:00A0;10.3389/fpsyg.2016.00009

Pham, M. T., & Avnet, T. (2004). Ideals and oughts and the reliance on affect versus substance in persuasion. *Journal of Consumer Research*, 30(4), 503–518.

Pham, M. T., & Avnet, T. (2009). Contingent reliance on the affect heuristic as a function of regulatory focus. *Organizational Behavior and Human Decision Processes*, 108(2), 267–278.

Piaget, J. (1965). *The moral judgment of the child*. New York: Free Press. (Original work published 1932.)

Piazza, J., & Landy, J. F. (2013). "Lean not on your own understanding": Belief that morality is founded on divine authority and non-utilitarian moral judgments. *Judgment and Decision Making*, 8(6), 639–661.

Pinillos, N. A., Smith, N., Nair, G. S., Marchetto, P., & Mun, C. (2011). Philosophy's new challenge: Experiments and intentional action. *Mind and Language*, 26(1), 115–139.

Pizarro, D. A., Uhlmann, E., & Bloom, P. (2003). Causal deviance and the attribution of moral responsibility. *Journal of Experimental Social Psychology*, 39(6), 653–660.

Plato. (1987). *The Republic and other works* (Trans. B. Jowett). Garden City, NY: Anchor Books.

Rand, D. G. (2016). Cooperation, fast and slow: Meta-analytic evidence for a theory of social heuristics and self-interested deliberation. *Psychological Science*, 27(9), 1192–1206.

Rand, D. G., Peysakhovich, A., Kraft-Todd, G. T., Newman, G. E., Wurzbacher, O., Nowak, M. A., & Greene, J. D. (2014). Social heuristics shape intuitive cooperation. *Nature Communications*, 5: 3677.

Rest, J. R. (1974). *Manual for the Defining Issues Test: An objective test of moral judgment*. Minneapolis, MN: University of Minnesota.

Rest, J. R., Narvaez, D., Thoma, S. J., & Bebeau, M. J. (1999). DIT2: Devising and testing a revised instrument of moral judgment. *Journal of Educational Psychology*, 91(4), 644–659.

Ritov, I., & Baron, J. (1990). Reluctance to vaccinate: Omission bias and ambiguity. *Journal of Behavioral Decision Making*, 3(4), 263–277.

Royzman, E. B., Goodwin, G. P., & Leeman, R. F. (2011). When sentimental rules collide: "Norms with feelings" in the dilemmatic context. *Cognition*, 121(1), 101–114.

Royzman, E., & Hagan, J. P. (2017). The shadow and the tree: Inference and transformation of cognitive content in psychology of moral judgment. In B. Trémolière & J.-F. Bonnefon (Eds.), *Moral inference* (pp. 56–74). Abingdon, UK: Routledge.

Royzman, E. B., Kim, K., & Leeman, R. F. (2015). The curious tale of Julie and Mark: Unraveling the moral dumbfounding effect. *Judgment and Decision Making*, 10(4), 296–313.

Royzman, E. B., Landy, J. F., & Goodwin, G. P. (2014). Are good reasoners more incest-friendly? Trait cognitive reflection predicts selective moralization in a sample of American adults. *Judgment and Decision Making*, 9(3), 176–190.

Royzman, E. B., Landy, J. F., & Leeman, R. F. (2015). Are thoughtful people more utilitarian? CRT as a unique predictor of moral minimalism in the dilemmatic context. *Cognitive Science*, 39(2), 325–352.

Royzman, E. B., Leeman, R. F., & Baron, J. (2009). Unsentimental ethics: Towards a content-specific account of the moral-conventional distinction. *Cognition*, 112(1), 159–174.

Schnall, S., Haidt, J., Clore, G. L., & Jordan, A. H. (2008). Disgust as embodied moral judgment. *Personality and Social Psychology Bulletin*, 34(8), 1096–1109.

Sheskin, M., & Baumard, N. (2016). Switching away from utilitarianism: The limited role of utility calculations in moral judgment. *PloS One*, 11: e0160084.

Starke, K., Ludwig, A.-C., & Brand, M. (2012). Anticipatory stress interferes with utilitarian moral judgment. *Judgment and Decision Making*, 7(1), 61–68.

Steele, C. M., & Josephs, R. A. (1990). Alcohol myopia: Its prized and dangerous effects. *American Psychologist*, 45(8), 921–933.

Suter, R. S., & Hertwig, R. (2011). Time and moral judgment. *Cognition*, 119(3), 454–458.

Tempesta, D., Couyoumdjian, A., Moroni, F., Marzano, C., De Gennaro, L., & Ferrara, M. (2012). The impact of one night of sleep deprivation on moral judgment. *Social Neuroscience*, 7(3), 292–300.

Trémolière, B., & Bonnefon, J.-F. (2014). Efficient kill-save ratios ease up the cognitive demands on counterintuitive moral utilitarianism. *Personality and Social Psychology Bulletin*, 40(7), 923–930.

Trémolière, B., De Neys, W., & Bonnefon, J.-F. (2012). Mortality salience and morality: Thinking about death makes people less utilitarian. *Cognition*, 124(3), 379–384.

Turiel, E. (1983). *The development of social knowledge: Morality and convention*. Cambridge, UK: Cambridge University Press.

Turiel, E., Hildebrandt, C., & Wainryb, C. (1991). Judging social issues: Difficulties, inconsistencies, and consistencies. *Monographs of the Society for Research in Child Development*, 56(2), 1–103.

Waytz, A., Dungan, J., & Young, L. (2013). The whistleblower's dilemma and the fairness-loyalty tradeoff. *Journal of Experimental Social Psychology*, 49(6), 1027–1033.

Weissenborn, R., & Duka, T. (2003). Acute alcohol effects on cognitive function in social drinkers: Their relationship to drinking habits. *Psychopharmacology*, 165(3), 306–312.

Wright, J. C., & Baril, G. (2011). The role of cognitive resources in determining our moral intuitions: Are we all liberals at heart? *Journal of Experimental Social Psychology*, 47(5), 1007–1012.

Youssef, F. F., Dookeeram, K., Basdeo, V., Francis, E., Doman, M., Mamed, D., … Legall, G. (2012). Stress alters personal moral decision making. *Psychoneuroendocrinology*, 37(4), 491–498.

6
INTUITION, REASON, AND CREATIVITY
An integrative dual-process perspective

Nathaniel Barr

Introduction

Long before psychology was a science, creativity was seen in many cultures as an essentially important yet difficult to understand aspect of human experience. Throughout history, to account for the mysterious inception of novel and useful ideas, appeals have often been made to supernatural forces and divine intervention. Decades ago, as psychology first began to approach, in earnest, the study of creativity from a scientific perspective, the perception that creativity was enigmatic persisted, with the construct being identified as amongst "the vaguest, most ambiguous, and most confused terms in psychology" (Ausubel, 1964, p. 344). Recent years have seen increasing amounts of research in the psychological literature aimed at understanding the nature of creative thought, yet this increased attention has done little to rectify the longstanding difficulty in characterizing the true nature of creative thought.

At the global level, creativity studies has been described as fractionated, with researchers from diverse academic disciplines and subfields of psychology, such as social, cognitive, and industrial/organizational areas, having little convergence in the way they approach the study of creativity (Hennessey & Amabile, 2010). Empirical exploration and theoretical development seems to exist within silos, and the opinion of some leading researchers diverges little from Ausubel's (1964) characterization, with contemporary research having been described as "murky but plentiful" (Hennessey & Amabile, 2010, p. 576). Confusion abounds within more local issues as well, with a particularly glaring inconsistency appearing in the cognitive literature regarding the extent to which executive cognition aids or hinders the creative process (e.g., Barr, Pennycook, Stolz, & Fugelsang, 2015; Smeekens & Kane, 2016).

The current chapter considers this local issue – the relative contribution of executive processing – in light of increasing amounts of evidence that reason is important in many types of creative thinking. Importantly, it is argued that such findings are not contradictory to results that find analytic thinking can hinder creative thought, nor are they in conflict with work that illuminates the importance of associative processing in insight problem solving. Rather, such evidence constitutes complementary qualifications surrounding a nuanced and dynamic psychological construct. Through consideration of the evidence surrounding the interaction of autonomous and controlled thinking in diverse forms of creativity, and the sorts of theoretical models required to account for such evidence, suggestions are made for how to conceptualize creativity more globally, with an eye for unifying some of the broader challenges faced by the study of creativity as a whole.

Thus, this chapter has several aims. First, it reviews the growing evidence implicating a central role of analytic thinking in certain types of creative thinking and considers the implications for local debates surrounding the utility of executive engagement in creative thought. It is concluded that different sorts of creative thinking require varying degrees of executive engagement and that more local theories of specific sorts of creative thinking are required. It is then argued that conceiving of this local issue from this perspective has implications for the sorts of broad conceptual frameworks that should be used to describe creative thought across subfields. In particular, it is suggested that researchers ought to adopt a meta-theoretical model that can account for the dynamic exchange between autonomous and controlled processing and the way that these modes of thought connect to generative and evaluative content in diverse contexts. To satisfy these requirements, creativity is argued to be best considered in the context of a broader dual-process meta-theoretical framework of human thinking, which has been explicated in the reasoning and decision-making literatures (cf., Evans & Stanovich, 2013). It is suggested that an important aspect of clarifying the nature of creative thinking is to strive for common conceptual language and frameworks across subfields wherever reasonable and feasible (see Silvia, 2014). The benefits of adopting such a perspective within the study of creativity are discussed, as are the positive implications for greater cross-pollination across reasoning and creativity research.

The rise of reason in creativity research

The genesis of novel and appropriate ideas has long been theorized to arise via autonomous activity within the associative "engine" of the mind. This perspective has resulted in creativity becoming a hallmark example of a subfield of psychology that historically has appealed heavily to intuitive and associative processes for explanatory mechanisms and to account for meaningful individual differences. Although a role has been carved for analytic thought in creativity, reflection and controlled processing has primarily been identified as important in the evaluation of ideas generated in the unconscious due to autonomous spread within semantic memory. Recent empirical evidence, however, suggests that analytic, executive, and reflective cognitive processes can play a more central role in creativity than has often been assumed. Such evidence includes correlational, experimental, and neuroscientific findings, and it spans several domains of creative thinking, including analogical reasoning, divergent thinking, making remote connections, and insight problem solving.

Consider one of the most venerable cognitive phenomena in the literature on creative thinking: the serial-order effect, which refers to the finding that when generating ideas, the number of ideas produced decreases over time (i.e., decreased fluency), but the ratings of creativity associated with ideas increase over time (i.e., increased originality; Christensen, Guilford, & Wilson, 1957). For instance, in a divergent-thinking test, fewer ideas would appear in the last minute than in the first minute of testing, but the ideas produced during the last minute are typically rated as more creative. This result is replicable and well studied across a number of paradigms. This pattern of results has long been considered to reflect the dynamics of the associative processes underlying idea generation. The nature of associative spread is presumed to be such that less creative, more semantically proximal ideas are active first, followed by more creative and more semantically distal ideas. Such an interpretation of this specific effect supported the broader view that most of the action in creative thought is done autonomously and unconsciously.

A related conception regarding the nature of creative ideation comes from Mednick's (1962) classic paper, "The associative basis of the creative process." Mednick considered the process of creative thinking to consist of "forming associative elements into new combinations which either meet specific requirements or are in some way useful. The more mutually remote the elements of the new combination, the more creative the process or solution" (1962, p. 221). Mednick developed an index of creativity called the Remote Associates Test (RAT), which is thought to tap this particular ability. During the RAT, participants are presented with three words that all hold independent connections with a fourth word, and participants are instructed to generate the fourth word (e.g., GOLF-NIGHT-SANDWICH-> CLUB). His account of superior performance on the RAT was connected to responses in word-association tasks and what he referred to as "associative hierarchies." He argued that individuals differ in the nature of these hierarchies: Whereas some individuals have steep associative hierarchies, meaning that their semantic networks are organized such that highly associated words are heavily weighted and readily come to mind, others have flatter associative hierarchies and less rigid associational organization in semantic memory, which allows them to fluently generate more semantically distant associates and makes them less biased toward conventional word associates. Flatter associative hierarchies have been shown to relate to better performance on the RAT (Mednick, Mednick, & Jung, 1964; Piers & Kirchner, 1971), suggesting that such a semantic organization is beneficial for creative thinking and for facilitating the autonomous spread of activation to unusual associates.

In recent years, such conceptions have been supplanted or expanded by more executively oriented explanations. For instance, in reconsidering purely associative factors and exploring a greater role for controlled processing, Benedek and Neubauer (2013) directly tested whether associative hierarchies of the sort described above predicted performance in divergent thinking and self-reported creative behaviors. In free-association tasks, more creative participants were indeed more fluent when generating responses, and overall their responses were less common. Interestingly, however, creativity was unrelated to the nature of one's associative hierarchy in association tasks. All participants began with less distal associates and became increasingly creative over time, counter to Mednick's argument that the more creative individuals should provide more distant, less common items earlier on. In describing the central difference between the creative and noncreative individuals in their study, Benedek and Neubauer (2013) note that although both groups started with very common responses and made progressively more uncommon responses with time, the more creative individuals were much faster at generating responses than their less creative counterparts, and accordingly they ended up retrieving a greater number of uncommon responses earlier on in the task. In other words, since the more creative individuals in the sample have greater associative fluency and make more responses in the same amount of time, they manage to exhaust the list of common items earlier on in the experiment and hence can proceed to retrieving more uncommon associates more quickly than less creative individuals. Importantly, however, the authors do not presume that this ability reflects individual differences in autonomous cognition, but instead interpret this evidence in the context of work that has found associational fluency of this sort to be connected to heightened adaptive executive function and greater cognitive control (e.g., Gilhooly, Fioratou, Anthony, & Wynn, 2007). They suggest that "creativity ... may not necessarily imply a special organization of associative memory, but it may rather rely on advanced executive abilities allowing for a highly effective access and processing of memory content" (Benedek & Neubauer, 2013, p. 287). That is, contrary to the classical assumption that differences in creativity ought to be attributed to the ease with which ideas spontaneously come to mind as a consequence of differences in semantic organization, Benedek and Neubauer (2013) argue that what is important is the ability to selectively retrieve uncommon associations through *controlled processing and retrieval mechanisms.*

In a similar vein, Beaty and Silvia (2012) revisited the serial-order effect in the context of a divergent-thinking task and replicated the primary effect: an increase in the creativity of responses (i.e., originality) and a decrease in the number of responses (i.e., fluency). These authors also questioned a purely associative understanding of the phenomenon and explored the nature of this effect as a function of individual differences. Specifically, they measured the general fluid intelligence of participants in their study and connected this measure to the creativity of the ideas offered over time. They found that whereas individuals with lower intelligence exhibited the classic serial-order effect, those higher in intelligence showed a diminished serial-order effect. This result suggests that the passive spread of activation to identify relations amongst items in memory is not the only way to be creative. It is possible to leverage intelligence to strategically intervene via top-down control and executive processes to find one's way to more creative ideas.

Such a supposition is also supported by recent evidence pertaining to the types of thinkers and factors that allow better performance in solving RAT problems.

Barr et al. (2015) administered a variety of cognitive ability and style measures to participants and related performance on these tasks to a number of creativity tests. The cognitive style measures indexed the extent to which a participant was disposed to engaging analytic or reflective thought. It was found that those who were (a) higher in cognitive ability and (b) more disposed to analytic thinking (based on both performance and self-report measures) solved more RAT problems than those who scored lower on these two measures. Insight problem solving on the RAT, or the sudden "illumination of solutions," has also even been related to executive processes. For instance, it has been found that articulatory suppression (i.e., repeating digits) impeded insight problem solving on difficult problems, whereas talking aloud (i.e., verbalizing one's thoughts about the task and inner-thoughts) facilitated performance (Ball & Stevens, 2009). In related work, Chein and Weisberg (2014) found that individual differences in attention and verbal working memory (WM) aided the solving of RAT problems.

Research has explored the strategies people use to solve RAT problems, revealing systematic tendencies that belie a purely passive spreading activation approach to solution. For instance, Smith, Huber, and Vul (2013) analyzed the way people tend to try and solve RAT problems and found that people

> use two systematic strategies to solve multiply-constrained problems: (a) people produce guesses primarily on the basis of just one of the three cues at a time; and (b) people adopt a local search strategy – they make new guesses based in part on their previous guesses.
>
> *(p. 64)*

In the context of the work above, it seems that people use controlled cognitive processing to direct their search in semantic space. In a paper that used both behavioral and computational modeling evidence, Gupta, Jang, Mednick, and Huber (2012) asserted that higher performance on the RAT was predicated upon an individual's ability to "recognize that a potential answer meets the specified requirements, and, more important, they must not be biased to consider only high-frequency candidate answers" (p. 293). It therefore seems that reflection and analytic thought could facilitate efficient search of semantic space, assessment of ideas generated autonomously through associative processes, and the ability to inhibit or override fluently accessed intuitive answers to arrive at the correct creative connection.

More support for the role of analytic thinking in creativity comes from research exploring the cognitive and neuroscientific correlates of creative analogical reasoning. To study creativity in the context of analogical reasoning, researchers have used the dimension of semantic distance to distinguish more creative, from less creative, analogies (e.g., Green, Cohen, Kim, & Gray, 2012). Analogical relations in which the constituent sub-relations are closer in semantic space and have a greater degree of superficial similarity are considered to be relatively less creative than analogies in which the underlying first-order relations are more semantically distant, share little in superficial similarity, and are united by only relational information. Although semantic-distance scores are computed as continuous values between 0 and 1, a dichotomy between cross- and within-domain analogies is often used. For example, in a within-domain analogy, the A:B pair is drawn from the same category (domain) as the C:D pair (e.g., Lamb chop is to Lamb as Pork chop is to Pig). In cross-domain analogies, however, the A:B and C:D pairs come from distinct categories (e.g., Lamb chop is to Lamb as Chapter is to Book).

In the work of Barr et al. (2015) discussed above, in addition to the RAT, participants also engaged in a speeded analogical reasoning task in which they were presented such four-term analogies of the form "A is to B as C is to D" and asked to identify as quickly as possible whether a valid analogy existed. Stimuli were a mixture of non-analogies, within-domain analogies (semantically near, noncreative), and cross-domain analogies (semantically distant, creative). Although overt responses in this task are identification based, success depends on covert generation of mappings between the constituent pairs and is accordingly considered a task of creative generation (see Green, Cohen et al., 2012, for a more detailed explanation of this logic). Participants were much more accurate and faster in this speeded analogical reasoning task at identifying noncreative, within-domain analogies than they were at correctly ascertaining creative, cross-domain analogies, providing further support for the idea that analyticity and reflection can be important for spanning semantic distance. In considering individual differences in this task, Barr et al. (2015) found that participants who were more willing and able to engage analytic thinking tended to be more successful at comprehending semantically distant creative analogies. Importantly, these participants also tended to be more successful at identifying invalid analogies, suggesting that this heightened performance was due to a greater ability to forge distant connections, rather than a general bias to respond affirmatively. Recall that the same relation with reasoning performance was true for the number of RAT problems solved (i.e., more analytic thinkers were more creative). Further, the number of RAT items solved was significantly positively correlated with creative analogical reasoning performance, suggesting a relation between these different types of creative thought. Such findings are consistent with Spellman, Holyoak and Morrison's (2001) observation that priming on the basis of relational information does not occur ballistically, but instead requires conscious attention toward that level of analysis. Together, this work suggests that making relationally complex creative connections requires analytic thinking.

The foregoing behavioral work is consistent with neuroimaging research that has explored creative analogical reasoning using the same stimuli described above in the work of Barr et al. (2015). The evidence supports a view that creative analogical reasoning relies heavily on frontal regions of the brain, specifically the frontopolar cortex (Bunge, Wendelken, Badre, & Wagner, 2005; Green, Fugelsang, Kraemer, Shamosh, & Dunbar, 2006; Green, Kraemer, Fugelsang, Gray, & Dunbar, 2010; Green, Fugelsang, Kraemer, Gray, & Dunbar, 2012). As semantic distance between the constituent pairs of an analogy parametrically increases, so too does activation in the frontopolar cortex, and this is true both in recognition and in generation tasks. This robust finding is presumed to occur as these regions are thought to underlie the relational integration required for understanding the complex creative connections, with more activation required for more semantically distant elements. Ramnani and Owen (2004) propose a model of the cognitive-anatomical architecture of prefrontal function and organization that implicates the frontopolar cortex as being crucial for the integration of items represented in relatively distal cortical space. In addition, neuropsychological work with frontotemporal dementia patients has shown that creative ability is contingent upon involvement of frontopolar cortex (de Souza et al., 2010), which provides convergent support for the conclusions of the neuroimaging results surrounding creative analogical reasoning. Green et al. (2006), in summarizing the key role of such regions in creative thinking, argue that

> highly developed frontal lobes – frontopolar cortex in particular – make the human brain unique in terms of its structure. It is perhaps not coincidental that the most advanced reaches of the evolved human brain should mediate function at the most advanced reaches of human cognition.
>
> (p. 134)

Considered in the context of research that finds a strong association between frontal lobe function and executive processes (e.g., Friedman & Miyake, 2016), work such as this, which connects frontal regions to creative thought, strongly supports accounts of creativity that emphasize analytic thinking.

Taken together, the evidence regarding the behavioral and neural correlates of creativity – whether from research examining creative analogical reasoning, divergent thinking, or making remote connections – strongly suggests a central connection between creative and analytic thinking. It is important to note, however, that the research discussed here represents a selective sampling of the studies that connect creativity and analyticity, and it is not an exhaustive recounting of the work in this area.

Intuitive and analytic processes in creativity

Despite an increasing impetus for conceptions of creativity to include an important role for analytic thinking, it is important to recognize that autonomous and intuitive thinking is also implicated in creativity. That is to say, an increased acknowledgment that analytic thinking is implicated in creative thought does not require a conception of creativity that is completely divorced from intuitive and autonomous cognitive processing, nor does it necessarily invalidate any existing research. Rather, creative thinking is best conceived as a dynamic interaction between autonomous and controlled processing.

In exploring the contributions of both types of thinking, Beaty, Silvia, Nusbaum, Jauk, and Benedek (2014) measured the contributions of both associative and executive processes in divergent thinking. In two studies, the authors indexed creativity using a classic divergent-thinking task (Alternative Uses of Objects, which is one of the most commonly used measures of creative ability; Kaufman, 2009) and related originality of ideas to associative and executive processes. Associative processes were measured through the use of two verbal-fluency tasks (Carroll, 1993) for which participants were asked to generate synonyms for common words. Using Latent Semantic Analysis (Landauer, Foltz, & Laham, 1998), participants' responses were then examined as a function of remoteness to the original prompt, which allowed the computation of a semantic-distance score that served as a measure of the relative associative differences across participants (see also Green, 2016). Executive abilities used were a measure of crystallized intelligence (Study 1) and a measure of fluid intelligence (Study 2). Across both studies, structural equation modeling revealed *both* associative and executive processes as significant independent predictors of creative thinking.

Beaty and colleagues have also provided neuroscientific evidence pertaining to the brain structures thought to underlie such an interaction between associative and executive processes, further providing evidence that to understand creativity, one must consider the interaction of analytic thinking and autonomous processes (see Beaty, Benedek, Silvia, & Schacter, 2016, for a review of this work). In one such study, Beaty, Benedek et al. (2014) explored resting-state connectivity between areas of the brain known to relate to controlled cognition (i.e., prefrontal cortex) and autonomous, associative processing (i.e., the default network). They found that those who scored higher on divergent-thinking tests had greater functional connectivity between the prefrontal cortex and default network than did the less creative participants. Such a result bolsters their behavioral work, cited above, and suggests that people who are more creative have "greater cooperation between brain regions associated with cognitive control and low-level imaginative processes" (p. 92). Beaty, Benedek, Kaufman, and Silvia (2015) found convergent evidence when exploring dynamic interactions between these brain regions while participants actually engaged in divergent-thinking tasks. Temporal connectivity analysis revealed that coupling between default network and dorsolateral prefrontal cortex was an important facet of creative thought. The researchers conclude that their results support a view in which creative thought depends on "cooperation between brain networks linked to cognitive control and spontaneous thought, which may reflect focused internal attention and the top-down control of spontaneous cognition during creative idea production" (p. 1). Both behavioral and neuroscientific evidence reach the same conclusions regarding the necessity of understanding both associative and executive processes in creativity.

Thus, given that individual differences in associative and executive abilities seem to be related to creative thinking, when one analyzes both discrepancies in results across studies (with some arguing that executive engagement is important and others arguing not) might, in part, be a consequence of what researchers elect to focus their attention on. Sowden, Pringle, and Gabora (2015), for example, note that Norris and Epstein (2011) reported that an experiential thinking style was related to performance on divergent-thinking tasks. However, they further note that this work only considered the number of responses given and not the originality scores, despite this information being available in the task. In another example of selective attention in analyzing and considering results, although Barr et al. (2015) found a positive relation between the number of RAT items solved and increased analytic cognitive style/cognitive ability, the solutions were not analyzed as a function of whether the participant solved the problem via insight or analytical processes, as could have been and is often measured.

Going the other direction, some researchers administering the RAT actively eliminate opportunities for more analytical strategies. For example, in Slepian and Ambady (2012), if participants did not produce a solution to a RAT problem within five seconds, they were asked to terminate their attempt. A time limit was "set to ensure that answers were discovered by connecting remotely associated concepts rather than by brute-force searching (see Dorfman, Shames, & Kihlstrom, 1996; Slepian, Weisbuch, Rutchick, Newman, & Ambady, 2010)" (Slepian & Ambady, 2012, p. 628). Such a set of parameters presupposes that creativity is an associative rather an executive process and/or that identical solutions created via insight and strategy are relatively different in their worthiness of interest to a creativity researcher. Choice of task and analysis seem to be quite important. Lin and Lien (2013) empirically supported this supposition by showing differential effects of WM load on closed-ended and open-ended creativity tasks. Accordingly, future research should, where reasonable, strive to focus on the joint relative contributions of associative and executive processes rather than simply seeking confirmation that one or the other process is implicated.

Dual-process theories of creativity

Although attempting to measure factors related to both associative and executive processes in creativity is an important step in correctly empirically documenting the nature of creativity, there remains a recognized need for a broader framework in which to articulate the relative contributions of these sorts of processes. For example, Beaty, Silvia et al. (2014), in light of their findings which showed joint contributions of associative and executive processes, suggest that to "further reconcile the associative and executive theories, a dual-process model may be the best approach" and that such a theory "provides a promising approach to understanding the relative contributions of automatic and controlled processes in creative thought" (p. 1195). Wiley and Jarosz (2012) agree that creative problem solving requires a mixture of "non-goal-directed processes and more controlled, attention-demanding processes" (p. 260). Moreover, they state that individual differences in the ability to shift between these two modes of thought may be useful in understanding creativity, but that "there is not yet a definitive paradigm that allows for the measurement of individual differences along these lines," and they overtly state that there is a "need for a dual-process model of problem solving that incorporates both analytic and nonanalytic processes" (p. 261). Given this, it seems that a dual-process theory of creativity is necessary to accommodate emergent evidence. An inspection of the literature reveals that many dual-process theories of creativity do exist, although as will be illustrated, they differ in important ways from cognitive perspectives on dual processes in reasoning more generally.

In a recent review article entitled "The shifting sands of creative thinking: Connections to dual-process theory," Sowden et al. (2015) thoroughly and insightfully explore the numerous theories of creativity that could be considered dual process in nature. Sowden et al. note that divergent thinking has oft been connected to the notion of associative thought, and convergent thinking is traditionally tied to more analytic thinking. Many prominent theories of creativity place the locus of creative genesis on the side of automatic and associative thought, arguing that controlled executive processes are related to evaluative components of the creative process. In other words, the associative engine of the mind autonomously, and often without intent, generates a creative idea, which is then scrutinized for utility and appropriateness in an evaluative mindset.

One of the most well-known examples of such a conception of the role of analytic thinking in creativity stems from Wallas' (1926) classic, *The Art of Thought*. Wallas identified four stages in the creative process: preparation, incubation, illumination, and verification. Such a model clearly suggests that a vacillation between unconscious and conscious or automatic and controlled processing is required for creativity to meaningfully emerge. However, the genesis of ideas (i.e., stages of incubation and illumination) seems to be more strongly associated with autonomous processes, and the evaluative components (i.e., stages of preparation and verification) are more connected to analytic and reflective cognitive processes.

Such a conception is also reflected in Guilford's (1950) famous distinction between divergent and convergent thinking outlined in his seminal Structure of Intellect model. In his framing, divergent thinking entails the generation of many ideas and convergent thinking involves focusing on a singular solution. Another classical model of creative thinking that has similar roles for autonomous and controlled thinking is Campbell's (1960) Blind-Variation and Selective-Retention model, which relates to Simonton's (1999) Darwinian theory of creativity. These models entail the generation of many ideas in a blind fashion, some of which are retained after evaluation for fitness. Several other models are discussed that mirror this distinction between generativity and evaluation – both Finke, Ward, and Smith's (1992) Genoplore model and Howard-Jones' (2002) dual-state model of creative thought place emphasis on the exchange between generation of ideas and subsequent exploration or analysis of the merits of the generated ideas.

It appears that there is no lack of dual-process theories in creativity studies, but there seems to be little in the way of agreement in the literature in terms of how to connect these theories within a broader framework. Sowden et al. (2015) conclude by noting that a means by which to reconcile these distinct but similar models is to integrate these views within the broader cognitive psychological literature on thinking:

> the time is ripe to develop an integrated dual-process model of creativity that clearly specifies the nature of this interaction [between modes of thought]

across different points in the creative process, and the mechanisms that underlie shifting between generative and evaluative thinking. An important part of this process will be to incorporate findings from more general dual-process theories of cognition.

(p. 60)

To understand how this might be accomplished, and to build on the insightful work of Sowden et al. (2015), it is worthwhile considering the nature of broader dual-process theories of cognition and how they relate to existing theories of creative thought.

Dual-process meta-theoretical model of cognition

One of the oldest and most ubiquitous approaches in the effort to understand human thinking is to distinguish two types, systems, or sorts of processes that together comprise the broader sphere of cognition. Conceptions of the mind and characterizations of thinking as being of two qualitatively distinct types have existed since antiquity (e.g., Aristotle) and were discussed by early pioneers of psychological science (e.g., William James; see Frankish & Evans, 2009). Neisser (1963) noted that the "psychology of thinking breeds dichotomies. Nearly everyone who has touched the subject has divided mental processing into two (or more) kinds" (p. 1). His observation was not only historically astute but prescient as well. Rather than dissipate over time, theories of this sort have proliferated and become more refined as increasing amounts of evidence come to support them in a wide variety of psychological domains, including reasoning, judgment, decision-making, and social cognition (see Evans, 2008; Evans & Stanovich, 2013).

Dual-process theories exist in many forms. One particularly influential instantiation, as conceived by Evans and Stanovich (2013), formalized the broad tradition of distinguishing between two qualitatively dissociable types of processing to understand how our minds work through the following simple defining characteristics: Type 1 processing is defined as autonomous, whereas the defining feature of Type 2 processing is the engagement of WM and the capacity for decoupling from the environment. One might reasonably ask: why adopt a dual-process meta-theoretical framework of this sort to understand creativity when there already exist more specific dual-process theories of creativity? Or, why not choose another broad dual-process model? A dual-process account that focuses on autonomy vs. WM dependency as defining features is useful for creativity studies for a number of reasons.

Such a conception of thinking has the capacity to characterize the moment-to-moment variation in cognitive processing states within an individual as well as meaningful differences at the trait-level across individuals both in terms of thinking styles (i.e., the relative disposition to engage Type 2 processing) and in terms of ability (i.e., the relative capacity to effectively use Type 2 processing/WM demanding processing). Accordingly, such theories have extremely broad import and exciting potential to account for variation in creativity at diverse levels of analysis, including both state and trait levels.

This framework also affords important depth in describing the nature of creative thought. Indeed, WM research has long divided visual and verbal WM, creating a taxonomy of modality that corresponds to a consequential component of creative experience (e.g., verbal fluency vs. artistic creation). Recent advances have found WM to be a non-unitary construct in more ways than modality. For instance, Unsworth and Engle (2007) describe a dual-component model of WM that provides evidence for a distinction between primary and secondary memory. Primary memory (PM) "serves to maintain a distinct number of separate representations active for ongoing processing by means of the continued allocation of attention" (Unsworth & Engle, 2007, p. 106) and has a capacity of approximately four items. Secondary memory (SM) consists of a "cue-dependent probabilistic search component" that retrieves information. In characterizing their account, Unsworth and Engle (2007) state that

> Representations are either maintained in PM through the continued allocation of attention or are retrieved through a cue-dependent search process from SM. Individual differences in WMC [working memory capacity] can occur either because of the efficiency of using PM or because of the efficiency of using cues to guide the search process of SM.
>
> (p. 126)

So, although distinguishing cognitive processing on the basis of whether WM is engaged or not might seem simple at first, in light of models of WM such as that explained above, it offers considerable depth in terms of the specificity of describing individual creative ideas and the nature of creativity more generally. For example, in articulating the different ways that one could achieve a creative solution, Mednick (1962) describes creativity by serendipity: "The requisite associative elements may be evoked contiguously by the contiguous environmental appearance (usually an accidental contiguity) of stimuli which elicit these associative elements" (p. 221). In such an instance, a creative idea could come about by the perceptual stream aligning elements in the environment in a meaningful and novel way. However, information could be retrieved from long-term memory via SM and fused with attended perceptual information arriving in PM, so long as capacity limits of PM are not exceeded. Such a framing can describe diverse modes by which reasoners might arrive at novel and useful ideas. It is also apparent that the nature of transmission into PM would depend on the nature of the task and stimulus. Much work remains to be done in articulating creativity in such specifics, but by connecting creativity to advances in WM research, this might yet be accomplished.

In this way, one of the most useful aspects of adopting such a framework would be the de-convolving of content and process in the creativity literature. A marked theme illuminated by Sowden et al. (2015) is the theoretical attention drawn between generativity and evaluation in the creativity literature. They note, however, that the divide in dual-process theories (generative vs. evaluative) diverges from the divide in more general dual-process models of cognition (autonomous vs. WM dependent), and that a clean mapping does not exist between generativity and autonomy, and evaluation and analyticity. Creativity seems to stand alone in its dual-process models, being divided by content (i.e., generation vs. evaluation) rather than process. To wit, it seems quite reasonable to assume that one could use WM-dependent resources to generate creative ideas in a controlled way (i.e., analytic generative cognitive processes) or autonomously reject or endorse an idea on the basis of an affective judgment (i.e., autonomous evaluative cognitive processes). There are a number of advantages afforded by incorporating a dual-process conception of creativity focused on process.

By taking a process-focused approach, one could enhance the temporal precision of the exchange between intuitive and analytic thought in the creative process. For instance, classical conceptions of creativity have centered on larger blocks of time defined by whether one is generating or evaluating. Allen and Thomas (2011) recently revisited these stages in the creative process from a modern dual-process framework, arguing in support of a view in which both autonomous and analytic thinking pervade all stages of the creative process. That is, although the overt goal of an individual may be to generate an idea, this does not mean that there are only associative processes going on. The vacillation between modes of thought in dual-process models of cognition can be subject to analysis at the millisecond level. It is important to acknowledge that this exchange is more precise than can be captured by appeal to the content of the thoughts and whether they are generative or evaluative in nature. WM is surely engaged and disengaged quite quickly as people vacillate between generation and evaluation, and mapping this interaction is an important avenue for future research in creative cognition.

Another advantage to adopting such a framework is the potential for connecting creativity research to other areas of cognitive inquiry. Dividing dual-process theories as a function of autonomy and controlled processing has a rich history in cognitive psychology (e.g., Shiffrin & Schneider, 1977). Theoretically making use of a qualitative distinction between thinking that is autonomous and that which is controlled is extremely common in reasoning and decision-making work, and also evidenced to be useful in other areas of cognition. By couching theory in creativity studies along a similar dimension, theories of creativity could be more strongly connected to research on human thinking more generally. For example, recent work on the phenomenon of mind wandering has revealed that there exists an important distinction between intentional/spontaneous and unintentional/deliberate mind wandering (Seli, Risko, Smilek, & Schacter, 2016). Similarly, Hintzman (2011) argues for researchers of the broad construct of memory to re-examine their emphasis on intentional remembering and, instead, shift their focus to studying spontaneous and unintentional memory, with many interesting avenues of research following. If creativity research attempted to connect to a broad meta-theoretical framework that permeates all of cognition, research on creativity could be both related to and distinguished from other sorts of thinking, reasoning, and decision-making.

Furthermore, by defining different sorts of thinking as a function of WM engagement, researchers interested in creativity could appeal to a deep and broad literature related to the impact of executive functions in many other areas of psychology (see Diamond, 2013). WM is one of the most central constructs in all of psychology, and by using a dual-process framework contingent upon this important factor, one can more effectively understand creativity in the context of other areas. Importantly, such theoretical framing can still be considered, in a complementary way, alongside classical distinctions between generation and evaluation.

Methodology, theory, and meta-theory

Some have critiqued the dual-process model articulated above as being unfalsifiable in the sense that such a characterization is sufficiently broad as to account for nearly any psychological phenomenon. In response, Evans and Stanovich (2013) argue that this framework should be considered a meta-theory to be used in the generation of testable hypotheses within specific tasks or contexts and that falsifiable questions should be oriented toward these task-level models. Accordingly, such a meta-theory in the context of creativity could afford precision and common ground in articulating predictions about the nature of the interplay between Type 1 and Type 2 processes across diverse domain-specific tasks and provide common language with which to create more specific theories of different sorts of creative thought. This holds promise for creativity research because a meta-theoretical framework of this sort can address many distinct manifestations of creativity measured in diverse contexts while still providing a common language and conceptual core through which diverse strands of research can be connected across domains and levels of analysis. Such discussion is connected to the issue of the extent to which creativity is domain-general or domain-specific. For instance, would one expect the same cognitive processes to subserve both an improvised interpretive dance and the genesis of a novel scientific theory? Would one who is creative in the arena of dance likely be a creative scientist? Although evidence exists for domain-general aspects of creativity, others contend that attempts to construct a grand theory of creativity can "distort, distract and disappoint" (Baer, 2011). Baer (2011) does suggest, however, that meta-theoretical perspectives can have some utility in guiding research of domain-specific instantiations of creativity.

Accordingly, such a meta-theory in the context of creativity could afford precision and common ground in articulating predictions about the nature of the interplay between Type 1 and Type 2 processes across diverse domain-specific tasks and in diverse populations. The notion that creativity research must account for both routine and special processes is well articulated in Gilhooly, Ball, and Macchi's (2015) introduction to a recent Special Issue of *Thinking & Reasoning* on Creativity and Insight Problem Solving. In summarizing the articles at hand, they note that the "themes that strongly emerge from the papers in the Special Issue include the relative roles of conscious and unconscious processes and the roles of special processes particular to insight as against routine processes found widely in problem solving" and suggest that in future research it would be "worth addressing more explicitly how the two broad types of processes do interact" (p. 3). More specific models that account for intentional or spontaneous creative ideas within specific domains can be generated. Such specificity is required as increasingly sophisticated qualifications emerge from the creativity literature. For instance, Rosen et al. (2016), using transcranial direct stimulation, showed that novice and expert jazz musicians differentially rely on Type 1 and Type 2 processing during creative improvisation.

Such a meta-theoretical framework can accommodate seemingly contradictory evidence through more specific theoretical models of particular sorts of creative thinking. For example, creativity researchers have thoroughly explored the cognitive neuroscience of insight and developed well-articulated and supported models of the way that creative insights arrive in consciousness (e.g., Bowden, Jung-Beeman, Fleck, & Kounios, 2005; Kounios et al., 2006). Salvi, Bricolo, Kounios, Bowden, and Beeman (2016) have also shown that across diverse problem types, insight solutions can be more accurate than analytical solutions. They also found support, on the basis of the errors apparent in their study, for the idea that insight solutions have "superior accuracy because they emerge into consciousness in an all-or-nothing fashion when the unconscious solving process is complete, whereas analytic solutions can be guesses based on conscious, prematurely terminated, processing" (p. 1). These researchers have provided strong support for the role of autonomous and unconscious processes that fit well with the diverse evidence under scrutiny in this chapter, and Kounios and Beeman (2014) also advocate methodologies attuned to detecting shifts between voluntary and involuntary modes of thought. Such a view affords a unique role for autonomous and non-WM-dependent processes in the generation of certain sorts of creative solutions, but does not demand that analyticity be deemed unimportant.

Similarly, contemporary work finds that executive engagement can be detrimental to creative thinking in some instances. Those holding the view that executive processing can hinder creative problem solving often point to evidence that high attentional control and/or high WM capacity does not benefit creative problem solving as it does analytic problem solving, because it often leads to fixation or undue focus on aspects of a problem that will not yield a solution (see Wiley & Jarosz, 2012, for a review). These researchers posit that a more dispersed or fuzzy state of attention, such as that associated with alcohol consumption (Jarosz, Colflesh, & Wiley, 2012), can allow for the type of mindset required to arrive at creative solutions. Such a view implies that relatively less executive engagement will generally lead to relatively more creativity, and it is supported by a large variety of empirical demonstrations (for other examples, see Aiello, Jarosz, Cushen, & Wiley, 2012; Ansburg & Hill, 2003; Kim, Hasher, & Zacks, 2007; Reverberi, Toraldo, D'Agostini, & Skrap, 2005; Schooler, Ohlsson, & Brooks, 1993; Sio & Ormerod, 2009; Wieth & Zacks, 2011; Zhong, Dijksterhuis, & Galinsky, 2008). Corgnet, Espín, and Hernán-González (2016) have also shown evidence that too much reflection can hinder creative thought.

Such findings, if only considered at a shallow level, seem at odds with the research above outlining the role of analytic thinking creativity and the growing evidence that executive control, WM capacity, and intelligence are associated with greater creativity (Beaty & Silvia, 2012, 2013; Benedek, Franz, Heene, & Neubauer, 2012; de Dreu, Nijstad, Baas, Wolsink, & Roskes, 2012; Jauk, Benedek, & Neubauer, 2014; Lee & Therriault, 2013; Silvia & Beaty, 2012; Süß, Oberauer, Wittmann, Wilhelm, & Schulze, 2002). Do these findings undermine accounts of creative thinking that rely prominently on executive involvement? Not necessarily. Rather than perceive such seemingly contradictory findings as irreconcilable, another option is to consider such observations as qualifications pertaining to factors of psychological importance. In other words, much of what seems contradictory can be seen as complementary if nuance in the studies of interest is considered. Kounios and Beeman, in assessing a recent review, effectively articulate the hazards that arise from a lack of precision in creativity studies:

> one recent review of cognitive neuroscience research on creativity and insight lumps together widely diverse studies characterized by a variety of definitions, assumptions, experimental paradigms, empirical phenomena, analytical methods, and stages of the solving process (and inconsistent experimental rigor). Unsurprisingly, because of such indiscriminate agglomeration, that review failed to find much consistency across studies, leading the authors to pronounce a negative verdict on the field (Dietrich & Kanso, 2010).
>
> *(Kounios & Beeman, 2014, p. 73)*

One important step that could be taken in creativity research would be to increasingly attempt to articulate individual studies with a common taxonomy of the cognitive correlates of creative thought. Of course, most creativity researchers are already quite sophisticated in this regard, but it remains clear that precision in the notion of what is meant by "creativity" is imperative, as is cataloging the range of cognitive processes involved. The dimensions here suggest that any taxonomy of a creative thought should be conceptualized by both process and content. Process, under a dual-process framework, would entail the nature of the interaction between Type 1 and Type 2 processes throughout the space of problem solving. Sowden et al. (2015) espouse the merits of a focused chronometric approach aimed at understanding the time course of the exchange between modes of thought. Gabora (2003, 2010) has undertaken important work in this direction by articulating a view of creativity centered on "contextual focus," a term used to refer to the shifting between a defocused and a more focused attentional state, but much remains to be known (see also Vartanian, 2009). An important topic is the mapping between autonomous and WM-dependent controlled thought and thought that is generative or evaluative in content at very precise time intervals and in the context of extant models of WM.

One might think that understanding creative thinking at this level would be difficult to ascertain, but there are ways to do so. The study of mind wandering often relies on the use of thought probes (e.g., Seli, Carriere, Levene, & Smilek, 2013), and creativity researchers could benefit from increased reliance on such a methodology. By periodically interrupting participants during an experiment and asking them about the current content of their thoughts, one can ascertain moment-to-moment variations in modes and content of thought. Relatedly, Jack and Roepstorff (2002) argue for increased assessments of subjective self-reports of phenomenal experience in the context of functional magnetic resonance imaging (fMRI) studies attempting to discern function in the frontal lobes, as this area is implicated in many types of executive-function-dependent behaviors. Creativity seems another area that could benefit from greater valuation of subjective self-reports from participants in understanding dynamic aspects of cognition that are difficult to pin down. By connecting objective task performance and neuroimaging measures in time to subjective self-reports and monitoring, we can hopefully advance our understanding of how autonomous and WM-dependent thoughts connect to generation and evaluation (see Sowden et al., 2015, for more ideas on this issue). Another interesting option is to engage in thinking-aloud protocols in order to monitor the internal subjective correlates of experience associated with the output of objectively creative ideas, and some creativity research has used such methodology (e.g., Gilhooly et al., 2007).

While Sowden et al. (2015) effectively identify this switch in modes of thought as an incredibly important aspect of creativity that must be more effectively understood going forward, this issue is also of central importance to current research in reasoning and decision-making. As such, common language and communication among creativity and cognitive researchers could be mutually beneficial. For example, Pennycook, Fugelsang, and Koehler (2012) explored the issue of analytic engagement in the context of conflict detection. The authors argue that detection of conflict can cue the onset of WM-dependent resources and that conflict detection is an important mechanism involved in analytic thinking. Interestingly, a parallel is seen in Nijstad, de Dreu, Rietzschel, and Baas' (2010) dual-pathway model, in which an "idea monitor" assesses autonomously generated ideas to see whether further analysis is warranted.

Another particularly interesting parallel concerns the types of intuitions that can be autonomously generated. For example, reasoning researchers are working to accommodate recent findings of "logical intuitions" in dual-process models of reasoning (e.g., Handley & Trippas, 2015). Given that most work on intuitions has been built upon the foundation of the study of heuristics and biases that can lead to errors and distortions in thinking, it is reasonable that theorizing about logical intuition is underdeveloped in the reasoning literature. However, consideration of evidence from creative insight that describes the way that novel, useful, and relatively well-formed ideas spontaneously emerge into consciousness could prove important in understanding such reasoning more generally.

As such, future development of extant theoretical and meta-theoretical models of reasoning should consider creative cognition as an important source of information pertaining to the nature of Type 1 processing and its sometimes surprising complexity and usefulness. While this chapter has primarily focused on the potential benefits that connecting creativity to cognition has for creativity studies, there are also important potential benefits for other areas of cognition. This is particularly true for reasoning research as significantly more evidence would be available for theoretical and meta-theoretical refinements if creativity researchers were to connect their work to the meta-theoretical dual-process models of cognition described here.

Connecting creativity research through common language

In assessing the current cohesiveness of the field of creativity studies, Hennessey and Amabile (2010) engaged in some interesting survey work in which they queried experts in the area as to what they believed were essential elements of the literature. Twenty-one experts were asked to nominate recent publications that they considered "must-have" references, resulting in 110 suggested books/volumes, chapters, and articles. Hennessey and Amabile (2010) were struck by the diversity of opinions, as evidenced by the considerable lack of overlap – "of the 110 nominated papers, only seven were suggested by two colleagues, and only one was suggested by three colleagues" (p. 571). Such diversity suggests that researchers in one sub-area of creativity studies can be entirely unaware of empirical and theoretical advances in others, with research lines which could be mutually informative going on concurrently but independently. The authors' perspective was subsequently supported by the research community, with others echoing their perception of a divide and expressing agreement that unification would be desirable (see also Glăveanu, 2014, for a similar perspective).

Not only do they identify and demonstrate the nature of this fractionation, Hennessey and Amabile (2010) also make prescriptions for how to remedy the situation (see also Hennessey & Watson, 2016). They argue that adoption of what they call "a systems view" would aid in unifying the field and assist in cross-disciplinary collaboration and understanding. Their model characterizes creativity as being a multilayered entity and posits that more progress will be made when more researchers recognize that "creativity arises through a system of interrelated forces operating at multiple levels, often requiring interdisciplinary investigation" (Hennessey & Amabile, 2010, p. 571). This model spans from the low-level neurological and cognitive correlates of creativity to the high-level cultural and societal factors that influence creative individuals and organizations.

Such an approach can elicit the important realization that areas beyond the scope of one's immediate paradigm can be informative, and this sort of an appreciation is an essential aspect of increasing our collective understanding of creativity, rendering their point an important one. However, although appreciation of the interrelated factors at varied levels of analysis that modulate creativity is a necessary step in this important direction, it is, on its own, not sufficient. What also seems necessary is some sort of means of common communication across various levels of the system. The philosopher of science Quine (1936) noted that "The less a science has advanced, the more its terminology tends to rest on an uncritical assumption of mutual understanding" (p. 90). What seems to be required in order to advance the science of creativity is not only a common understanding that parallel work is being conducted at varied levels of analysis, but a common language with which to transcend the boundaries that exist as consequence of the varied levels of the systems-view model. Some clarity could come to those attempting to make sense of the murkiness inherent in the current understanding of creativity by more clearly connecting emergent empirical evidence and theoretical frameworks within creativity to broader models of human cognition and reasoning. Dual-process theories of thinking are pervasive in cognitive and social psychology and can be calibrated to consider low-level neural and cognitive correlates of creativity (e.g., neural correlates of creative insight) to high-level social and cultural factors (e.g., the emphasis on critical thinking in an educational system); accordingly, they offer a promising means by which to orient creativity studies toward a common currency of technical terms.

Promoting effective communication across this vast chasm in level of analysis confers unique responsibilities to those studying at different levels of the system. For those studying the cognitive and neural correlates of creativity, it is important to recall that it might well be possible to connect even the most basic research back to the societal and cultural aims pertaining to the enhancement and proliferation of innovative and creative thought. By attempting to articulate, while staying clear about the limits of reasonable interpretation, how cognitive and neuroscientific models of basic aspects of creative thinking might relate to higher-order institutions, researchers studying the lower levels can aid in generating higher-order interventions and educational policies surrounding creativity. For those at the higher-order levels of analysis, it would be worthwhile to attempt to continually connect interventions meant to promote creativity to potential underlying cognitive mechanisms. By orienting educative or non-educative nudges (Sunstein, 2016), training programs, and educational efforts to enhance creativity and innovation to lower-level correlates, one makes theories more precise and heightens the ability to infer which aspects of the education, choice architecture, or training are most productive. Many popular and longstanding educational programs and interventions meant to induce change are not only unproductive, but they can in fact be harmful, and evidence is the key to improving outcomes. One example of such a persistent yet empirically debatable practice meant to evoke positive change in creativity studies is the emphasis on brainstorming in teaching creativity (see Torr, 2008). By orienting discussion of such programs to cognitive and neural evidence surrounding creativity studies, we can strive toward more precise and well-articulated conceptions of how to teach and train people to be more creative (e.g., Vartanian, 2013).

If all creativity researchers took on a responsibility to attempt to reach across the chasms created by the subfield silo system, there would be several advantages. Both groups might be more inclined to transcend the boundaries of their typical citation circle and read more widely. Many creative ideas and innovations have emerged when humans have set aside differences and connected deep underlying relations, as in creative analogies. This broadening of focus, with a common eye towards how cognition relates to creation at the highest levels, might help to alleviate the fractured nature of the literature of one of the most important constructs in all of psychology. Silvia (2014) notes that the great diversity in creativity studies can be taken as a "sign of healthy pluralism, not lamentable fragmentation" (p. 233) and that varied methods, approaches, and types of theory are ideal. This is true, and optimism is certainly warranted given the exciting current state of research. However, some unification seems possible given the large number of extant dual-process theories in creativity and the ever-growing evidence on the exchange between generative and evaluative modes of thought via interaction between autonomous and controlled thought. There is considerable convergence in both evidence and theory within the diverse subfields that comprise creativity studies, so it seems possible to engage in at least some large-scale synthesis, although plurality remains important. Consideration of such diverse but convergent evidence through common meta-theoretical frameworks could serve the useful function of facilitating transfer across levels, and this process should be taken to reflect the emergence of a cohesive and interconnected body of research pertaining to creativity, in some ways ready for further integration through common terminology, where appropriate.

Summary and conclusions

This chapter reviewed evidence that strategic, reflective, and analytic processes can facilitate creativity, accentuating the extent to which executive involvement is important in this area of research. This evidence demands a framework for understanding creativity that can account for the relative contributions of intuitive and analytical thought. It is argued that the adoption of a meta-theoretical dual-process account of creativity that is strongly grounded in contemporary cognitive and neuroscientific work could mark a useful step in the development of more interconnected theories of diverse forms of creativity. This chapter reviewed the advantages that adoption of dual-process meta-theoretical frameworks can offer as well as suggesting new avenues for research in this area, which both inform our understanding of creativity and make suggestions for refinement of dual-process theories more generally. Given that the field of creativity studies is far from unified, a particular advantage of a common meta-theoretical framework is the possibility of connecting disconnected literatures, although it is nevertheless important to recognize the advantages afforded by diversity and decentralization (Silvia, 2014).

Although it is not novel to consider creativity in terms of basic cognitive processes, recent theoretical and empirical advances in cognitive and neuroscientific research have potentiated new specificity in discussion of the mechanisms that underlie thinking generally and creativity more specifically. In all, adoption of a dual-process meta-theoretical framework can address many distinct manifestations of creativity measured in diverse contexts while still providing a common language and conceptual core through which diverse strands of research can be connected across domains and levels of analysis. By aligning the study of creativity with other cognitive subfields, emerging work in creativity can continually be kept up to date in light of parallel advances in understanding more basic aspects of human cognition.

A major advantage of adopting such a framework is the emphasis placed on a mechanistic approach in which the cognitive and neural processes that underlie thinking and reasoning are applied to understanding the means by which a creative connection is forged or creative ideas are generated. Such an approach grounds creativity in the broader cognitive and neuroscientific literature, allows the process to be characterized at a fine temporal resolution, and affords greater integration across domains of creativity research. Such a conceptualization that accommodates analytic thinking is compatible with extant theoretical frameworks focused on the types of thinking in various stages of the creative process (Allen & Thomas, 2011), the interplay between associative and analytic thinking at the neural level (Gabora, 2010; Beaty, Benedick et al., 2014; Beaty et al., 2016), the interaction between associative and executive processes in creativity (Silvia & Beaty, 2012), theories that describe different paths to creative ideas (de Dreu et al., 2012), the emergence and evolution of creative thinking in the human species (Gabora & Kaufman, 2010), and eminent and real-world creativity (Dunbar & Blanchette, 2001; Holyoak & Thagard, 1995), and it can help connect creativity to other types of cognition thought to be uniquely human (Penn, Holyoak, & Povinelli, 2008).

Given the many complexities of our future and the associated challenges we collectively face, continued creativity in the scientific, artistic, economic, environmental, and social domains is a necessity (see Barr & Pennycook, 2018, this volume). An imperative is thus continuing our momentum in relating the study of creativity to issues of applied importance. Leveraging methodological advance, rigorous empirical exploration, and cross-disciplinary theoretical refinement, our understanding of creativity in diverse domains could be used to craft interventions and education that can lead to further innovation. In light of the extant theory and evidence surrounding the behavioral and neural correlates of creativity reviewed here, it seems likely that research into analytic thinking will play a central role in the strategic advance of our collective creative potential and that meta-theoretical frameworks centered on the interplay between autonomous and controlled thinking can prove a useful means by which to unify the disparate facets of creativity research.

References

Aiello, D., Jarosz, A. F., Cushen, P. J., & Wiley, J. (2012). Firing the executive: When an analytic approach does and does not help problem solving. *Journal of Problem Solving*, 4: 6.

Allen, A. P., & Thomas, K. E. (2011). A dual process account of creative thinking. *Creativity Research Journal*, 23(2), 109–118.

Ansburg, P. I., & Hill, K. (2003). Creative and analytic thinkers differ in their use of attentional resources. *Personality and Individual Differences*, 34(7), 1141–1152.

Ausubel, D. P. (1964). Creativity, general creative abilities, and the creative individual. *Psychology in the Schools*, 1(4), 344–347.

Baer, J. (2011). Why grand theories of creativity distort, distract, and disappoint. *IJCPS-International Journal of Creativity and Problem Solving*, 21(1), 73–100.

Ball, L., & Stevens, A. (2009). Evidence for a verbally-based analytic component to insight problem solving. In N. Taatgen & H. van (Eds.), *Proceedings of the 31st Annual Conference of the Cognitive Science Society* (pp. 1060–1065). Austin, TX: Cognitive Science Society.

Barr, N., & Pennycook, G. (2018). Why reason matters: Connecting research on human reason to the challenges of the Anthropocene. In G. Pennycook (Ed.), *The New Reflectionism in Cognitive Psychology* (pp. 119–142). Abingdon, UK: Routledge.

Barr, N., Pennycook, G., Stolz, J. A., & Fugelsang, J. A. (2015). Reasoned connections: A dual-process perspective on creative thought. *Thinking & Reasoning*, 21(1), 61–75.

Beaty, R. E., Benedek, M., Kaufman, S. B., & Silvia, P. J. (2015). Default and executive network coupling supports creative idea production. *Scientific Reports*, 5: 10964. doi:00A0;10.1038/srep10964

Beaty, R. E., Benedek, M., Silvia, P. J., & Schacter, D. L. (2016). Creative cognition and brain network dynamics. *Trends in Cognitive Sciences*, 20(2), 87–95.

Beaty, R. E., Benedek, M., Wilkins, R. W., Jauk, E., Fink, A., Silvia, P. J., Hodges, D. A., Koschutnig, K., & Neubauer, A. C. (2014). Creativity and the default network: A functional connectivity analysis of the creative brain at rest. *Neuropsychologia*, 64, 92–98.

Beaty, R. E., & Silvia, P. J. (2012). Why do ideas get more creative across time? An executive interpretation of the serial order effect in divergent thinking tasks. *Psychology of Aesthetics, Creativity, and the Arts*, 6(4), 309–319.

Beaty, R. E., & Silvia, P. J. (2013). Metaphorically speaking: Cognitive abilities and the production of figurative language. *Memory & Cognition*, 41(2), 255–267.

Beaty, R. E., Silvia, P. J., Nusbaum, E. C., Jauk, E., & Benedek, M. (2014). The roles of associative and executive processes in creative cognition. *Memory & Cognition*, 42(7), 1186–1197.

Benedek, M., Franz, F., Heene, M., & Neubauer, A. C. (2012). Differential effects of cognitive inhibition and intelligence on creativity. *Personality and Individual Differences*, 53–334(4), 480–485.

Benedek, M., & Neubauer, A. C. (2013). Revisiting Mednick's model on creativity-related differences in associative hierarchies: Evidence for a common path to uncommon thought. *Journal of Creative Behavior*, 47(4), 273–289.

Bowden, E. M., Jung-Beeman, M., Fleck, J., & Kounios, J. (2005). New approaches to demystifying insight. *Trends in Cognitive Sciences*, 9(7), 322–328.

Bunge, S. A., Wendelken, C., Badre, D., & Wagner, A. D. (2005). Analogical reasoning and prefrontal cortex: Evidence for separable retrieval and integration mechanisms. *Cerebral Cortex*, 15(3), 239–249.

Campbell, D. T. (1960). Blind variation and selective retention in creative thought as in other knowledge processes. *Psychological Review*, 67, 380–400.

Carroll, J. B. (1993). *Human cognitive abilities: A survey of factor analytic studies*. New York: Cambridge University Press.

Chein, J. M., & Weisberg, R. W. (2014). Working memory, insight, and restructuring in verbal problems: Analysis of compound remote associate problems. *Memory & Cognition*, 42(1), 67–83.

Christensen, P. R., Guilford, J. P., & Wilson, R. C. (1957). Relations of creative responses to working time and instructions. *Journal of Experimental Psychology*, 53(2), 82–88.

Corgnet, B., Espín, A. M., & Hernán-González, R. (2016). Creativity and cognitive skills among millennials: Thinking too much and creating too little. *Frontiers in Psychology*, 7: 1626. doi:00A0;10.3389/fpsyg.2016.01626

de Dreu, C. K. W., Nijstad, B. A., Baas, M., Wolsink, I., & Roskes, M. (2012). Working memory benefits creative insight, musical improvisation and original ideation through maintained task-focused attention. *Personality and Social Psychology Bulletin*, 38(5), 656–669.

de Souza, L. C., Volle, E., Bertoux, M., Czernecki, V., Funkiewiez, A., & Levy, R. (2010). Poor creativity in frontotemporal dementia: A window into the neural bases of the creative mind. *Neuropsychologia*, 48(13), 3733–3742.

Diamond, A. (2013). Executive functions. *Annual Review of Psychology*, 64, 135–168.

Dietrich, A., & Kanso, R. (2010). A review of EEG, ERP, and neuroimaging studies of creativity and insight. *Psychological Bulletin*, 136(5), 822–848.

Dorfman, J., Shames, V. A., & Kihlstrom, J. F. (1996). Intuition, incubation, and insight: Implicit cognition in problem solving. In G. Underwood (Ed.), *Implicit cognition* (pp. 257–296). Oxford, UK: Oxford University Press.

Dunbar, K., & Blanchette, I. (2001). The in vivo/in vitro approach to cognition: The case of analogy. *Trends in Cognitive Sciences*, 5(8), 334–339.

Evans, J. St. B. T. (2008). Dual-processing accounts of reasoning, judgment, and social cognition. *Annual Review of Psychology*, 59, 255–278.

Evans, J. St. B. T., & Stanovich, K. E. (2013). Dual-process theories of higher cognition: Advancing the debate. *Perspectives in Psychological Science*, 8(3), 223–241.

Finke, R. A., Ward, T. B., & Smith, S. M. (1992). *Creative cognition: Theory, research, and applications*. Cambridge, MA: MIT Press.

Frankish, K., & Evans, J. St. B. T. (2009). The duality of mind: An historical perspective. In J. St. B. T. Evans & K. Frankish (Eds.), *In two minds: Dual processes and beyond* (pp. 1–30). Oxford, UK: Oxford University Press.

Friedman, N. P., & Miyake, A. (2016). Unity and diversity of executive functions: Individual differences as a window on cognitive structure. *Cortex*, 86, 186–204. doi:10.1016/j.cortex.2016.04.023

Gabora, L. (2003). Contextual focus: A cognitive explanation for the cultural transition of the Middle/Upper Paleolithic. In R. Alterman & D. Hirsch (Eds.), *Proceedings of the 25th Annual Meeting of the Cognitive Science Society* (pp. 432–437, Boston MA, July 31–August 2). Hillsdale NJ: Lawrence Erlbaum Associates.

Gabora, L. (2010). Revenge of the "neurds": Characterizing creative thought in terms of the structure and dynamics of human memory. *Creativity Research Journal*, 22(1), 1–13.

Gabora, L., & Kaufman, S. (2010). Evolutionary perspectives on creativity. In J. Kaufman & R. Sternberg (Eds.), *Cambridge handbook of creativity* (pp. 279–300). Cambridge, UK: Cambridge University Press.

Gilhooly, K. J., Ball, L. J., & Macchi, L. (2015). Insight and creative thinking processes: Routine and special. *Thinking & Reasoning*, 21(1), 1–4.

Gilhooly, K. J., Fioratou, E., Anthony, S. H., & Wynn, V. (2007). Divergent thinking: Strategies and executive involvement in generating novel uses for familiar objects. *British Journal of Psychology*, 98(4), 611–625.

Glăveanu, V. P. (2014). The psychology of creativity: A critical reading. *Creativity: Theories – Research – Applications*, 1(1), 10–32. doi:00A0;10.15290/ctra.2014.01.01.02

Green, A. E. (2016). Creativity, within reason semantic distance and dynamic state creativity in relational thinking and reasoning. *Current Directions in Psychological Science*, 25(1), 28–35.

Green, A. E., Cohen, M. S., Kim, J. U., & Gray, J. R. (2012). An explicit cue improves creative analogical reasoning. *Intelligence*, 40(6), 598–603.

Green, A. E., Fugelsang, J. A., Kraemer, D. J. M., Gray, J. R., & Dunbar, K. N. (2012). Neural correlates of creativity in analogical reasoning. *Journal of Experimental Psychology: Learning, Memory, & Cognition*, 38(2), 264–272.

Green, A. E., Fugelsang, J., Kraemer, D., Shamosh, N., & Dunbar, K. (2006). The dynamic role of prefrontal cortex in reasoning and abstract thought. *Brain Research*, 1096, 125–137.

Green, A. E., Kraemer, D. J. M., Fugelsang, J. A., Gray, J. R., & Dunbar, K. N. (2010). Connecting long distance: Semantic distance in analogical reasoning modulates frontopolar cortex activity. *Cerebral Cortex*, 20(1), 70–76.

Guilford, J. P. (1950). Creativity. *American Psychologist*, 5(9), 444–454.

Gupta, N., Jang, Y., Mednick, S. C., & Huber, D. E. (2012). The road not taken: Creative solutions require avoidance of high-frequency responses. *Psychological Science*, 23(3), 288–294.

Handley, S. J., & Trippas, D. (2015). Dual processes and the interplay between knowledge and structure: A new parallel processing model. *Psychology of Learning and Motivation*, 62, 33–58.

Hennessey, B. A., & Amabile, T. M. (2010). Creativity. *Annual Review of Psychology*, 61, 569–598.

Hennessey, B. A., & Watson, M. W. (2016). The defragmentation of creativity: Future directions with an emphasis on educational applications. In G. E. Corazza & S. Agnoli (Eds.), *Multidisciplinary contributions to the science of creative thinking* (pp. 21–31). London: Springer.

Hintzman, D. L. (2011). Research strategy in the study of memory: Fads, fallacies, and the search for the "coordinates of truth." *Perspectives on Psychological Science*, 6(3), 253–271.

Holyoak, K. J., & Thagard, P. (1995). *Mental leaps: Analogy in creative thought*. Cambridge, MA: MIT Press.

Howard-Jones, P. A. (2002). A dual-state model of creative cognition for supporting strategies that foster creativity in the classroom. *International Journal of Technology and Design Education*, 12(3), 215–226.

Jack, A. I., & Roepstorff, A. (2002). Introspection and cognitive brain mapping: From stimulus–response to script–report. *Trends in Cognitive Sciences*, 6(8), 333–339.

Jarosz, A. F., Colflesh, G. J. H., & Wiley, J. (2012). Uncorking the muse: Alcohol intoxication facilitates creative problem solving. *Consciousness and Cognition*, 21(1), 487–493.

Jauk, E., Benedek, M., & Neubauer, A. C. (2014). The road to creative achievement: A latent variable model of ability and personality predictors. *European Journal of Personality*, 28(1), 95–105.

Kaufman, J. C. (2009). *Creativity 101*. New York: Springer.

Kim, S., Hasher, L., & Zacks, R. T. (2007). Aging and a benefit of distractability. *Psychonomic Bulletin & Review*, 14(2), 301–305.

Kounios, J., & Beeman, M. (2014). The cognitive neuroscience of insight. *Annual Review of Psychology*, 65, 71–93.

Kounios, J., Frymiare, J. L., Bowden, E. M., Fleck, J. I., Subramaniam, K., Parrish, T. B., & Jung-Beeman, M. (2006). The prepared mind neural activity prior to problem presentation predicts subsequent solution by sudden insight. *Psychological Science*, 17(10), 882–890.

Landauer, T. K., Foltz, P. W., & Laham, D. (1998). Introduction to latent semantic analysis. *Discourse Processes*, 25(2–3), 259–284.

Lee, C. S., & Therriault, D. J. (2013). The cognitive underpinnings of creative thought: A latent variable analysis exploring the roles of intelligence and working memory in three creative thinking processes. *Intelligence*, 41(5), 306–320.

Lin, W. L., & Lien, Y. W. (2013). The different role of working memory in open-ended versus closed-ended creative problem solving: A dual-process theory account. *Creativity Research Journal*, 25(1), 85–96.

Mednick, M. T., Mednick, S. A., & Jung, C. C. (1964). Continual association as a function of level of creativity and type of verbal stimulus. *The Journal of Abnormal and Social Psychology*, 69(5), 511–515.

Mednick, S. A. (1962). The associative basis of the creative process. *Psychological Review*, 69(3), 220–232.

Neisser, U. (1963). The multiplicity of thought. *British Journal of Psychology*, 54(1), 1–14.

Nijstad, B. A., de Dreu, C. K. W., Rietzschel, E. F., & Baas, M. (2010). The dual pathway to creativity model: Creative ideation as a function of flexibility and persistence. *European Review of Social Psychology*, 21(1), 34–77.

Norris, P., & Epstein, S. (2011). An experiential thinking style: Its facets and relations with objective and subjective criterion measures. *Journal of Personality*, 79(5), 1043–1079. doi:00A0;10.1111/j.1467-6494.2011.00718.x

Penn, D. C., Holyoak, K. J., & Povinelli, D. J. (2008). Darwin's mistake: Explaining the discontinuity between human and nonhuman minds. *Behavioral and Brain Sciences*, 31(2), 109–178.

Pennycook, G., Fugelsang, J., & Koehler, D. (2012). Are we good at detecting conflict during reasoning? *Cognition*, 124(1), 101–106.

Piers, E. V., & Kirchner, E. P. (1971). Productivity and uniqueness in continued word association as a function of subject creativity and stimulus properties. *Journal of Personality*, 39(2), 264–276.

Quine, W. V. (1936). Truth by convention. In *Philosophical essays for Alfred North Whitehead* (pp. 90–124). New York: Longmans, Green & Co.

Ramnani, N., & Owen, A. M. (2004). Anterior prefrontal cortex: Insights into function from anatomy and neuroimaging. *Nature Reviews Neuroscience*, 5(3), 184–194.

Reverberi, C., Toraldo, A., D'Agostini, S., & Skrap, M. (2005). Better without (lateral) frontal cortex? Insight problems solved by frontal patients. *Brain*, 128(12), 2882–2890.

Rosen, D. S., Erickson, B., Kim, Y. E., Mirman, D., Hamilton, R. H., & Kounios, J. (2016). Anodal tDCS to right dorsolateral prefrontal cortex facilitates performance for novice jazz improvisers but hinders experts. *Frontiers in Human Neuroscience*, 10: 579. doi:10.3389/fnhum.2016.00579

Salvi, C., Bricolo, E., Kounios, J., Bowden, E., & Beeman, M. (2016). Insight solutions are correct more often than analytic solutions. *Thinking & Reasoning*, 22(4), 1–18.

Schooler, J. W., Ohlsson, S., & Brooks, K. (1993). Thoughts beyond words: When language overshadows insight. *Journal of Experimental Psychology: General*, 122(2), 166–183.

Seli, P., Carriere, J. S., Levene, M., & Smilek, D. (2013). How few and far between? Examining the effects of probe rate on self-reported mind wandering. *Frontiers in Psychology*, 4: 430.

Seli, P., Risko, E. F., Smilek, D., & Schacter, D. L. (2016). Mind-wandering with and without intention. *Trends in Cognitive Sciences*, 20(8), 605–617.

Shiffrin, R. M., & Schneider, W. (1977). Controlled and automatic human information processing: II. Perceptual learning, automatic attending, and a general theory. *Psychological Review*, 84(2), 127–190.

Silvia, P. J. (2014). Why big theories are fruitless, fragmentation is ideal, defining creativity is overrated and method-driven research is urgent: Some thoughts on the flourishing state of creativity science. *Creativity: Theories – Research – Applications*, 1(2), 233–239.

Silvia, P. J., & Beaty, R. E. (2012). Making creative metaphors: The importance of fluid intelligence for creative thought. *Intelligence*, 40(4), 343–351.

Simonton, D. K. (1999). Creativity as blind variation and selective retention: Is the creative process Darwinian? *Psychological Inquiry*, 10(4), 309–328.

Sio, U. N., & Ormerod, T. C. (2009). Does incubation enhance problem solving? A meta-analytic review. *Psychological Bulletin*, 135(1), 94–120.

Slepian, M. L., & Ambady, N. (2012). Fluid movement and creativity. *Journal of Experimental Psychology: General*, 141(4), 625–629.

Slepian, M. L., Weisbuch, M., Rutchick, A. M., Newman, L. S., & Ambady, N. (2010). Shedding light on insight: Priming bright ideas. *Journal of Experimental Social Psychology*, 46(4), 696–700.

Smeekens, B. A., & Kane, M. J. (2016). Working memory capacity, mind wandering, and creative cognition: An individual-differences investigation into the benefits of controlled versus spontaneous. *Psychology of Aesthetics, Creativity, and the Arts*, 10(4), 389–415.

Smith, K. A., Huber, D. E., & Vul, E. (2013). Multiply-constrained semantic search in the Remote Associates Test. *Cognition*, 128(1), 64–75.

Sowden, P. T., Pringle, A., & Gabora, L. (2015). The shifting sands of creative thinking: Connections to dual-process theory. *Thinking & Reasoning*, 21(1), 40–60.

Spellman, B. A., Holyoak, K. J., & Morrison, R. G. (2001). Analogical priming via semantic relations. *Memory & Cognition*, 29(3), 383–393.

Süß, H.-M., Oberauer, K., Wittmann, W. W., Wilhelm, O., & Schulze, R. (2002). Working-memory capacity explains reasoning ability – and a little bit more. *Intelligence*, 30(3), 261–288.

Sunstein, C. R. (2016). Do people like nudges? *Administrative Law Review*, Forthcoming. doi:10.2139/ssrn.2604084

Torr, G. (2008). *Managing creative people: Lessons in leadership for the ideas economy*. West Sussex, UK: John Wiley & Sons Ltd.

Unsworth, N., & Engle, R. W. (2007). The nature of individual differences in working memory capacity: Active maintenance in primary memory and controlled search from secondary memory. *Psychological Review*, 114(1), 104–132.

Vartanian, O. (2009). Variable attention facilitates creative problem solving. *Psychology of Aesthetics, Creativity, and the Arts*, 3(1), 57–59.

Vartanian, O. (2013). Fostering creativity: Insights from neuroscience. In O. Vartanian, A. Bristol, & J. C. Kaufman (Eds.), *Neuroscience of creativity* (pp. 257–271). Cambridge, MA: MIT Press.

Wallas, G. (1926). *The art of thought*. New York: Harcourt Brace.

Wieth, M., & Zacks, R. (2011). Time of day effects on problem solving: When the non-optimal is optimal. *Thinking & Reasoning*, 17(4), 387–401.

Wiley, J., & Jarosz, A. (2012). Working memory capacity, attentional focus, and problem solving. *Current Directions in Psychological Science*, 21(4), 258–262.

Zhong, C.-B., Dijksterhuis, A., & Galinsky, A. D. (2008). The merits of unconscious thought in creativity. *Psychological Science*, 19(9), 912–918.

7

WHY REASON MATTERS

Connecting research on human reason to the challenges of the Anthropocene

Nathaniel Barr and Gordon Pennycook

Introduction

The capacity to reason has improved the life of human beings in innumerable ways through the innovations it has wrought and the experiences it affords. Culture, art, music, literature, science, and engineering are all products of reason that enrich our collective experience and well-being. Although these benefits are intuitively apparent, a reflective analysis reveals that the same advances that better our lives also have come to threaten them. George Miller famously made this observation in his 1969 APA address, arguing that the "most urgent problems of our world today are the problems we have made for ourselves. ... They are human problems whose solutions will require us to change our behavior and our social institutions" (p. 1063). This chapter aims to unpack this assertion by mapping the relations between human reason, innovation, and some of the biggest obstacles to the continued success of the human species. A review of contemporary societal and environmental problems in the context of modern reasoning research and applications of behavioural science reveals much in the way of interconnection. Reason is intimately bound to both the causes of and solutions to modern risks like climate change and large-scale conflict.

In this chapter we argue that the empirical study of how we think, what we believe, and how we behave, and the practical application of lessons from such research, have the potential to play an important role in how we address our most threatening global problems. The study of morality, cooperation, creativity, belief formation, and how thinking relates to technology are identified as particularly pressing areas for researchers and practitioners to focus upon. It is argued that the pursuit of advancing and applying reasoning research must be elevated from an important area of psychological research to an urgent matter of global priority. In light of the strong ties between thinking, beliefs, and behaviours of relevance to large-scale challenges, the study of human reasoning and its application holds a particularly potent position in our navigation of the novel risks we now face. To survive and flourish, we must study human reason and apply what we learn to how we live our lives.

The Anthropocene

Tens of thousands of years ago, in what is now known as the Upper Paleolithic Revolution, the archaeological record reveals an eruption of human innovation. This explosion marked a shift from a relatively static state of progress within our species to a steep climb; "unlike previous eras, when stasis dominated, innovation [became] the essence of culture, with change being measured in millennia rather than hundreds of millennia" (Leakey, 1984, pp. 93–94). These changes spanned all facets of life, ranging from advances in hunting strategies, increased sophistication in art and jewellery, changes in social structure, and ritualized burial and religious rites (see Gabora, 2003). This surge was not short-lived, and our lives remain defined by the acceleration of our innovative output.

From the onset of the first explosive surges of collective creative output around the globe, the pace of progress has continually increased and the mark of the human mind upon the planet has become increasingly apparent. In illustrating this heightened pace of innovation, Ronald Wright points out that "from the first chipped stone to the first smelted iron took nearly 3 million years; from the first iron to the hydrogen bomb took only 3,000" (2004, p. 14). Such furious acceleration continues into the contemporary. For example, from the time of the Wright brothers' famous first flight at Kitty Hawk to the first time humans set foot on the moon, a mere 66 years had passed. Within a lifetime, humans progressed from skimming across the surface of the Earth, an incredible accomplishment in itself, to setting foot on an orbiting satellite some 384,400 km from our planet. In describing the marked acceleration of technological and scientific advance in the modern era, Ray Kurzweil (1999) argues that

> during the 19th century [the pace of] technological progress was equal to that of the ten centuries that came before it. Advancement in the first two decades of the 20th century matched that of the entire nineteenth century. Today significant technological transformations take just a few years.

That human action has a significant impact upon Earth has long been recognized by scholars (e.g., Marsh, 1864) and remains an active topic of discussion in diverse academic fields. However, the last few decades are unique in the intensity of human impact. Since 1950, in what has been called 'The Great Acceleration', a sharp increase in population, economic activity, and human pressures on Earth has occurred (Steffen, Broadgate, Deutsch, Gaffney, & Ludwig, 2015). The collective innovation that emerged as a consequence of our incredible capacity to think and reason has so drastically influenced the Earth that many have called for the current post-industrial geologic era to be defined in terms of our impact on the planet: the Anthropocene (see Steffen, Grinevald, Crutzen, & McNeill, 2011).

Though our innovations have afforded us countless benefits, they are not without costs and have led to an unprecedented era in terms of risk. The risks that could destroy or significantly degrade our collective future well-being are diverse and range from "volcanic eruptions to pandemic infections, nuclear accidents to worldwide tyrannies, out-of-control scientific experiments to climatic changes, and cosmic hazards to economic collapse" (Bostrom & Ćirković, 2008, p. 1). Though we've long faced naturalistic risks, Bostrom (2013), in an article entitled "Existential Risk Prevention as Global Priority", argues that the most threatening risks are anthropogenic and related to technological advances. *The Global Risks Report 2017* by the World Economic Forum (2017) converges with this assessment. The report identifies environmental concerns, disruptions as a consequence of emerging technology, economic inequality, and societal polarization as critical contemporary challenges for humanity. Thus, modern analysis of the risks that most threaten us echoes the sentiments of Miller (1969), found at the beginning of this chapter; for him, "our most pressing problems are of our own creation" (p. 1063).

The avoidance of naturalistic risks, such as volcanic eruptions or cosmic hazards, are largely out of our control. However, those problems that we have created, such as environmental disaster and large-scale conflict, might be within our sphere of influence. For instance, some estimates suggest that a large proportion, up to 40%, of the per capita greenhouse gas emissions contributing to climate change can be connected to choices made by individual citizens (MacKay, 2008). Individual voters can in part determine the sort of geopolitical policies enacted by nation states related to international conflict by virtue of the leaders they elect. Although we face collective catastrophe, individual psychology is at the forefront of minimizing such risk. Bostrom (2013) suggests that our ability to detect and avert potential catastrophe at our own hands can occur by way of "improvements in society's ability to recognise and act on important truths" (p. 27) and through "advances in science and philosophy, spread of rationality culture, and biological cognitive enhancement" (p. 28), which can all be traced back to human reason.

In describing the Upper Paleolithic Revolution, which sparked our ascent into the Anthropocene, Leakey (1984) argues that "this collective archaeological signal is unmistakable evidence of the modern human mind at work" (pp. 93–94). What spurred this shift? What made the mind modern? Other major shifts in human intelligence and cultural history have often coincided with neuroanatomical changes, but no evidence exists that the influx of innovative output in the Upper Paleolithic was correlated with changes to our brains. It has been argued, in accounting for this surge of creativity, that this era is associated with the "onset of symbolic thinking, cognitive fluidity, and the capacity to shift between convergent and divergent or explicit and implicit modes of thought. Also, the emergence of metacognition enabled our ancestors to reflect on and even override their own nature" (Gabora & Kaufman, 2010, p. 293). Accordingly, Gabora and Kaufman

(2010) argue that the innovation in the Upper Paleolithic came about not as a result of changes to the structure of our brains, but rather as a consequence of a change in how we used our brains.

In concordance with Miller's (1969) argument, it would seem that the same intellectual evolution which afforded humans many benefits in the modern era is also responsible for many of the complex and serious challenges to our collective well-being that we must now face. To conquer the challenges that we face in the Anthropocene, we must again change the way we use our brains. We must improve our understanding of how we think such that we can leverage that understanding to improve our collective ability to reason, and we must also think differently about the extent to which reason matters. Studying human reason, and applying lessons from that research, must be conceptualized not just as an important area of psychological inquiry, but as a global priority for the success of our species.

Creativity and innovation

Difficult problems require innovative solutions, so perhaps the most obvious antidote in the quest to avoid catastrophe from our own reason is to continue to increase creativity. An imperative thus exists for humankind to expand extant basic and applied research programmes in traditional areas of scientific and engineering that yield practical outcomes. In addition, art, literature, music, and other creative pursuits are important avenues for influencing individual behaviour. In order to maximize our creative potential in these areas, not only should society dedicate large resources toward innovative activities, we should also be investing heavily in understanding the cognitive and social mechanisms of creativity to best understand how to structure society and education to foster it.

Despite the well-recognized need for further creativity in society, and decades of concerted psychological research in this area, a replete understanding of the nature of creativity and how to enhance it have remained elusive. Part of the challenge is that although much work has been done in this area, there are many essentially independent but concurrent streams of research that span the many levels of analysis which comprise creativity studies (see Hennessey & Amabile, 2010). Although there are many benefits to such a decentralized structure (see Silvia, 2014), an important avenue for theoretical development is to generate models of creativity that allow for understanding the relation between cognitive and neural correlates of creativity and the higher-order organizational- and societal-level factors that influence whether creative ideas are translated to meaningful innovation.

Extensive amounts of behavioural and neuroscientific evidence converge to suggest that creativity is best understood as an interplay between autonomous and controlled thinking. Beaty, Silvia, Nusbaum, Jauk, and Benedek (2014b) demonstrated that individual differences in both associative (Type 1) processing and executive (Type 2) processing were predictive of variance in creative ability, and in convergent neuroscientific research, they have shown that creative thought required "cooperation between brain regions associated with cognitive control and low-level imaginative processes" (Beaty et al., 2014a, p. 92).

Given such findings, calls have been made for creativity studies to become more strongly aligned with reasoning research. For example, Sowden, Pringle, and Gabora (2015) suggest that creativity research should be contextualized in the broader cognitive psychological literature on thinking and that reasoning research on the interaction between different modes of thought is a promising area for integration. To accommodate evidence surrounding the interplay between autonomous and controlled thinking in creativity, and to address the disarray in theoretical development in this area, Barr (2018, this volume) maps dual-process meta-theoretical frameworks of human reasoning to creativity research. He argues that such models hold great potential as they are ubiquitous in both low-level cognitive research and in higher-order societal-level interventions and education, allowing for a common language that can span levels of analysis. It is argued that more thinking, reasoning, and decision-making researchers should be investing time and effort toward integrating and expanding their research streams into the arena of creative cognition.

Human scientific and technological advance are, of course, already being leveraged to combat problems of our own creation. Although scientific advance has created new risks, it simultaneously is able to answer many of the new questions that it has posed. Disconcertingly though, despite the need for scientific innovation being arguably more important than ever before, anti-science attitudes are prevalent and appear to be increasing in some quarters (such as among Republicans in the United States; see Gauchat, 2012). Thus, a priority in the Anthropocene is finding ways to increase attention and appreciation of science through effective communication. One means to address this issue is to creatively communicate scientific facts surrounding the risks we face in ways that are more amenable to popular understanding than technical reports or scientific papers. For example, the Doomsday Clock (http://thebulletin.org/three-minutes-and-counting7938) was created to illustrate the likelihood of a human-caused global catastrophe. Similar initiatives are underway at Concordia University with the Human Impact Lab (www.humanimpactlab.com), which aims to develop creative means to illustrate the nature of modern risks. Interestingly, and perhaps disturbingly, this pursuit is not merely a matter of educating the public, as people's views on at least some scientific issues appear to be strongly associated with ideology as well – a point discussed later in this chapter.

Understanding creativity in the context of human reason is important both for facilitating the genesis of new and useful ideas and in finding ways to convince the public to adopt and endorse such ideas. Interestingly, in the Anthropocene, some of our most powerful creations interact with the substrate that created them – technology and thinking are enmeshed. Thus, understanding thinking in the modern era necessarily entails consideration of how our cognitive capacity and reasoning now interacts with and relates to some of the most influential innovations in the history of our species – computing technology and the internet.

The extended mind: process and content

In considering the impact of technology in our lives, it has long been recognized that many of the most important innovations in the history of our species are those that enhance our natural physical and cognitive abilities: "Most of the greatest advances of modern technology have been instruments which extended the scope of our sense organs, our brains or our limbs. Such are telescopes and microscopes, wireless [sets], calculating machines, typewriters, motor-cars, ships and aeroplanes" (Craik, 1967, p. 61).

Marshall McLuhan articulated the implications that such technological advances have for our daily lives when arguing that "the medium is the message" (1964, p. 81). In *Understanding Media: The Extensions of Man*, McLuhan (1964) considered the impact of inventions such as the telephone and radio, and how they have modified the landscape of our experience and routines. More recently, philosophers and psychologists have focused increasing attention on the ways that different media interact with the way we think. In the Anthropocene, an important aspect of understanding thinking entails studying how our thinking may be modified by or interact with technological advance to shape human thought and the way humans engage with the world.

In 1998, Clark and Chalmers published their seminal work, "The Extended Mind", providing a philosophical perspective on how artifacts in the world can be conceived as allowing us to extend our thinking beyond our brains. Their work is relevant for a range of behaviours, from offloading arithmetic to paper to more complex interactions like cybernetic neural enhancements. Interestingly, although the internet existed at the time, and many foresaw its impending rise, the ubiquity and centrality of this medium in human life in the 21st century had yet to become clear. In 1995, but a few years before the notion of the extended mind became extensively discussed, 86% of American adults did not use the internet, but by 2013 this proportion flipped, with 86% reporting they used the internet (Pew Research Center, 2016). As such, Clark and Chalmers' (1998) work has arguably become increasingly important with time, with more complex and important extensions of the mind emerging as computing technology continued to accelerate rapidly.

Of particular importance in spurring conversations and empirical research into the way that thinking and internet use interacts was David Carr's (2008) essay "Is Google Making Us Stupid?" His introspective work reflected on the way that reading online inspires relatively shallow thought when compared to consumption of longer physical texts. Although his work was not empirical, the anecdotes he recounted and the ideas he espoused resonated with a world increasingly interconnected by the internet. In a landmark study, Sparrow, Liu, and Wegner (2011) empirically assessed the role that the internet had in the way people remember information. Sparrow et al. demonstrated that individuals offloaded memory to the internet in a way akin to the manner in which people rely on transactive memories of other individuals. Priming experiments showed that when faced with difficult, but not easy, trivia questions, people readily thought of the internet. They also found that rather than remember content, people were prone to remember where that information was accessible. Together, these data support empirically some of what Carr (2008) proposes; people were using the internet to limit cognitive effort.

Since Sparrow et al.'s (2011) work was published, the internet has only gained a more prominent role in the daily affairs of the average human. Empirical investigations exploring the relation between the internet, memory, and reasoning are likewise becoming more frequent. For example, Fisher, Goddu, and Keil (2015) showed that searching for information online inflated estimates of internal knowledge. Ferguson, McLean, and Risko (2015) showed that the internet can influence metacognitive processes and modulate the willingness of an individual to offer answers. Barr, Pennycook, Stolz, and Fugelsang (2015b) looked at individual differences in reliance on search engines, with an emphasis on smartphones. They found that less reflective, less intelligent, and more intuitive reasoners were more likely to rely on their device for information in daily life, and they suggested that this pattern of results is indicative of people offloading their thinking to technology and that this offloading constitutes a modern type of cognitive miserliness. Vujic (2017) showed that the number of computing hours per day was negatively related to sustained attention and rational thinking, that the proportion of time on smartphones was negatively related to rational thinking style, and that trait mindfulness did not act as a protective factor. Ward, Duke, Gneezy, and Bos (2017) showed that the mere presence of a smartphone can reduce cognitive capacity. An important aspect of human reasoning research in the modern era will be keeping pace with the way that such technology is used in daily life and continually expanding our understanding of the relation between how we think and how we use technology.

Another important line of research in this area surrounds the nature of the content online and how it is transferred. Rather than rely on a standardized central encyclopaedia, the internet represents an ever evolving dynamic knowledge store. If humans are, as argued by Sparrow et al. (2011) and others, offloading memory and cognition to the internet, then consideration of online content in relation to human reasoning is increasingly important. For example, research into the way information travels in the context of social networks suggests that many of us operate in what are called echo chambers, which often facilitate the spread of misinformation (see Del Vicario et al., 2016). Echo chamber refers to the phenomenon of people primarily sharing and consuming content that coincides with information which they already believe, often amplifying those beliefs. Rather than procuring information from diverse sources across the ideological spectrum, the average member of our species relies on a curated, convergent set of friends and sources for information. Network analyses conducted by Williams, McMurray, Kurz, and Lambert (2015) showed that on Twitter, most users "interact only with like-minded others, in communities dominated by a single view" (p. 126), and that activist and sceptic circles are largely echo chambers. Del Vicario et al. (2016) analyzed how Facebook users consume information about scientific and conspiracy news and showed that selective exposure to content created homogeneous clusters of information in distinct circles. Misinformation online comes not only from individual citizens, but governments as well, making this area of research even more consequential. As part of a project on computational propaganda, Bradshaw and Howard (2017) outlined how dozens of countries, both authoritarian and democratic, engaged in social media manipulation meant to manage public opinion using 'cyber troops', which are military and political teams meant to shape the way citizens see and understand contemporary issues.

As the internet's ubiquity rises, it will be important to uncover how the internet facilitates the spreading of and belief in things like conspiracy theories (Swami, 2018, this volume), bullshit (Pennycook, Cheyne, Barr, Koehler, & Fugelsang, 2014), and fake news (Pennycook, Cannon, & Rand, 2017). Interestingly, belief in conspiracies (Swami, 2018, this volume) and seeing profundity in bullshit (Pennycook et al., 2014) are both associated with decreased analytic thinking, as is reliance on the internet for information (Barr et al., 2015b). As such, it may be the case that those who are most prone to endorsing such questionable views might be most often encountering them online. Conspiracist ideation is a particularly consequential area to understand as there are well-documented negative consequences of such beliefs that pervade diverse domains of everyday life (for reviews, see Swami, 2018, this volume; Douglas, Sutton, Jolley, & Wood, 2015). Limiting the spread of misinformation is clearly important, but social and cognitive psychologists should be especially concerned with understanding the mechanisms by which individuals assess information they encounter and how to limit potential bias as a consequence of group relations. For example, Swire, Berinsky, Lewandowsky, and Ecker (2017) conducted a study aimed at understanding how people process political misinformation and found that judgements of truth or falsity were influenced by whether or not it was attributed to Donald Trump and whether participants supported him.

In general, continued exploration into how people recognize fake news and other forms of bullshit (see Frankfurt, 2005) should be an important future direction for behavioural, social, and cognitive research, as what citizens consume and believe has direct connection to the most pressing problems in the Anthropocene, like lack of belief in climate change and extreme political views. The correction of misinformation and successful debiasing of erroneously held beliefs across all levels of society constitutes one of the great challenges of the information age (see Lewandowsky, Ecker, Seifert, Schwarz, & Cook, 2012). By better understanding the ways that people find information, how they assess whether it is valid, and how they act upon that information, we can better understand the true nature of the social and psychological obstacles to our collective success.

Traditional beliefs and moral tribes in the modern era

Although humans now enjoy the modern affordances of advanced innovation, many of our most ancient and deeply seated dispositions and beliefs remain a central aspect of contemporary life. Religion remains a powerful force in shaping human belief and behaviour, with estimates suggesting that up to 90% of the world's population believes in some sort of deity (Saad, 2011). Secularity and atheism have often been predicted to increase due to the rise of the internet and increases in scientific and rational thinking. However, taking a biologically informed perspective, some recent work suggests that so long as believers continue to have more children than non-believers, secularity will not subsume the whole of society in the immediate future (Ellis, Hoskin, Dutton, & Nyborg, 2017). These authors actually argue for a contra-secularization hypothesis whereby secularism will see a decline in industrialized nations in the 21st century. In assessing the persistence of supernatural belief in the face of ever increasing scientific education and knowledge, Lindeman (2018, this volume) cites Gilovich's (1991) observation that despite having the best universities in the world, there are significantly more astrologers than astronomers in the United States; she also recounts The Church Research Institute's (2016) observation that despite Finland having one of the best education systems on Earth, almost half of the populace believe in angels and entertain the idea of an afterlife. Atheists often report intellectual, rational, and scientific reasons for religious disbelief (Hunsberger & Altemeyer, 2006), but it seems clear that even as society advances scientifically, supernatural beliefs are not likely to uniformly extinguish as a result. Although human reason has ushered in an era of unprecedented advances, many traditional beliefs remain a fixture of contemporary society.

As globalization marches on, The Great Acceleration continues, and people of diverse beliefs continually come together, it is important to understand both the psychology of group dynamics and the psychology of beliefs. Of particular interest is the relation between cognitive and social factors in the context of religious belief. Social foundations theory specifically addresses this relation (see Morgan, Wood, & Caldwell-Harris, 2018, this volume). This theory argues that to more fully understand the well-documented relation between analytic thinking and religiosity, one must consider the societal factors in which this relation occurs. Specifically, the social foundations hypothesis articulates a view in which social density, cognitive style, and religiosity interact, with different sorts of societies encouraging different sorts of thinking styles, which in turn can result in different levels of religiosity. Social density is a broad concept that considers a number of facets of society, including the relative emphasis on independent or interdependent construal, the relative need to respect hierarchy and authority, and differences in the extent to which one seeks to appease in-group members. Societies high in social density, that more highly prize interdependence, respect for authority, and reliance on social rules, are thought to encourage more intuitive, rather than analytic, thinking styles.

Interestingly, Morgan et al. (2018, this volume) posit that behaviours associated with high social density are especially important when living conditions are difficult, harsh, and precarious, like when natural disasters occur, and people must extensively rely on social relations for support and resources. To support this supposition, Morgan et al. cite evidence that religiosity increases after economic crises and natural disasters (Chen, 2010; Norris & Inglehart, 2011; Sibley & Bulbulia, 2012). Given the challenges of the Anthropocene – the potentially disastrous consequences of anthropogenic climate change, other environmental disasters, the ongoing increase in economic inequality, and the fallout if large-scale conflict were to occur – the social foundations hypothesis might predict another relation between the risks of this era and human reason: Not only might a failure to understand and change our thinking precipitate changes to the planet and economy, changes to the planet and economy might yet change our thinking.

Although the forces of globalization mean more diverse groups than ever before are living together, this has not necessarily resulted in greater unification of ideals, and polarization of belief is a considerable issue to address. One major factor in accounting for such polarization relates to our moral beliefs. Greene (2014) has documented the way in which humans organize into moral tribes, privileging those in our in-group. Research in this area has catalogued and explored how individuals differ in the way they conceptualize moral transgressions. Moral foundations theory (see Haidt, 2012) has articulated differences across individuals in what they view to be the critical determinants of what constitutes right or wrong. For instance, liberals and conservatives differ in their relative valuation of tradition and respect for authority as factors driving moral decisions. Research has also shown that disgust can play a role in moral judgments, with conservatives being more easily disgusted than liberals, which can have consequences for issues of tolerance and acceptance (e.g., Inbar, Pizarro, & Bloom, 2009).

Importantly, in terms of the broader argument articulated in this chapter, such moral reasoning has strong connections to reasoning research. For instance, Pennycook et al. (2014) showed that analytic thinking style is related to differences in binding moral values, and that the extent to which disgust influences moral judgments is also dependent upon differences in analytic thinking style (see also Pizarro & Bloom, 2003). In accounting for such relations, Landy and Royzman (2018, this volume) put forth the Moral Myopia Model (MMM), which articulates a novel formulation of the relation between reason and moral judgements. These authors reviewed research in this area and developed a view in which deliberate and analytic thinking is related to more complex conceptions of moral issues and consideration of a number of normative factors, whereas intuitive processing is more oriented to singular factors of consequence. Thus, in their view, deliberate thinking promotes a measured, weighted approach that considers multiple factors, and intuitive thinking promotes dogmatic adherence to but one normative factor, such as individual rights or utilitarian gains.

In an increasingly complex world, it seems likely that singular focus on any one factor in moral reasoning could be disadvantageous to group harmony, particularly when the work of Haidt (2012) and others has shown that different groups value different factors. As such, in the context of the MMM, an interesting possible means by which to facilitate reductions in the odds of cultural violence as a function of moral tribalism is to focus on increasing deliberate thinking, rather than to focus solely on the content of disagreements.

And it is not just conflict – moral reasoning research also intersects with issues pertaining to consumption that connects to pollution, climate change, and environmental challenges. Mazar and Zhong (2010) showed that although priming green products makes people more altruistic than being primed by conventional products, purchasing such green products can have detrimental consequences. Relative to conventional products, those that bought green products were more likely to subsequently steal, cheat, and act less altruistically. In other cases, moral appeals can be positive. For instance, Bernedo, Ferraro, and Price (2014) demonstrated in a large population that a one-time nudge combining technical information, moral persuasion, and social comparisons can have significant benefits in convincing individuals to reduce their water consumption over long periods of time. Teaching people how to live more sustainable lives interacts with cognitive biases, and an important task is to leverage morality in the pursuit to save the planet, as giving people tips on how to be more environmentally friendly is more complex than it appears (see Grolleau, Midler, & Mzoughi, 2017).

Individual differences in reasoning and group affiliation are also of consequence for climate change. For instance, although an overwhelming majority of scientists agree that climate change is a real and present danger and that humans are to blame, the issue is highly politicized in the United States. Party lines and personal cultural affiliations are more predictive in determining views about climate change and other scientific issues than are differences in intelligence, reflectiveness, or scientific knowledge (Kahan, Jenkins-Smith, & Braman, 2011; Kahan et al., 2012; Kahan, 2013). Indeed, much of the rejection of science in general is a consequence of motivated cognition, such that people do not accept findings which threaten their beliefs or view of the world (Lewandowsky & Oberauer, 2016). Kahan et al. (2012) undertook a large-scale study to assess if the idea that the reason for disbelief in anthropogenic climate change was a lack of knowledge or education, and they found no support for that position. Rather, they found that social ties were of extreme consequence. The most intelligent and knowledgeable about climate change were not the most concerned – rather, they were the most polarized. In summarizing their work, the authors suggest that

> public divisions over climate change stem not from the public's incomprehension of science but from a distinctive conflict of interest between the personal interest individuals have in forming beliefs in line with those held by others with whom they share close ties and the collective one they all share in making use of the best available science to promote common welfare.
>
> *(Kahan et al., 2012, p. 732)*

In all, research into moral reasoning constitutes an incredibly important avenue for psychological research in the Anthropocene. Reasoning researchers should increasingly explore the intersection of cultural cognition, moral tribalism, traditional beliefs, motivated reasoning, and social network dynamics in the context of human conflict and political polarization. As technological advances increase the ease and scale with which both individuals and nation states can inflict violence, an increasingly important task for reasoning researchers will be to better understand how best to encourage cooperation across moral tribes in daily life and in the pursuit of solving problems that threaten us collectively at the broadest scale.

Importance of cooperation

How to manage the diverse beliefs that make up the global landscape in a truly globalized age, particularly those that seem to contradict contemporary demands in favour of traditional standards, remains a huge ethical and practical challenge. For instance, some have argued that religious beliefs which suggest an afterlife can be antithetical to efforts aimed at recognizing the importance of self-preservation on the planet, and in solving the sorts of problems discussed in this chapter. Steven Pinker (2011), for example, argues that "The doctrine of the sacredness of the soul sounds vaguely uplifting, but in fact is highly malignant. It discounts life on earth as just a temporary phase that people pass through, indeed, an infinitesimal fraction of their existence" (p. 143). Although rates of religiosity are in decline, it remains clear that even in the modern era, human belief structures rooted in ancient traditions are powerful in shaping both the individual and the collective, and efforts to shift such ideologies drastically in short order would likely be unsuccessful in addition to being hugely unethical. Thus, a challenge for the scientific community will be to align matters of global concern to be complementary with pre-existing belief structures and ideologies. That is, the literature on the psychology of belief suggests that many of the long-standing beliefs that shape society today are likely to remain entrenched, and efforts at shifting public opinion to policies that minimize the threat of anthropogenic risks must complement, rather than replace, existing views to be both ethical and practically useful. In short, people with diverse ideologies must cooperate.

Cooperation and compromise is especially difficult in a world wrought with inequity. Although the 'Great Acceleration' is associated with sharp rises in GDP globally, analyses reveal that much of the economic growth has occurred in the wealthier OECD countries, whereas the population growth is largely driven by increases in the less wealthy, non-OECD nations (Steffen et al., 2015). Evidence suggests that economic development, inequality, war, and state violence are connected (Nafziger & Auvenin, 2002). Such socio-economic inequality, and the consequent extremism and violence with which it can be associated, is particularly perilous in the modern era. Not only are we at risk from the environmental by-products of consumption-heavy lifestyles afforded by innovations, but technological advances also figure prominently in overt aggression and large-scale conflict. From the discovery of how to harness the power of the atom through the Cold War and into the present, the risks posed by nuclear weapons continually increases, whether it be through accident or intentional aggression (Schlosser, 2013). In assessing the need to arrive at peace in the nuclear age, Lemon (1946) warned that "unless [peace] can be accomplished, the darkest of all ages surely lies ahead; the rare joy that in the past has gone with the acquisition of knowledge will be known no more" and that the accomplishments of the past seem insignificant, "compared to achievements that now must promptly be attained in other fields of human activity" (p. 441).

Philosophers, psychologists, scientists, other academics, politicians, religious and cultural leaders, and citizens must extensively discuss means by which to accommodate traditional views with contemporary risk analysis and align the goals of diverse groups. The World Economic Forum (2017), in concluding their analysis of global risks, implores those in positions of power to "redouble ... efforts to protect and strengthen our systems of global collaboration. Nowhere is this more urgent than in relation to the environment" (p. 58). In assessing the prospect of world peace, Martin Luther King Jr. (1967/1986) famously argued for the importance of global cooperation: "our loyalties must transcend our race, our tribe, our class, our nation; and this means we must develop a world perspective" (p. 253). Cooperation is not only desirable, but essential in this precarious age.

Some trends in this direction are encouraging; for example, organizations such as the Evangelical Environmental Network are rallying religious Americans to support the fight against climate change. The Pope has also declared that anthropogenic climate change marks a true threat, and he has made calls for believers to act sustainably. Indigenous philosophies are seeing increasing recognition in the public sphere as environmentally threatening industries continue to encroach upon ancestral lands (e.g., the Dakota Access Pipeline). These views have long emphasized spiritual and traditional beliefs that align with the modern warnings of contemporary scientists. For instance, the seventh-generation principle advocates considering all decisions with an eye for the consequences for future descendants, and many Indigenous North American languages have a word that translates to "we are all related to and respect everything in life" (e.g., '*mitakuye oyasion*' in Lakotan, '*Nogomaq*' in Algonquian, and '*Ea Nigade Qusdi Idaddavhn*' in Cherokee). Cooperatively integrating such views with the empirical evidence of contemporary science is an important avenue for approaching environmental issues and large-scale conflict.

Thankfully, many strides have been made in recent years that advance our understanding of the relation between cooperation and reasoning and hold promise in applied interventions. The pursuit of cooperation is not only a practical priority for businesses, governments, and citizens, but a fruitful area for academic research as well. Some of the most influential work aimed at understanding the cognitive and social underpinnings of cooperation adopts a dual-process framework and explores the relative contributions of intuition and analytic thinking. In assessing whether intuition or analyticity yields greater cooperation, the results are clear; more deliberation leads to less cooperation, with humans disposed to "spontaneous giving and calculated greed" (Rand, Greene, & Nowak, 2012; Rand & Nowak, 2013; Rand et al., 2014; Rand, 2016). Given that cooperation seems to be facilitated by intuitive thinking, advice from psychologists to be more intuitive constitutes a deviation from the standard refrain from reasoning researchers that humans would do well to reflect more often and to engage analytic thinking more frequently.

For example, Bear and Rand (2016) present an evolutionary model in which intuition acts as a social heuristic and deliberation does not increase cooperation. They suggest that reflection often leads people to override their initial intuition to collaborate, and that our impulses are not typically selfish. Jordan, Hoffman, Nowak, and Rand (2016) demonstrated that cooperating without calculation and taking less time to decide to work together acts as a signal of trustworthiness and is actually associated with being more trustworthy as well. Stagnaro, Arechar, and

Rand (2017) researched the influence of top-down incentives to cooperate and demonstrated that institutions which reward working together can have power in shaping cultures of cooperation.

Finding ways to promote intuitive cooperation but foster critical reflection in other domains is a considerable challenge in the current climate. Given that deliberate reasoning seems a remedy in moral tribalism but a hindrance to cooperation, prescriptions for peace and togetherness at both the interpersonal and societal levels seem complex at best and impossible at worst. Striking the balance between intuition and reason, both as individuals and as a society, is increasingly important as risks increase in scope and severity. Important work awaits in mapping the relation between individual psychology, group dynamics, and societal structure in the context of cooperation and the Anthropocene.

The future of research on human reason: basic and applied approaches

For generations, psychologists have argued that the application of lessons from psychology could yield massive dividends for society. Behaviourists, particularly B. F. Skinner, argued that by modifying and reinforcing behaviour, we could shape a more cohesive and functional society. Skinner's (1948) novel, *Walden Two*, described a society which was structured to align with insights about human psychology and social dynamics. George Miller, in his famous 1969 APA address, argued, "if we were ever to achieve substantial progress toward our stated aim – toward the understanding, prediction and control of mental and behavioural phenomena – the implications for every aspect of society would make brave men tremble" (p. 1065).

The contemporary era has seen similar admonishments from psychologists to take the lessons from the science of behaviour and find ways to apply them in meaningful and practical ways. For example, Lilienfeld, Ammirati, and Landfield (2009) echo Miller's (1969) urging to give psychology away by arguing that disseminating research on debiasing could hold great promise in promoting human welfare, asserting that "research on combating extreme confirmation bias should be among psychological science's most pressing priorities" (Lilienfeld et al., 2009, p. 390). An inspection of global commitments in applied behavioural science suggests that the world is increasingly heeding this call.

Since the publication of Ariely's (2008) *Predictably Irrational*, Thaler and Sunstein's (2008) *Nudge*, and Kahneman's (2011) *Thinking, Fast and Slow*, the notion that behavioural science and the psychology of reasoning, judgement, and decision-making can be leveraged in business and policy has increasingly entered the public consciousness (see Thaler, 2015, for a history). Around the world, governments are housing behavioural science teams and engaging in the direct application of insights, nudges, and rigorous experimentation. In the United Kingdom, the Behavioural Insights Team, which is jointly owned by the UK government, Nesta (a charity), and the employees, has achieved considerable success. Another example, ideas42, is a group that aims "to use the power of behavioral science to design scalable solutions to some of society's most difficult problems" (www.ideas42.org/about-us/). Obama (2015) issued an executive order that directed the federal government to leverage insights from behavioural science. In Canada, the Province of Ontario has been piloting behavioural-insights-based projects, and the federal Privy Council Office is engaging in behavioural science work within the Innovation Hub. Such centres are not confined to Europe and North America either – the Busara Center for Behavioral Economics primarily focuses on poverty alleviation and boasts offices in the United States, Kenya, Uganda, and Ethiopia. These represent a fraction of the organizations and initiatives that are leveraging psychological and behavioural science in the pursuit of problems related to our collective well-being on the planet. As the scope and number of such groups increase, so too do our odds of success in addressing the challenges of the Anthropocene. Field experiments, randomized control trials, and other sorts of studies that examine how people reason in the real world are increasingly being used in many areas (see Shafir, 2012). As governments, businesses, and other organizations around the world increasingly rely on insights and methods germane to reasoning research, the impetus for investment in such research also increases (see Benartzi et al., 2017).

As vital as such applied work is, it is also imperative that society supports basic research into human reason. The applied work that has proven successful is scaffolded on the foundation of basic research and theoretical models of human reason developed over decades of psychological research. As noted by Lewin (1951), "there is nothing so practical as a good theory" (p. 169). For example, the seminal works of Kahneman and Tversky, including prospect theory, have been cited as key in inspiring the behavioural economics explosion in the applied realm (e.g., Camerer, 1999). The world is noisy, and in order to increase our ability to craft effective interventions and understand human reason in these complex environments, we must concurrently refine and develop our theories of reasoning in the lab, where we can isolate causal factors. Importantly, as reasoning research increasingly extends its reach in the real world, applied outcomes can be used to guide basic research. Descriptive studies, normative analysis, and prescriptive interventions all should constitute areas of priority (see Fischhoff, 2010). Increasingly sophisticated theoretical models are required in an increasingly challenging and complex world, and they must be functional in their application to anthropogenic issues. Fischhoff, echoing Baddeley's (1979) call for increased intermingling between the basic and applied, foresees the future of research in this area as defined by interaction between "*applied basic* research, testing theory by its application, and *basic applied* research, creating theory from new phenomena observed through those tests" (Fischhoff, 2010, p. 733). A back and forth between researchers and practitioners is, in our opinion, an essential aim for those interested in human reason in the Anthropocene.

If more researchers engage in a mixture of basic and applied research focused on real-world challenges, interdisciplinary approaches will be increasingly required. For instance, in work outlining how to correct misinformation, experts draw on political science, education, and computer science (see Cook, Ecker, & Lewandowsky,

2015). The rise of artificial intelligence and computing technology not only pervades individual psychology, but also intersects with economic and workplace issues across many sectors. J. P. Guilford (1950), in his famous APA address about creativity, recognized that as such technologies progressed, humankind must

> develop an economic order in which sufficient employment and wage earning would still be available. This would require creative thinking of an unusual order and speed. In the second place, eventually about the only economic value of brains left would be in the creative thinking of which they are capable.
>
> *(p. 448)*

Thus, the trend toward increased reliance on smartphones and computing technology intersects with economic, business, moral, ethical, and environmental challenges that require collaborative and interdisciplinary research. The Organisation for Economic Co-operation and Development's report *Behavioural Insights and Public Policy: Lessons from Around the World* illustrates the breadth of topics already covered in contemporary applied research. The report features a large number of case studies and outlines how insights and experimentation are applied in a multitude of areas, including "consumer protection, education, energy, environment, finance, health and safety, labour market policies, public service delivery, taxes and telecommunications" (OECD, 2017, p. 3). Extending the reach of reasoning research into such diverse sectors will require ongoing collaboration with nearly the full spectrum of professional domains and academic areas.

Another important point is that for basic and applied research to be as fruitful as possible, reasoning researchers must employ methods and approaches that draw on the innovations of this age. In recounting the history of the cognitive revolution, which was foundational for the evolution of the sort of research discussed in this chapter, Miller (2003) identifies cross-discipline collaboration as critical, particularly areas connected to emergent technology. He cites Norbert Wiener's work on cybernetics, Marvin Minsky and John McCarthy's pioneering work on artificial intelligence, Chomsky's work on linguistics, and Alan Newell and Herb Simon's use of computers to simulate cognitive processes as catalytic in crystallizing new ways of conceiving of thinking.

Today, similar revolutions are afoot in that the use of technology is transforming the way that we understand and address the challenges of the modern era from a cognitive perspective. For example, Medimorec and Pennycook (2015) used text analysers to compare the language of climate change proponents and deniers in order to reveal the ways that denial is manifest linguistically. Brady, Wills, Jost, Tucker, and Van Bavel (2017) used a large sample of social media communications to understand how highly polarizing policy-relevant issues are spread in the context of real political discourse. Chen et al. (2016) leveraged advanced neuroimaging technologies to longitudinally assess future creative cognitive ability as a function of alterations in frontoparietal and frontotemporal brain networks. Seth Stephens-Davidowitz's

(2017) book, *Everybody Lies: Big Data, New Data, and What the Internet Can Tell Us About Who We Really Are*, illustrates the potency of Google search data in illuminating how people think about core issues of our time. Rand, Tomlin, Bear, Ludvig, and Cohen (2017) apply "a formal theoretical approach that applies mathematical methods from non-linear dynamical systems analysis and population biology together with numerical methods and computational simulations" (p. 3) to show the way that automatic and controlled thinking cycle in a society over time. They argue that societal progress due to increased cognitive control can allow for automaticity to increase, which in turn undermines the advances made as a function of the era of heightened control. Illumination of such a cycle can explain historical and contemporary trends and inform our quest to address the challenges of the Anthropocene.

The list of such work goes on, and it must grow, as reasoning research has an imperative to keep pace with the technological advances afforded by human innovation to truly understand thinking in the modern age. Much as computing technology has extended the mind of the average human, it has extended the ways to study and understand the relation between human reason and the challenges we face as a species. As impressive as the threats we face now are in scope and severity, they are arguably matched by the remarkably advanced tools, methods, and theories available to those interested in studying the very mind that brought about those threats.

The future of reasoning research is bright, and it is our hope that the continued advancement and application of this body of work can result in a concomitant brightening of our future prospects of success as a species. Improving our basic understanding of the nature of moral belief, religious belief, conspiratorial thinking, how thinking interacts with technology, creativity, understanding and belief in the power of science, and cooperation has the potential to yield immense rewards by informing applied interventions and policy. As we progress into the future, research into human reason must leverage advanced technology and be connected to the challenges we collectively face.

Risk and (not) investing in research on human reason

Decision science and reasoning research has a long history of studying risk tolerance. Much of this work has been conducted in the context of relatively small gambles that are not strongly related to individual or collective well-being, but instead map onto financial scenarios meant to emulate less dire choices in the real world. Overall, this work finds that humans are quite loss averse, favouring avoiding loss than making equivalent gains (Kahneman, Knetsch, & Thaler, 1991). Interestingly, although this work finds that people tend to be very loss averse in such scenarios, it appears that we as a species are more tolerant, perhaps illogically so, of larger, even existential risks. Bostrom (2013) argues that we are dangerously myopic on longer timescales with greater risks in that we underestimate the massive benefits of even tiny reductions in the odds that we either end our collective existence or so damage the environment as to jeopardize the future possibility that our species attains its full potential. If we preserve the planet for future generations, we can have a hand in preserving human life on this planet, and perhaps beyond (see Dick, 2003). Given the relation of such risks to human reason, it is apparent that we must engage in conversations about the risk of not exploring the way human reasoning interacts with such extreme risks. That is, although historically research into human reason has investigated risk tolerance of individuals in society, it is time for society to consider reasoning research in the context of risk. Our species is perched precariously on our sole planet in an unprecedentedly risky time. It is important for individuals, organizations, and governments to invest heavily in learning about human reason and leveraging insights from that research to address pressing problems.

In considering investment in such research in the context of the immediate existential threats we face as a consequence of our own reason, it seems clear that the cost of not investing in such research outweighs the investment that would be required to facilitate such research and its applications. We implore those who agree with this conclusion to advocate strongly and publicly for funding and investment in the areas discussed in this chapter. Never before has reasoning research been this advanced or applied this widely, yet never before has there been a stronger imperative for further advancement and wider application. Reason matters.

Conclusion

Humans are unique amongst animals on Earth in the diversity, complexity, and impact of our cultural and physical artifacts – language, art, science, and technology are unparalleled amongst other animals. The development of the human capacity to reason and the ability to manipulate not just objects but also symbols have long been identified as playing a central role in our differentiating ourselves cognitively, technologically, and creatively from other species on our planet (Barr, Pennycook, Stolz, & Fugelsang, 2015a; Penn, Holyoak, & Povinelli, 2008; Stanovich, 2005). We are uniquely situated as a species that has shaped the face of the planet so significantly that we now face challenges that are a consequence of our creations (Steffen et al., 2011).

In this era, in order to ensure the perpetuation and progress of the human species and avoid anthropogenic existential risk (Bostrom, 2013), we collectively must attempt to minimize large-scale human conflict, social injustice, and environmental destruction and pollution, including climate change. Technological advances and globalization, emergent properties of human reason, have created novel and complex issues that now demand our reflection and analysis.

A change in our thinking led us into the Anthropocene. Now, in order to survive and progress in this era, we need to change our thinking to be more creative and less extreme in our beliefs, to leverage the advantages of emergent technology, and to cooperate more. We also need to change how we think about the prioritization of applying and advancing research on human reason. Work in this area must be recast from an important area of cognitive research to an urgent global priority. Cognitive and behavioural economic research has shown that people often tend to be short-sighted in their reasoning and decision-making, and researchers, universities, governments, and funding agencies must not mirror this myopia in the allocation of resources and attention dedicated to further understanding human reasoning and rationality in a bid to address our most important societal issues. By bettering our understanding of human cognition, belief, and behaviour, we can reason our way to a more secure future.

References

Ariely, D. (2008). *Predictably irrational*. New York: HarperCollins.
Baddeley, A. D. (1979). Applied cognitive and cognitive applied psychology: The case of face recognition. In L. Nilsson (Ed.), *Perspectives on memory research* (pp. 367–388). Abingdon, UK: Routledge.
Barr, N. (2018). Intuition, reason, and creativity: An integrative dual-process perspective. In G. Pennycook (Ed.), *The new reflectionism in cognitive psychology: Why reason matters* (pp. 93–118). Current Issues in Thinking and Reasoning. Abingdon, UK: Routledge.
Barr, N., Pennycook, G., Stolz, J. A., & Fugelsang, J. A. (2015a). Reasoned connections: A dual-process perspective on creative thought. *Thinking & Reasoning*, 21(1), 61–75.
Barr, N., Pennycook, G., Stolz, J. A., & Fugelsang, J. A. (2015b). The brain in your pocket: Evidence that Smartphones are used to supplant thinking. *Computers in Human Behavior*, 48, 473–480.
Bear, A., & Rand, D. G. (2016). Intuition, deliberation, and the evolution of cooperation. *Proceedings of the National Academy of Sciences*, 113(4), 936–941.
Beaty, R. E., Benedek, M., Wilkins, R. W., Jauk, E., Fink, A., Silvia, P. J., … & Neubauer, A. C. (2014a). Creativity and the default network: A functional connectivity analysis of the creative brain at rest. *Neuropsychologia*, 64, 92–98.
Beaty, R. E., Silvia, P. J., Nusbaum, E. C., Jauk, E., & Benedek, M. (2014b). The roles of associative and executive processes in creative cognition. *Memory & Cognition*, 42(7), 1186–1197.
Benartzi, S., Beshears, J., Milkman, K. L., Sunstein, C. R., Thaler, R. H., Shankar, M., Tucker, W., Congdon, W. J., & Galing, S. (2017). Should governments invest more in nudging? *Psychological Science*, 28(8), 1041–1055.
Bernedo, M., Ferraro, P. J., & Price, M. (2014). The persistent impacts of norm-based messaging and their implications for water conservation. *Journal of Consumer Policy*, 37(3), 437–452.
Bostrom, N. (2013). Existential risk prevention as global priority. *Global Policy*, 4(1), 15–31.
Bostrom, N., & Ćirković, M. (2008). *Global catastrophic risks*. Oxford: Oxford University Press.
Bradshaw, S., & Howard, P. N. (2017). *Troops, trolls and troublemakers: A global inventory of organized social media manipulation*. Working Paper 2017.12. Oxford, UK: Project on Computational Propaganda. Available at: http://comprop.oii.ox.ac.uk/
Brady, W. J., Wills, J. A., Jost, J. T., Tucker, J. A., & Van Bavel, J. J. (2017). Emotion shapes the diffusion of moralized content in social networks. *Proceedings of the National Academy of Sciences*, 114(28), 7313–7318.
Camerer, C. (1999). Behavioral economics: Reunifying psychology and economics. *Proceedings of the National Academy of Sciences*, 96(19), 10575–10577.

Carr, D. (2008). Is Google making us stupid? *The Atlantic*, July/August. Available at: https://www.theatlantic.com/magazine/archive/2008/07/is-google-making-us-stupid/306868/

Chen, D. (2010). Club goods and group identity: Evidence from Islamic resurgence during the Indonesian financial crisis, earlier version with model. *Journal of Political Economy*, 118(2), 300–354.

Chen, Q., Beaty, R. E., Wei, D., Yang, J., Sun, J., Liu, W., & Qiu, J. (2016). Longitudinal alterations of frontoparietal and frontotemporal networks predict future creative cognitive ability. *Cerebral Cortex*. doi:00A0;10.1093/cercor/bhw353

Clark, A., & Chalmers, D. (1998). The extended mind. *Analysis*, 58(1), 7–19.

Cook, J., Ecker, U., & Lewandowsky, S. (2015). Misinformation and how to correct it. In R. A. Scott & S. M. Kosslyn (Eds.), *Emerging trends in the social and behavioral sciences: An interdisciplinary, searchable, and linkable resource* (pp. 1–17). Hoboken, NJ: John Wiley & Sons.

Craik, K. J. W. (1967). *The nature of explanation* (Vol. 445). Cambridge University Press Archive.

Del Vicario, M., Vivaldo, G., Bessi, A., Zollo, F., Scala, A., Caldarelli, G., & Quattrociocchi, W. (2016). Echo chambers: Emotional contagion and group polarization on Facebook. *Scientific Reports*, 6: 37825. doi:00A0;10.1038/srep37825

Dick, S. J. (2003). Cultural evolution, the postbiological universe and SETI. *International Journal of Astrobiology*, 2(1), 65–74.

Douglas, K. M., Sutton, R. M., Jolley, D., & Wood, M. J. (2015). The social, political, environmental, and health-related consequences of conspiracy theories. In M. Bilewicz, A. Cichocka, & W. Soral (Eds.), *The psychology of conspiracy* (pp. 183–200). Abingdon, UK: Routledge.

Ellis, L., Hoskin, A. W., Dutton, E., & Nyborg, H. (2017). The future of secularism: A biologically informed theory supplemented with cross-cultural evidence. *Evolutionary Psychological Science*, 3(3), 1–19.

Ferguson, A. M., McLean, D., & Risko, E. F. (2015). Answers at your fingertips: Access to the Internet influences willingness to answer questions. *Consciousness and Cognition*, 37, 91–102.

Fischhoff, B. (2010). Judgment and decision making. *Wiley Interdisciplinary Reviews: Cognitive Science*, 1(5), 724–735.

Fisher, M., Goddu, M. K., & Keil, F. C. (2015). Searching for explanations: How the Internet inflates estimates of internal knowledge. *Journal of Experimental Psychology: General*, 144(3), 674–687.

Frankfurt, H. G. (2005). *On bullshit*. Princeton, NJ: Princeton University Press.

Gabora, L. (2003). Contextual focus: A cognitive explanation for the cultural transition of the Middle/Upper Paleolithic. In R. Alterman & D. Kirsh (Eds.), *Proceedings of the 25th annual meeting of the Cognitive Science Society* (pp. 432–437, July 31–August 2, Boston, MA). Hillsdale, NJ: Lawrence Erlbaum Associates.

Gabora, L., & Kaufman, S. B. (2010). Evolutionary approaches to creativity. In J. C. Kaufman & R. J. Sternberg (Eds.), *The Cambridge handbook of creativity* (pp. 279–300). Cambridge: Cambridge University Press.

Gauchat, G. (2012). Politicization of science in the public sphere: A study of public trust in the United States, 1974 to 2010. *American Sociological Review*, 77(2), 167–187.

Gilovich, T. (1991). *How we know what isn't so: The fallibility of human reason in everyday life*. New York: The Free Press.

Greene, J. (2014). *Moral tribes: Emotion, reason, and the gap between us and them*. New York: Penguin.

Grolleau, G., Midler, E., & Mzoughi, N. (2017). Behavioral insights for the analysis of green tips. *Ecological Economics*, 134, 258–262.

Guilford, J. P. (1950). Creativity. *American Psychologist*, 5(9), 444–454.
Haidt, J. (2012). *The righteous mind: Why good people are divided by politics and religion*. New York: Vintage.
Hennessey, B. A., & Amabile, T. M. (2010). Creativity. *Annual Review of Psychology*, 61, 569–598.
Hunsberger, B. E., & Altemeyer, B. (2006). *Atheists: A groundbreaking study of America's nonbelievers*. Amherst, NY: Prometheus Books.
Inbar, Y., Pizarro, D. A., & Bloom, P. (2009). Conservatives are more easily disgusted than liberals. *Cognition and Emotion*, 23(4), 714–725.
Jordan, J. J., Hoffman, M., Nowak, M. A., & Rand, D. G. (2016). Uncalculating cooperation is used to signal trustworthiness. *Proceedings of the National Academy of Sciences*, 113(31), 8658–8663.
Kahan, D. M. (2013). Ideology, motivated reasoning, and cognitive reflection. *Judgment and Decision Making*, 8(4), 407–424.
Kahan, D. M., Jenkins-Smith, H., & Braman, D. (2011). Cultural cognition of scientific consensus. *Journal of Risk Research*, 14(2), 147–174.
Kahan, D. M., Peters, E., Wittlin, M., Slovic, P., Ouellette, L. L., Braman, D., & Mandel, G. (2012). The polarizing impact of science literacy and numeracy on perceived climate change risks. *Nature Climate Change*, 2(10), 732–735.
Kahneman, D. (2011). *Thinking, fast and slow*. New York: Farrar, Strauss, Giroux.
Kahneman, D., Knetsch, J. L., & Thaler, R. H. (1991). Anomalies: The endowment effect, loss aversion, and status quo bias. *The Journal of Economic Perspectives*, 5(1), 193–206.
King, M. L., Jr. (1967/1986). A Christmas sermon on peace. In *A testament of hope: The essential writings and speeches of Martin Luther King, Jr* (pp. 253–258). New York: HarperCollins.
Kurzweil, R. (1999). *The coming merging of mind and machine*. New York: Scientific American, Incorporated. Available at: https://www.scientificamerican.com/article/merging-of-mind-and-machine/
Landy, J. F., & Royzman, E. B. (2018). The Moral Myopia Model: Why and how reasoning matters in moral judgment. In G. Pennycook (Ed.), *The new reflectionism in cognitive psychology: Why reason matters* (pp. 70–92). Current Issues in Thinking and Reasoning. Abingdon, UK: Routledge.
Leakey, R. (1984). *The origins of humankind*. New York: Science Masters Basic Books.
Lemon, H. B. (1946). *From Galileo to the nuclear age: An introduction to physics*. Chicago: University of Chicago Press.
Lewandowsky, S., Ecker, U. K., Seifert, C. M., Schwarz, N., & Cook, J. (2012). Misinformation and its correction: Continued influence and successful debiasing. *Psychological Science in the Public Interest*, 13(3), 106–131.
Lewandowsky, S., & Oberauer, K. (2016). Motivated rejection of science. *Current Directions in Psychological Science*, 25(4), 217–222.
Lewin, K. (1951). *Field theory in social science: Selected theoretical papers* (Ed. Dorwin Cartwright). New York: Harper.
Lilienfeld, S. O., Ammirati, R., & Landfield, K. (2009). Giving debiasing away: Can psychological research on correcting cognitive errors promote human welfare? *Perspectives on Psychological Science*, 4(4), 390–398.
Lindeman, M. (2018). Towards understanding intuition and reason in paranormal beliefs. In G. Pennycook (Ed.), *The new reflectionism in cognitive psychology: Why reason matters* (pp. 33–55). Current Issues in Thinking and Reasoning. Abingdon, UK: Routledge.
MacKay, D. (2008). *Sustainable energy – without the hot air*. Cambridge: UIT.

Marsh, G. P. (1864). *Man and nature, or, physical geography as modified by human action*. New York: Scribner.

Mazar, N., & Zhong, C. B. (2010). Do green products make us better people? *Psychological Science*, 21(4), 494–498.

McLuhan, M. (1964). *Understanding media: The extensions of man*. New York: McGraw Hill.

Medimorec, S., & Pennycook, G. (2015). The language of denial: Text analysis reveals differences in language use between climate change proponents and skeptics. *Climatic Change*, 133(4), 597–605.

Miller, G. A. (1969). Psychology as a means of promoting human welfare. *American Psychologist*, 24(12), 1063–1075.

Miller, G. A. (2003). The cognitive revolution: A historical perspective. *Trends in Cognitive Sciences*, 7(3), 141–144.

Morgan, J., Wood, C., & Caldwell-Harris, C. (2018). Reflective thought, religious belief, and the social foundations hypothesis. In G. Pennycook (Ed.), *The new reflectionism in cognitive psychology: Why reason matters* (pp. 10–32). Current Issues in Thinking and Reasoning. Abingdon, UK: Routledge.

Nafziger, E. W., & Auvinen, J. (2002). Economic development, inequality, war, and state violence. *World Development*, 30(2), 153–163.

Norris, P., & Inglehart, R. (2011). *Sacred and secular: Religion and politics worldwide*, 2nd Edition. Cambridge: Cambridge University Press.

Obama, B. (2015). *Executive order – Using behavioral science insights to better serve the American people*. Washington, DC: The White House. Available at: https://www.whitehouse.gov/the-press-office/2015/09/15/executive-order-usingbehavioral-science-insights-better-serve-american

OECD (2017). *Behavioural insights and public policy: Lessons from around the world*. Paris: OECD Publishing.

Penn, D. C., Holyoak, K. J., & Povinelli, D. J. (2008). Darwin's mistake: Explaining the discontinuity between human and nonhuman minds. *Behavioral and Brain Sciences*, 31(2), 109–178.

Pennycook, G., Cannon, T. D., & Rand, D. G. (2017). *Prior exposure increases perceived accuracy of fake news*. Available at: https://ssrn.com/abstract=2958246

Pennycook, G., Cheyne, J. A., Barr, N., Koehler, D. J., & Fugelsang, J. A. (2014). The role of analytic thinking in moral judgements and values. *Thinking & Reasoning*, 20(2), 188–214.

Pew Research Center. (2016). *Internet/broadband fact sheet*. Available at: www.pewinternet.org/data-trend/internet-use/internet-use-over-time/

Pinker, S. (2011). *The better angels of our nature: The decline of violence in history and its causes*. London: Penguin UK.

Pizarro, D. A., & Bloom, P. (2003). The intelligence of the moral intuitions: A comment on Haidt (2001). *Psychological Review*, 110(1), 193–196.

Rand, D. G. (2016). Cooperation, fast and slow: Meta-analytic evidence for a theory of social heuristics and self-interested deliberation. *Psychological Science*, 27(9), 1192–1206.

Rand, D. G., Greene, J. D., & Nowak, M. A. (2012). Spontaneous giving and calculated greed. *Nature*, 489(7416), 427–430.

Rand, D. G., & Nowak, M. A. (2013). Human cooperation. *Trends in Cognitive Sciences*, 17(8), 413–425.

Rand, D. G., Peysakhovich, A., Kraft-Todd, G. T., Newman, G. E., Wurzbacher, O., Nowak, M. A., & Green, J. D. (2014). Social heuristics shape intuitive cooperation. *Nature Communications*, 5: 3677. doi:00A0;10.1038/ncomms4677

Rand, D. G., Tomlin, D., Bear, A., Ludvig, E. A., & Cohen, J. D. (2017). Cyclical population dynamics of automatic versus controlled processing: An evolutionary pendulum. *Psychological Review*. doi:00A0;10.1037/rev0000079

Saad, L. (2011). U.S. political ideology stable with conservatives leading. *Gallup*, August 1. Available at: www.gallup.com/poll/148745/political-ideology-stable-conservatives-leading.aspx

Schlosser, E. (2013). *Command and control: Nuclear weapons, the Damascus accident, and the illusion of safety*. New York: Penguin.

Shafir, E. (2012). *The behavioral foundations of public policy*. Princeton, NJ: Princeton University Press.

Sibley, C. G., & Bulbulia, J. (2012). Faith after an Earthquake: A longitudinal study of religion and perceived health before and after the 2011 Christchurch New Zealand earthquake. *PLOS ONE*, 7(12): e49648. doi:00A0;10.1371/journal.pone.0049648

Silvia, J. P. (2014). Why big theories are fruitless, fragmentation is ideal, defining creativity is overrated, and method-driven research is urgent: Some thoughts on the flourishing state of creativity science. *Creativity: Theories – Research – Applications*, 1(2), 233–239. doi:00A0;10.15290/ctra.2014.01.02.10

Skinner, B. F. (1948). *Walden two*. New York: Macmillan.

Sowden, P. T., Pringle, A., & Gabora, L. (2015). The shifting sands of creative thinking: Connections to dual-process theory. *Thinking & Reasoning*, 21(1), 40–60.

Sparrow, B., Liu, J., & Wegner, M. (2011). Google effects on memory: Cognitive consequences of having information at our fingertips. *Science*, 333(6043), 776–778.

Stagnaro, M. N., Arechar, A. A., & Rand, D. G. (2017). *From good intentions to good norms: Top-down incentives to cooperate foster prosociality but not norm enforcement*. Mimeo.

Stanovich, K. E. (2005). *The robot's rebellion: Finding meaning in the age of Darwin*. Chicago: University of Chicago Press.

Steffen, W., Broadgate, W., Deutsch, L., Gaffney, O., & Ludwig, C. (2015). The trajectory of the Anthropocene: The great acceleration. *The Anthropocene Review*, 2(1), 81–98.

Steffen, W., Grinevald, J., Crutzen, P., & McNeill, J. (2011). The Anthropocene: Conceptual and historical perspectives. *Philosophical Transactions of the Royal Society of London A: Mathematical, Physical and Engineering Sciences*, 369(1938), 842–867.

Stephens-Davidowitz, S. (2017). *Everybody lies: Big data, new data, and what the internet can tell us about who we really are*. New York: HarperCollins.

Swami, V. (2018). The Earth is flat! Or is it?: How thinking analytically might just convince you the Earth isn't flat. In G. Pennycook (Ed.), *The new reflectionism in cognitive psychology: Why reason matters* (pp. 56–69). Current Issues in Thinking and Reasoning. Abingdon, UK: Routledge.

Swire, B., Berinsky, A. J., Lewandowsky, S., & Ecker, U. K. (2017). Processing political misinformation: Comprehending the Trump phenomenon. *Royal Society Open Science*, 4(3): 160802.

Thaler, R. H. (2015). *Misbehaving: The making of behavioral economics*. New York: W. W. Norton & Company.

Thaler, R. H., & Sunstein, C. R. (2008). *Nudge: Improving decisions about health, wealth, and happiness*. New Haven, CT: Yale University Press.

The Church Research Institute. (2016). *Osallistuva luterilaisuus. Suomen evankelis-luterilainen kirkko vuosina 2012–2015* [Partaking Lutheranism. The Finnish Evangelical-Lutheran Church of Finland in 2012–2015]. Kuopio: Grano.

Vujic, A. (2017). Switching on or switching off? Everyday computer use as a predictor of sustained attention and cognitive reflection. *Computers in Human Behavior*, 72, 152–162.

Ward, A. F., Duke, K., Gneezy, A., & Bos, M. W. (2017). Brain drain: The mere presence of one's own smartphone reduces available cognitive capacity. *Journal of the Association for Consumer Research*, 2(2), 140–154.

Williams, H. T., McMurray, J. R., Kurz, T., & Lambert, F. H. (2015). Network analysis reveals open forums and echo chambers in social media discussions of climate change. *Global Environmental Change, 32*, 126–138.

World Economic Forum. (2017). *The global risks report 2017*, 12th Edition. Geneva: World Economic Forum.

Wright, R. (2004). *A short history of progress*. Edinburgh: Canongate Books.

INDEX

Aarnio, K. 10
Actively Open-minded Thinking scale (AOT) 39–40, 42, 43
alcohol, effects of 71, 75, 107
algorithmic processes 38–39, 40–41
Amabile, T. M. 110
Ambady, N. 101
analogies 97–98
analytical thought 13, 107; in conflict detection 109; and conspiracy theories 56–69, 126; and convergent thinking 102; and cooperation 131; and creativity 97–101, 105, 113; and intuition 14–15; and paranormal belief/religiosity 10, 11–14, 23–24, 37, 39–40, 43, 48, 127; and social cognition 20; and social density 18, 25; in WEIRD cultures 15–16; see also cognitive-experiential self-theory (CEST); critical thinking; reasoning
Anthropocene 119–142
Argument Evaluation Test (AET) 39
articulatory suppression 97
associative thought 36, 94–96, 99–100, 101, 105, 122–123; see also dual-process theory
astrology 48–49
atheism 11, 21, 126–127
attentional control 107, 108, 125; see also working memory (capacity), WM(C)
Attentional Myopia Model 71
attitude polarisation 61
Ausubel, D. P. 93

automacity 135
autonomous thinking 3, 38; see also associative thought; dual-process theory; intuition

Ball, L. J. 106
Baron, J. 74, 75, 76
Barr, N. 98, 101, 123
Bartels, D. M. 82
Bear, A. 23, 131
Beaty, R. E. 96, 99–100, 101, 122–123
Beeman, M. 108
behavioural science 132–133
belief bias 2–3, 11
Benedek, M. 95–96
Bernedo, M. 129
bias 48, 61–62, 64, 109, 126, 132; see also belief bias; heuristics
blame 82
Bloom, P. 3–4, 82
Bostrom, N. 121, 135–136
Bradshaw, S. 126
brain anatomy, and executive processes 98–99, 100
brainstorming 111
Brotherton, R. 61
Brown, Michael S. 43
Browne, M. 12–13, 15

Calvinism, and individualism 21
Campbell, D. T. 102
Carr, David 124–125
category mistakes 44–46

Catholicism, and collectivist values 21
Chalmers, D. 124
children 44–45, 70
China, cognitive styles 15–16, 25
choices, individual 121
Clark, A. 124
Clark, B. A. 76
Clarke, S. 6
climate change 121, 128–129, 131
cognitive abilities 62, 63, 72, 79, 81; and creativity 97; and religiosity 13, 48; *see also* algorithmic processes
cognitive control 21, 96, 100, 123, 135
cognitive development 70
cognitive inhibition 41, 47
cognitive load 47, 71, 74, 82, 83
cognitive mode 16–17
Cognitive Reflection Test (CRT) 11–14, 16, 41, 43, 74, 75, 82, 84
cognitive style 13, 14, 15–18, 72, 97, 127
cognitive-experiential self-theory (CEST) 35–37
coherency 59
Cokely, E. T. 84
collaboration, cross-discipline 134
collectivistic cultures 15–16, 17, 21, 22, 25
computing technology 124–126, 134–135
conflict, international 121, 130
conflict sensitivity 4, 12–13, 48, 75, 109
conjunction fallacy 61
conscious reasoning, in moral judgment 83
conspiracy theories 56–69, 126
content, and the internet 124–126
continuum theory of thinking 33
control, illusion of 59
controlled processing and retrieval 94, 96
conventional violations 70–71, 77–78, 80–81
convergent thinking 102
cooperation 22–24, 85, 130–132
core knowledge confusions 44–48
correlations, caveats 42
counter-normativity, and morality 77–81
creativity, creativity research 93–118, 134; dual-process models/meta-theory 101–110, 112, 123; and innovation 122–123; intuitive and analytic processes 99–101; promoting communication in 110–112; reason in 94–99; taxonomy for 108
critical thinking 40, 49, 63–64, 132; *see also* analytical thought
cross-cultural studies, on thinking styles 15–17
cultural differences, and cognitive style/mode 15–17

culture, and paranormal beliefs 48
Cushman, F. 83

decision-making 34–35, 38, 103, 105
Defining Issues Test 81
deliberate thinking 71–73; *see also* analytical thought; reasoning
dieting 71
disgust 78, 79, 128
dispositional inferences 61
divergent thinking 95–96, 100, 102
Doomsday Clock 123
dress codes 77–78
dual-process theory 3, 14, 34–44, 72–73, 75, 86; and creativity 101–110, 111

East Asian cultures, cognitive style 15–17, 25
economic crises and inequality 121, 127, 130
education: and conspiracist beliefs 64; and paranormal beliefs 33, 42
Einstein, Albert 43
emotions, regulation of 38
empathy 20–21, 25–26
Engle, R. W. 104
environmental concerns 121–123
Epsteinian approach 35–38
errors 40; *see also* core knowledge confusions
evaluation 102–103, 104–105, 108
Evans, J. St. B. T. 2–3, 38, 103, 106
experiential system *see* Rational-Experiential Inventory
external reasoning 72

Facebook 61, 125
Faith in Intuition 37–38, 43, 79
fake news 126
Ferguson, A. M. 125
financial crisis (2008), and conspiracy theories 57, 64–65
Finke, R. A. 102
Finland 10, 33, 127
Finley, A. J. 13–14
flat Earth theory 56
footbridge dilemma 73–77
Frazer, James 33
fundamental attribution error 61

Gabora, L. 108, 123
generativity 102–103, 104–105, 108
Gilhooly, K. J. 106
globalization, and diversity 128
Goertzel, T. 60
Google 124, 135
Greene, J. D. 11, 72–73, 74, 128

group identity 19–20, 126, 129; see also social foundations hypothesis
Guilford, J. P. 102, 134
Gupta, N. 97

Haidt, J. 73, 86
harmful violations 77, 78, 80
Hauser, M. 83
Hennessey, B. A. 110
heuristics 2, 4, 34–35, 48, 109
hierarchy 17–18
historical context 1–3
Hofstadter, R. 58, 59
holistic thinking 16–17, 21; see also magical thinking
Howard-Jones, P. A. 102
Huber, D. E. 97
Human Impact Lab 123
hypothetical thinking 38

ideas 42 132–133
incest 78–79
Indigenous philosophies 131
individual differences 60, 71, 72, 96, 101; see also cognitive abilities
individualism, and cognitive style 15–16, 17–18, 21, 25
informational framing 64
information/misinformation, online 124–126
insights 97, 106–107, 108, 109–110, 133
intellectual abilities see algorithmic processes
intentionality 44–45, 47, 82
internal reasoning, in moral judgment 72
internet 124–126
intuition 3–5, 10; and cooperation 131–132; and creativity 99–101; and the internet 125; logical 109; and moral judgment 73, 79, 82; and ontological confusions 47–48; and paranormal belief/religiosity 11, 17, 22–26, 37–38, 43–44; and reflective thought 14–15; see also cognitive-experiential self-theory (CEST)

Jack, A. I. 20–21
Jarosz, A. F. 101
jazz 107
JFK (film) 61
Jordan, J. J. 131
Judaism, and collectivist values 21

Kahan, D. M. 129
Kahane, G. 75
Kahneman, D. 2, 3, 4, 34–35, 132, 133
Kane, M. J. 76

Kelemen, D. 47
Kelley, C. M. 84
Kennedy assassination 61
Kohlberg, Lawrence 70
Kounios, J. 108
Kurzweil, Ray 120

Leakey, R. 121
learning processes, implicit 38
Lemon, H. B. 130
Lilienfeld, S. O. 132
Lindeman, M. 10, 127
loss aversion 135
Luther King Jr., Martin 131

Macchi, L. 106
magical thinking 36, 40
Malinowski, B. 36
marginalisation, and conspiracy theories 59
master rationality motive (MRM) 43
McCauley, R. N. 14
McHoskey, J. W. 60–61
McLuhan, Marshall 124
media, technological advances 124–126
Mednick, S. A. 95, 96, 104
memory 104, 105–106, 124–125; see also working memory (capacity), WM(C)
mentalizing 20, 21
message bias 64
metacognitive processes, and the internet 125
Miller, George 119, 132, 134
mind wandering 105, 108–109
mistakes, category 44–46
moon landing 64
Moore, A. B. 76, 84
moral concern 20–21; see also norms, moral/social
moral dilemmas 73–77
Moral Foundations Theory 80, 128
Moral Myopia Model (MMM) 70–92, 128
Moral-Conventional Distinction Task (MCDT) 77–78, 80
Morgan, J. 127
multiple moral considerations 71–73, 76–77

natural disasters 18, 127
Need for Cognition 37–38
Neubauer, A. C. 95–96
neuroimaging 99, 109
neuroticism, and cognitive inhibition 41
New Age spiritualism 36
New Guinea, ethnographic studies 36
norms, moral/social 17, 19, 20–21, 22–24
nudges 129, 132

Obama, Barack 57
offenses 77–81, 85; *see also* Moral Myopia Model (MMM)
Oliver, J. E. 57, 64
ontological confusions 46–48
open-minded thinking 39–40
order effect 14
Organisation for Economic Co-operation and Development 134
Owen, A. M. 99

paranoia 58
paranormal beliefs 33–55; *see also* religiosity
Pascal, Blaise 34
Paxton, J. M. 74, 79
Pennycook, Gordon 11–13, 14–15, 109, 128
perceptual/cognitive styles, and religiosity 21–22
personality 42, 60
philosophy 34, 49, 110–111, 124, 131
physical phenomena 44
Piaget, Jean 44, 70
Pinker, Steven 130
Pizarro, D. A. 82
political orientation 128; and cognitive style 15–16; and conspiracy theories 57, 58
political propaganda, online 126
poverty alleviation 133
prevention focus 79
priming effects 62–63, 74, 79, 98, 124–125, 128–129
Pringle, A. 123
prior beliefs 2
process *see* dual-process theory; metacognitive processes
promotion focus 79
propaganda 126
psychopathology, and conspiracy theories 58
purity violations 78–79, 80

Quine, W. V. 110–111

Ramnani, N. 99
Rand, D. G. 11, 23, 131, 135
Rasch model 76
Rational-Experiential Inventory 10, 35, 37–38, 82
Razmyar, S. 13
reasoning 1–3, 125, 132–136; in the Anthropocene 119–142; and creativity research 94–99; and moral judgment 70–92; *see also* analytical thought
Reeve, C. L. 13

reflective thought 11, 39–40, 94, 97; and individualism 25; and moral judgment 74–75, 77–78, 85; and religious disbelief 13, 14, 26, 41
religiosity 10–32, 126–127, 130–131; *see also* paranormal beliefs
Remote Associates Test (RAT) 95, 96–98, 101
Risen, J. L. 40
risk 121–123, 130–131, 135–136
Rosen, D. S. 107
Russell, Bertrand 49

Salvi, C. 107
schizotypy 41, 58, 64
science education 33, 37, 122–123
scientific work, thinking styles 43
search engines 124, 125, 135
secularity 126–127
self-reports on thinking 109
semantic distance 97–99, 100
serial-order effect 95–96
Shenhav, A. 11
"side effect" effect 74
Silvia, P. J. 96, 100, 101, 112
Skinner, B. F. 132
sleep deprivation 74–75, 76–77, 81
Slepian, M. L. 101
smartphones 125
Smith, K. A. 97
social authority 19
social cognition 20–21
social density *see* social foundations hypothesis
social foundations hypothesis 17–18, 20–25, 127–128
Social Heuristics Hypothesis 85
Social Intuitionist Model (SIM) 73, 83, 86
social media networking 125–126
social selection effects 25
Sowden, P. T. 102–103, 104, 108, 109, 123
Sparrow, B. 124
spirits 48
spiritual epistemology 12, 15
Stanovich, K. E. 38–40, 43, 103, 106
stories 48
stressful events 59, 64, 74
Subbotsky, E. 36
supernatural belief 34, 127; *see also* paranormal beliefs; religiosity
superstitions 37, 40
sustainability 129
Swire, B. 126
syllogisms 11–12

technological progress, and impacts/risks 120–126, 134–135
Tempesta, D. 76
Theory of Mind 20–21, 25
time pressure 47, 74, 98, 101
trolley dilemma 73–77
trust 22, 23
Turiel, E. 77, 78
Tversky, A. 2, 3, 4, 34–35, 133
Twitter 125
Type 1 and 2 processes *see* analytical thought; associative thought; dual-process theory; intuition; reasoning

Uhlmann, E. 82
Ungar, L. 74
Unsworth, N. 104
Upper Paleolithic Revolution 121–122
utilitarianism 73, 74–77, 82–83

vaccines 64
Varnum, M. E. W. 15

violations: conventional 70–71, 77–78, 80–81; moral 77–80; ontological 46–48; *see also* Moral Myopia Model (MMM)
Vujic, A. 125

Wallas, G. 102
Ward, A. F. 125
Western European (WEIRD) cultures, cognitive style 15–16
Wiley, J. 101
William of Ockham 34
Williams, H. T. 125
Wood, T. J. 57, 64
working memory (capacity), WM(C) 38, 41, 76, 77, 84; and creativity 97, 103–106, 107, 108, 109
World Economic Forum (2017) 131; *The Global Risks Report* 121
Wright, Ronald 120

Young, L. 83

Taylor & Francis eBooks

Helping you to choose the right eBooks for your Library

Add Routledge titles to your library's digital collection today. Taylor and Francis ebooks contains over 50,000 titles in the Humanities, Social Sciences, Behavioural Sciences, Built Environment and Law.

Choose from a range of subject packages or create your own!

Benefits for you
- Free MARC records
- COUNTER-compliant usage statistics
- Flexible purchase and pricing options
- All titles DRM-free.

REQUEST YOUR FREE INSTITUTIONAL TRIAL TODAY

Free Trials Available
We offer free trials to qualifying academic, corporate and government customers.

Benefits for your user
- Off-site, anytime access via Athens or referring URL
- Print or copy pages or chapters
- Full content search
- Bookmark, highlight and annotate text
- Access to thousands of pages of quality research at the click of a button.

eCollections – Choose from over 30 subject eCollections, including:

Archaeology	Language Learning
Architecture	Law
Asian Studies	Literature
Business & Management	Media & Communication
Classical Studies	Middle East Studies
Construction	Music
Creative & Media Arts	Philosophy
Criminology & Criminal Justice	Planning
Economics	Politics
Education	Psychology & Mental Health
Energy	Religion
Engineering	Security
English Language & Linguistics	Social Work
Environment & Sustainability	Sociology
Geography	Sport
Health Studies	Theatre & Performance
History	Tourism, Hospitality & Events

For more information, pricing enquiries or to order a free trial, please contact your local sales team:
www.tandfebooks.com/page/sales

Routledge Taylor & Francis Group

The home of Routledge books

www.tandfebooks.com